Negotiating a Preferential Trading Agreement

Negotiating a Preferential Trading Agreement

Issues, Constraints and Practical Options

Edited by

Sisira Jayasuriya

School of Economics and Finance, La Trobe University, Melbourne, Australia

Donald MacLaren

Department of Economics, University of Melbourne, Melbourne, Australia

Gary Magee

School of Economics and Finance, La Trobe University, Melbourne, Australia

Edward Elgar

Cheltenham, UK • Northampton, MA, USA

Published by
Edward Elgar Publishing Limited
The Lypiatts
15 Lansdown Road
Cheltenham
Glos GL50 2JA
UK

Edward Elgar Publishing, Inc.
William Pratt House
9 Dewey Court
Northampton
Massachusetts 01060
USA

A catalogue record for this book is available from the British Library

Library of Congress Control Number: 2009921522

Mixed Sources
Product group from well-managed forests and other controlled sources
www.fsc.org Cert no. SA-COC-1565
© 1996 Forest Stewardship Council

ISBN 978 1 84720 481 3

Printed and bound by MPG Books Group, UK

Contents

Figures

Tables

Contributors

Philip Adams, Centre of Policy Studies, Monash University, Melbourne, Australia

Philippa Dee, Crawford School of Economics and Government, Australian National University, Canberra, Australia

Christopher Findlay, School of Economics, University of Adelaide, Adelaide, Australia

Russell Hillberry, School of Economics, University of Melbourne, Melbourne, Australia

Sisira Jayasuriya, School of Economics and Finance, La Trobe University, Melbourne, Australia

Peter Lloyd, Department of Economics, University of Melbourne, Melbourne, Australia

Nicolas J.S. Lockhart, Sidley Austin Brown & Wood LLP, Sydney, Australia

Donald MacLaren, Department of Economics, University of Melbourne, Melbourne, Australia

Gary Magee, School of Economics and Finance, La Trobe University, Melbourne, Australia

Yinhua Mai, Centre of Policy Studies, Monash University, Melbourne, Australia

Andrew D. Mitchell, Melbourne Law, University of Melbourne, Melbourne, Australia

Neville Norman, Department of Economics, University of Melbourne, Melbourne, Australia

Martin Richardson, School of Economics, Australian National University, Canberra, Australia

Jeff Waincymer, Faculty of Law, Monash University, Melbourne, Australia

Dashu Wang, Department of Public Finance, Peking University, Beijing, China

Kimberlee Weatherall, TC Beirne School of Law, University of Queensland, Brisbane, Australia

Abbreviations

ABARE	Australian Bureau of Agricultural and Resource Economics
ABS	Australian Bureau of Statistics
ACP	African, Caribbean and Pacific
ACS	Australian Customs Service
AD	Anti-dumping
ACFTA	ASEAN–China Free Trade Agreement
AFTA	ASEAN Free Trade Area
AGE	Applied general equilibrium
AIG	Australian Industry Group
ANZCERTA	Australia New Zealand Closer Economic Agreement
APEC	Asia-Pacific Economic Cooperation
ARDL	Auto-regressive distributed lag
ASEAN	Association of Southeast Asian Nations
AUSFTA	Australia–United States Free Trade Agreement
BITs	Bilateral investment treaties
CAFTA	China–Australia Free Trade Agreement
CARICOM	Caribbean Community and Common Market
CDI	China Development Institute
CER	Closer Economic Relations
CES	Constant elasticity of substitution
CGE	Computable general equilibrium
cif	Cost, insurance and freight
CRTA	Committee on Regional Trade Agreements
CSE	Consumer support estimate
CTC	Change in tariff classification
CTF	Clothing, textiles and footwear
CTH	Change of tariff heading
CUSFTA	Canada–United States Free Trade Agreement
CVD	Countervailing duty
DFAT	Department of Foreign Affairs and Trade
DRM	Dispute resolution mechanism
DS	Dispute resolution/settlement
DSB	Dispute settlement body

DSU	Understanding on rules and procedures governing the settlement of disputes
EFTA	European Free Trade Agreement
EPA	economic partnership agreement
ETM	Elaborately transformed manufactured
EU	European Union
FDI	Foreign direct investment
fob	Free on board
FTA	Free trade agreement
GATS	General Agreement on Trade in Services
GATT	General Agreement on Tariffs and Trade
GSSE	General services support estimate
GTAP	Global Trade Analysis Project
HS	Harmonized commodity description and coding system
ICSID	International Centre for Settlement of Investment Disputes
IICJ	International Islamic Court of Justice
IMF	International Monetary Fund
IP	Intellectual property
IPRS	Intellectual property rights
MERCOSUR	Mercado Comun del Sur (Southern Common Market in South America)
MFA	Multi Fibre Arrangement
MFN	Most-favoured nation
MMC	Monash multi-country
MOFCOM	Ministry of Commerce, China
NAFTA	North American Free Trade Agreement
n.e.c.	Not elsewhere classified
NGO	Non-government organization
NME	non-market economy
NPC	Nominal rate of protection
NRA	Nominal rate of assistance
OECD	Organization for Economic Co-operation and Development
ORCs	Other regulations of commerce
ORRCs	Other restrictive regulations of commerce
PANEURO	system of rules of origin in the European Union
PRC	Peoples Republic of China
PSE	Producer support estimate
PTA	Preferential trade agreement
ROO	Rule of origin
ROW	Rest of the world

RTA	Regional trade agreement
SAFTA	Singapore–Australia Free Trade Agreement
SCM	Subsidies and countervailing measures
SG	Safeguards
SOE	State-owned enterprise
SPS	Sanitary and phytosanitary
STM	Simply transformed manufactured
TAFTA	Thailand–Australia Free Trade Agreement
TBTs	Technical barriers to trade
TPAD	third party anti-dumping
TQ	Tariff quota
TRIPS	Agreement on Trade-Related Aspects of Intellectual Property Rights
TSE	Total support estimate
UNCITRAL	United Nations Commission on International Trade Law
UNIDROIT	International Institute for the Unification of Private Law
USTR	US Trade Representative
VER	voluntary export restraint
WIPO	World Intellectual Property Organization
WTO	World Trade Organization

Preface

The initial stimulus for this volume came at a conference two years ago on aspects of the proposed Australia–China Free Trade Agreement. We were involved in the organization of the conference at the time as members of the Asian Economics Centre, University of Melbourne in partnership with the China Development Institute (CDI) in Shenzhen, China, with support from the Australian Department of Foreign Affairs and Trade (DFAT). It brought together academics, industry leaders, key members of the negotiating teams and political leaders, including the prime minister of Australia. The chance to interact closely with negotiators was particularly instructive for us as academic researchers. We gained some insight into the concrete realities of the negotiating process and an appreciation of the viewpoint of negotiators who have to attempt to reach agreement on a multitude of complex issues within a framework quite tightly constrained by political and institutional factors that determined the scope and range of the Agreement.

Academic specialists in international trade have focused most attention on issues related to the desirability and consequences of Free Trade Agreements (FTAs) or, more correctly, Preferential Trading Agreements. The inescapable reality, however, is that most countries have shifted emphasis from World Trade Organization (WTO) multilateralism onto the FTA path. Our discussions and interactions with participants of the FTA negotiation process convinced us that academics could – without prejudice to their positions on the wider issue of multilateralism – make useful contributions on how to improve outcomes of negotiated agreements.

We are fortunate that a group of eminent international trade economists and lawyers – some of whom were participants at the Shenzhen Conference – have contributed chapters on relevant aspects of the Australia–China economic relationship and on the key technical issues, such as Rules of Origin, Dispute Resolution Mechanisms etc that comprise an integral part of any FTA negotiating process. All chapters were subjected to a refereeing process and revised in the light of comments. A leading Chinese academic, Professor Dashu Wang, who is actively engaged in China's FTA initiatives made a special contribution from a Chinese perspective. We are very grateful for their contributions and for their cooperation. It is natural that there is a diversity of views among the contributors on many issues and it should be noted that views expressed in the chapters are to be attributed strictly to their respective authors.

We accumulated many other debts in putting together this volume. Without in any way implicating them in the views expressed in this volume, we wish to thank the following in particular for their contributions:

- Professor Professor Li Luo Li, President (CDI), Shenzhen (China) and his colleagues, Professor Guo Wanda (Vice-President, CDI), Dr Carol Feng, Director International Department (CDI) and their team, who provided research support and warm hospitality during our visits to Shenzhen and also co-organized the FTA Conference.
- Mr Ric Wells, Lead Negotiator of the Australian FTA negotiating team and his colleagues for their assistance and cooperation.
- Mr Kevin Magee, then Australian Consul-General, Guangzhou (currently, Australian Ambassador to Saudi Arabia) and his team at the Consulate for hospitality and assistance and for playing the pivotal role in the organization of the FTA Conference.
- Mr Kenny Zhang, Managing Director, Waratah International, for assisting us in numerous ways including providing generous sponsorship for the conference and our research.
- Professor Richard Pomfret, University of Adelaide, for reading through the entire manuscript and giving detailed comments.
- Professor Glyn Davis, Vice Chancellor, Melbourne University, for strong support throughout, including attendance at the FTA conference.
- Ms Cherie Millerick, Manager, Department of Economics, University of Melbourne for very efficient administrative support.
- Ms Lee Smith for her editorial assistance.

We also thank our respective spouses, Sreeni, Eileen and Min Mee, for their love and patience.

Sisira Jayasuriya
Donald MacLaren
Gary Magee

PART I

Introduction and overview

1. Introduction

Sisira Jayasuriya and Gary Magee

Preferential trading agreements (PTAs) – often misleadingly called Free trade agreements (FTAs) – have been proliferating at an accelerating pace in recent years (given the wide usage of the latter, both terms are used in this volume). In July 2007 there were 380 agreements that had been notified to the World Trade Organization (WTO) (not all had been notified) and it is expected that there will be some 400 in operation by 2010.[1] Almost every WTO member is also a member of one or more PTAs. There are PTAs comprising developed countries, developing countries, North–South combinations, near neighbours and distant members, and most countries appear to be either involved in (or preparing for) PTA negotiations. Those who have caught the PTA fever now include several countries that have in the past been staunch supporters of multilateralism, eschewing PTAs as a diversion from the difficult but ultimately productive path of deep and meaningful non-discriminatory trade liberalization through the General Agreement on Tariffs and Trade (GATT)/WTO process.

Australia is a notable example. Though it has had a long-standing close bilateral relationship with New Zealand – culminating in the Australia–New Zealand Closer Economic Relations (CER) agreement – until quite recently it was firmly committed to multilateralism as the way to achieve freer trade. In regional fora such as APEC, Australia espoused the so-called open regionalism which was basically a mechanism that aimed to extend any regional trade liberalization to non-members, thereby linking any regional liberalization to the wider goal of broader non-discriminatory liberalization. However, all that has changed in the last few years. In addition to the CER agreement with New Zealand, Australia has signed three PTAs since 2003, starting with the Australia–Singapore FTA, followed by the Australia–Thailand FTA and the Australia–US FTA which came into effect in 2005. By early 2008, it was involved in substantive negotiations or scoping/feasibility studies for several other PTAs, including PTAs with China, India, ASEAN (as a grouping) and New Zealand, Chile, the Gulf Cooperation Council, Japan, Korea, Indonesia and Malaysia.

Australia's enthusiastic embrace of PTAs only confirms what has become quite evident in recent years at the global level. Despite protestations to the contrary, there is a clear shift in emphasis by most major countries away from the WTO multilateral process towards PTAs and this has, in turn, led other smaller countries to follow suit, partly to ensure that they are not 'cut out' of the benefits of membership in discriminatory PTAs. But the perceived economic benefits from membership of these exclusionary clubs are only one factor, sometimes not even the main factor, in the accelerated drive to sign (often criss-crossing) PTAs. Not surprisingly, governments generally emphasize the positive aspects of PTAs because political and strategic imperatives underpin many of the agreements. The successful conclusion of an FTA – however limited its scope is – often comes to be seen as the test of the strength of the political relationship between the parties, with political implications for the government leaders who had committed themselves to achieving it. Further, FTA negotiations are naturally the focus of interest for potentially affected parties; these include, in particular, relatively small (and well organized) groups of producers/ suppliers who stand to gain substantially from expanded market access to the foreign market or to lose a great deal from import competition from foreign exporters. This political context places both severe constraints and strong pressures on negotiators to achieve a successful outcome in the form of an agreement that can claim to be a source of major benefits while protecting vital areas of national interest from foreign competitors. But what constitutes a desirable PTA? How can PTA negotiators deliver a successful outcome?

It is now common in political fora to discuss the PTA as a potential vehicle for achieving significant reductions in barriers to trade, not only in goods but also in services and other areas (particularly in the sense of enhancing free movement of capital – investment liberalization). But ever since Jacob Viner (1950) pointed out that, in principle, the net (static) welfare effect of a PTA is ambiguous because a PTA has the potential for both trade creation and trade diversion, economists have recognized that discriminatory trade liberalization is not necessarily welfare improv- ing. Trade creation occurs if the PTA leads to closer aligning of domestic prices with international prices inducing production shifts from a high cost partner to a low cost partner or from welfare-increasing consump- tion increases in response to such price changes. On the other hand, trade diversion occurs if production shifts from a low cost non-partner country to a higher cost partner. The overall benefit then depends on which of these dominate. In theory, it is possible to set up a PTA that will (largely) elim- inate trade diversion (thus ensuring that welfare would be enhanced) by suitable adjustments to the overall structure of tariffs with non-members.

This has spawned intense controversy and debate about the desirability of PTAs and the nature of the link between PTAs and multilateral liberalization: are PTAs 'building blocks' (facilitators) or 'stumbling blocks' (obstacles) to the achievement of global trade liberalization? Those who see PTAs as building blocks highlight the weaknesses of the WTO, the difficulties of achieving agreements in multilateral trade negotiations and the ease with which groups of like-minded countries can agree among themselves to advance the liberalization process faster and in greater depth. In political economy terms, sometimes it is argued that even limited and partial liberalization can strengthen support for wider and deeper liberalization. On the other hand, opponents point to the 'spaghetti bowl' effect of overlapping and criss-crossing PTAs that lead to the limited scope of PTAs due to avoidance of 'sensitive sectors', costly administrative complexities produced by a multiplicity of trade regulations and procedures (differential tariffs, technical standards, rules of origin, and so on) and the possibility of competing trade blocs. The literature on this topic is already vast and rapidly expanding but the issues remain intensely contentious; the economics profession itself has become quite polarized.[2]

Nevertheless, there seems to be a general consensus emerging that ideally PTAs should aim to be broad in terms of sectoral coverage, stronger than standard WTO commitments (WTO-plus) and more extensive in terms of 'behind the border' – internal market-liberalization permitting deeper economic integration. Sally (2008, pp. 126–7) summarizes the key features of a desirable PTA as follows:

> For PTAs to make economic sense, they should have comprehensive sectoral coverage, be consistent with relevant WTO provisions [in Article XXIV GATT and Article V GATTS – General Agreement on Trade in Services] and preferably go beyond both WTO commitments and applied practice at home. In other words, they should involve genuine and tangible, not bogus, liberalisation. There should be strong provisions for non-border regulatory cooperation, especially to improve transparency in domestic laws and regulations in order to facilitate market access and boost competition. Rules of Origin [ROO] requirements must be as simple, generous and harmonised as possible to minimise trade diversion and red tape. Strong, clean 'WTO-plus' PTAs should reinforce domestic economic and institutional reforms to remove market distortions and extend competition. Finally, non-preferential [MFN] tariffs should be low in order to minimise any trade diversion resulting from PTAs.

Though official statements are full of lofty words proclaiming a commitment to achieve such deep and comprehensive agreements, actual PTA negotiations typically take place within a framework that most economists would consider to be fundamentally flawed. It is a framework rooted in strong mercantilist ethos. The starting point of the negotiating (bargaining) process is that gains from trade accrue only to the exporter; hence by reducing 'our' trade barriers and providing them access to 'our' market we are granting the 'other side' a favour. This is a 'concession' that in turn demands a quid pro quo concession from the other side in the form of a reciprocal offer of greater market access for our exporters. This particular stance adopted by negotiators is rationalized in several ways. A common political economy rationale is based on the view that reciprocity facilitates domestic acceptance of 'concessions' to the foreigners, while other justifications are based on bargaining tactics with game-theoretic underpinnings. However, it is widely observed that the interests of domestic consumers are typically downplayed, if not ignored altogether in these negotiations; even when they are recognized, producer interests typically dominate. Resistance to liberalization almost invariably comes from strong producer groups who find it easier to exercise political clout and constrain governments in PTA negotiations than in multilateral negotiations. This is perhaps not surprising: if governments were genuinely committed to consumer welfare there would be no need to follow a PTA (or even a multilateral) route; consumer benefits from cheaper imports can be easily gained by unilateral liberalization. It is also not surprising that many PTAs, driven by political motives and negotiated under severe domestic lobby group pressures and constraints, are weak, partial and ineffective (if not actually harmful) in terms of achieving trade liberalization and market integration.

Though the gains from multilateralism may be greater and the costs of the shift towards PTAs may prove to be high, the reality of PTAs makes it imperative that analysts give careful consideration to how better PTAs can be negotiated. This, for example, is a challenge that official negotiators cannot avoid. The particular domestic political economy constraints and the relative bargaining power of the negotiating partners are certainly key factors that influence the final shape of agreements. For negotiators, an appreciation of the implications of adopting different technical options can nevertheless be quite helpful in attempting to enhance the scope and value of a PTA and to minimize any negative impacts within the given political constraints. But, while there is a growing literature on the implications of specific aspects of PTAs, such as the impact of complex rules of origin, the literature that can be used as a general guide in addressing the concrete negotiating issues involved is relatively sparse.

Our aim in this volume is primarily to contribute to this task of presenting useful guidelines for negotiating better PTAs. We do not undertake or present an in-depth benefit–cost assessment of an Australia–China PTA, though there is some discussion about the potential gains from certain liberalization measures. The contributing authors are international trade experts from the twin disciplines of economics and law who focus on the issues of interest in PTA negotiations in the wider context of the Australia–China economic relationship. China and Australia are relative newcomers to PTAs, though they both appear to be racing to make up for lost time. They are natural trading partners with strong complementarities whose economic links have strengthened enormously in recent years. China – whose industrialization and rapid growth has made it the driving force in generating the global commodity boom – is now the main trading partner of resource and land (agriculture) rich Australia. The two countries seem ideal candidates for a deep and comprehensive PTA. Even analysts sceptical of the desirability of Australia's FTAs with countries such as the USA, Thailand and Singapore, have been generally favourably disposed towards a PTA with China. From China's point of view, the need for reliable and secure resource supplies seems to make it a very attractive proposition. But the negotiations have not proved easy and have exposed differences over a wide range of issues. We believe that this quite protracted and difficult negotiation process between Australia and China for a Free Trade Agreement – a PTA – provides a very handy and illustrative case study to look at several key issues and areas of interest to all those involved in negotiating PTAs.

The structure of this book is as follows. Section I comprises, in addition to this chapter, two other chapters. In Chapter 2, Russell Hillberry presents a review of recent ex post analysis of the empirical experience of FTAs, with some discussion of implications for FTA design. On the basis of this review, he suggests that regional agreements containing multiple countries are the best alternative to unilateral/multilateral reforms, while interlocking bilateral agreements are best avoided. Further, governments should seek to harmonize policy commitments across past, current and future PTAs. Though the availability of applied (computable) general equilibrium models have popularized ex ante assessments of PTAs, he points out that both the proliferation of preferential trade agreements and their broadening policy scope make it substantially more difficult for economists to quantify the economic impacts of the agreements. As a result, a greater burden is placed on policy makers' judgement. Hillberry emphasizes the importance of unilateral liberalization and that PTAs should not be treated as substitutes for domestic policy reforms. Chapter 3 is a special contribution by a Chinese economist, Professor Dashu Wang from Peking University, who is actively involved in China's FTA negotiations, providing a Chinese perspective and emphasizing the political context in which these negotiations take place. China has strong political objectives in pursuing PTAs; in particular, it aims to challenge US supremacy in Asia and Japan's position as the dominant economic power, and wants to avoid being outmanoeuvred by Japan in the Asian region.

Section II comprises Chapters 4–7, which are focused on the sector-specific issues in manufacturing, agriculture, services and resources. Neville Norman in his survey of the Australian manufacturing sector issues in Chapter 4 explains why the potential threat of Chinese import competition continues to make this a sensitive area. In agriculture, where Australia has a clear comparative advantage in most products, Donald MacLaren (Chapter 5) argues that while there are barriers constraining Australian agricultural exports into China, there may be little that Australia can offer China in return for enhanced market access into China; thus any bargaining on this will need to offer incentives for China in other sectors. Further, the kinds of reforms that can improve market access for Australia in agriculture will require 'behind-the-border' reforms in China, and these are difficult to achieve on a preferential basis and hence unlikely to be successfully negotiated in a bilateral PTA. This introduces both the importance of non-border reforms and the difficulties associated with achieving them in PTAs.

Philippa Dee and Christopher Findlay in Chapter 6 look at the services sector issues. This is where existing links are weakest, though there has been significant growth in areas such as travel and education. They point out that China has so far been unwilling to include services provisions in its PTAs at all, or has been unwilling to go beyond its existing WTO accession commitments. This is an area where the issue of 'behind-the-border' regulatory reforms is most acutely posed with the previously mentioned problems related to bilateral negotiations. Australia is seeking a first mover advantage for its services in China, or in some cases a second mover advantage (behind Hong Kong and Macao). Dee and Findlay argue that the consequences of any preferential access for Australian suppliers will depend partly on whether supply conditions from the Australian end are competitive. In particular, in this context they highlight the implications of an aspect of PTA negotiations that is not often recognized: the 'client focus' of trade officials that sees them happy to negotiate on behalf of individual services suppliers, rather than necessarily ensuring open entry for all suppliers from the country. If supply conditions in Australia are not competitive, selected Australian producers may capture greater rents with no benefit to Chinese users. They suggest that an Australia–China free trade agreement will do nothing to further the cause of domestic regulatory reform in China. Indeed, it may even create a subset of Australian services suppliers earning rents in China, who then have an interest in opposing further regulatory reform.

The resources sector, as Yinhua Mai and Philip Adams point out in Chapter 7, is perhaps the most critical from a bilateral viewpoint. It is where natural complementarities are strongest. They see significant gains from an FTA which liberalizes further border trade liberalization in this sector, but fuller gains can accrue if this is accompanied by investment liberalization. But this is likely to be a more difficult area of negotiation than relaxing border protection. Foreign ownership in the resources sector is a sensitive topic. The implementation of investment facilitation measures is also likely to be more difficult than the removal of tariffs on the resource products, because it involves institutional and legislative changes.

Section III comprises five chapters that address key technical issues that arise in choosing rules and institutional designs in the design of successful PTAs: intellectual property, rules of origin, business law and enforcement, trade remedies and dispute settlement procedures and PTA compliance with the WTO. Each chapter surveys the basic issues, main alternatives and an evaluation based on both theory and international experience, taking into account the particular legal, institutional and political circumstances facing the negotiating partners. The discussions illustrate how these general principles in each case are applied to the concrete circumstances of an Australia–China agreement.

In Chapter 8, Kimberlee Weatherall raises the issue of intellectual property (IP) in the context of China and Australia, where domestic regulatory regimes are very different (and, in China's case, also changing very rapidly). This is an area where bilateral agreements that raise standards are almost bound to become multilateralized. Though cooperation or dispute settlement provisions would not legally be required to be extended to other WTO members, they would nevertheless be seen as precedents. Hence, any agreement would be seen as having a much wider impact and not confined to the two negotiating partners. Given the relatively weak bargaining power of Australia, getting a completely satisfactory agreement would be difficult. On the other hand, this is an area where China would need to move forward in any case. Weatherall discusses various options and proposes a combination of defensive, cooperation, and dispute settlement approaches incorporating a dynamic element. The issues and options are clearly of relevance for any PTA where partners have significantly different IP regimes, as would typically be the case when negotiations are between a developing and developed country.

Peter Lloyd and Donald MacLaren address issues related to rules of origin (ROOs) in Chapter 9. ROOs are one of the most critical technical issues in any PTA. With increasing product fragmentation, almost no good is wholly produced in one country and, unless clear guidelines are laid down to establish eligibility for trade preferences under a PTA, the system becomes costly and unworkable, and preferences are largely eroded. While there is a general consensus that simple, 'generous' ROOs are essential if a PTA is to achieve true liberalization in goods trade, choosing between different options is not a simple task. It is recognized that all ROO systems are necessarily trade restrictive to some extent in order to prevent trade deflection. However, Lloyd and MacLaren argue that most ROO systems are much more trade restrictive than they need to be. They describe and analyse the advantages and disadvantages of major ROO systems and specific characteristics, and explain how a system can be chosen in order to minimize trade restrictiveness and, as far as possible, other untoward effects on the costs of compliance, uncertainty and the pattern of trade.

Mechanisms for enforcement of agreements and dispute resolution (DS) procedures are important to any well-designed agreement. In Chapter 10, Jeff Waincymer addresses legal issues related to business law and enforcement involving both trade and investment in the context of PTAs. In Chapter 11 Martin Richardson focuses on economic aspects of trade remedies and dispute settlement procedures. Waincymer reviews the wide variety of systems and approaches in existing PTAs which range from near informal procedures for dispute resolution to tightly specified procedures. There is tension between advocates of a legalist approach and those who prefer international organizations to behave in a more pragmatic manner. There are trade-offs involved in practice and compromises are almost unavoidable. However, arguably, moving to a more legalist approach may help resist domestic protectionist pressures. Richardson presents a trench-ant and fundamental critique of the underlying rationale for most so-called trade remedies, arguing that ideally the complete abolition of administered protection in a PTA would be the most desirable outcome. However, as many may consider such an approach too drastic, he proposes alternative procedures that are simple, WTO consistent and impose lower efficiency costs.

In the final chapter, Andrew Mitchell and Nicolas Lockhart take up the issue of how a PTA can ensure broad compliance with relevant WTO provisions. They point out that, in legal terms, the coexistence of the WTO and PTAs among WTO members creates a complex system of competing international rights and obligations. Of course this is a tension that has been present from the very inception of GATT when PTAs were allowed to operate in violation of the fundamental most-favoured nation (MFN) principle of non-discrimination. For PTAs to comply with WTO rules they must fall within one of the exceptions valid under WTO law; hence, each WTO member must ensure that any PTA to which it is a party complies with the conditions of the relevant WTO exception. Unfortunately, as Mitchell and Lockhart point out, the proliferation of PTAs has created a situation where no one is willing to challenge the legality of any PTA, so that there is de facto acceptance of any type of PTA, thus increasing the likelihood that PTAs may increasingly undermine the fundamental principles of WTO and the rules-based multilateral trading system.

NOTES

1. Information from the WTO website: www.wto.org.
2. The literature on this subject is quite large; a good introduction to the issues, debates and the literature can be found in World Bank (2005) and Schott (2004). Sally (2008) provides an excellent discussion of the key issues and the related political economy considerations. See also, Hoekman and Winters (2007).

REFERENCES

Hoekman, B. and A. Winters (2007), 'Multilateralizing "deep regional integration": a developing country perspective', paper presented at the Conference on Multilateralizing Regionalism, sponsored and organized by WTO/HEI, co-organized by the Centre for Economic Policy Research (CEPR), 10–12 September 2007, Geneva, Switzerland.

Sally, R. (2008), *Trade Policy, New Century: the WTO, FTAs and Asia Rising*, London: The Institute of Economic Affairs.

Schott, J.J. (2004), 'Free trade agreements: boon or bane of the world trading system?', accessed 12 February 2008, at www.petersoninstitute.org/publications/chapters_preview/375/01iie3616.pdf.

Viner, Jacob (1950), *The Customs Union Issue*, New York: Carnegie Endowment for International Peace.

World Bank (2005), *Global Economic Prospects: Trade, Regionalism and Development*, Washington, DC: The World Bank.

2. Review of international experience: ex post studies of other PTAs and implications for PTA design

Russell Hillberry[1]

The last decade has seen remarkable growth in the number of preferential trade agreements (PTAs). One hundred and seven goods agreements and 34 preferential services agreements have been notified to the WTO since the implementation of the Uruguay Round in 1995. Figure 2.1 illustrates the recent nature of this phenomenon.[2]

There are a number of explanations for the rapid growth in the number of PTAs. First, growth in the number of WTO members, and in the scope of their economic interests, has made it more difficult to identify mutually agreeable multilateral commitments. As a result, multilateral negotiations have slowed down, and trade ministries have shifted their attention toward PTAs. Second, the international goods trade is becoming more complex, requiring policy makers to address a more comprehensive set of issues than they once did. Third, governments are increasingly using PTAs to pursue non-economic objectives. The United States, for example, appears to have embraced PTAs as a foreign policy tool. Finally, the shift by large countries toward PTAs has had a destabilizing effect on the multilateral process. The subsequent proliferation of PTAs follows, in part, from the absence of credible large country support for the multilateral process.

Both the growth in the number of PTAs and the expansion of their policy scope have complicated economists' efforts to inform trade policy. When policy makers negotiated occasional, multilateral agreements that focused primarily on tariff reductions, economists could fully endorse the agreements, and support them with plausible quantitative estimates of their likely impact. Recent PTAs are much harder to evaluate, for two reasons. First, the newer agreements are broad in policy scope – including commitments on intellectual property, investment, dispute settlement and more. The economic effect of these commitments can be difficult to quantify. Second, PTAs are no longer occasional one-off agreements that can be treated analytically as policy ends; they are part of a process in which each agreement affects, and

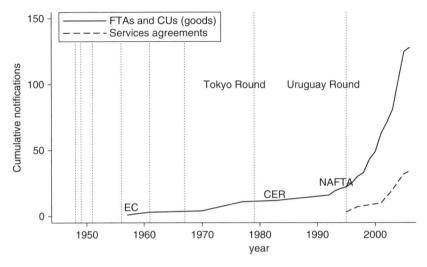

Source: World Trade Organization.

Note: Vertical lines are GATT round implementation dates.

Figure 2.1   Cumulative notifications of PTAs to the WTO

is affected by, all other PTAs. Evaluating the effects of any given negotiation on subsequent negotiations is, so far, beyond the scope of applied theory.

A side benefit of the flurry of recent PTAs is that it provides economists with a variety of experiments with which to evaluate the economic effects of PTAs. Large, comprehensive agreements such as the North American Free Trade Agreement (NAFTA) have now been in place for a sufficiently long time to allow rigorous ex post analysis. Quantitative tools have been developed for evaluating non-traditional policy commitments in areas such as intellectual property rights. Hypotheses about the implications of non-economic policy objectives have been developed, and their consequences for trade negotiations evaluated.

The purpose of this chapter is to review the recent empirical literature on PTAs. The emphasis is on ex post analysis of PTAs and involves (primarily) econometric work. There is a large theoretical literature on PTAs that will only get brief attention. The vast ex ante literature using applied general equilibrium models as a primary tool for assessing PTAs is referenced only in passing.

One explanation for the increased scope of modern trade agreements is the growing complexity of the international goods trade. The first section of the chapter attempts to illuminate this trend. The second part reviews the recent empirical literature documenting the effects of trade policy measures on trade flows. The following section investigates empirical studies of broader PTA policy commitments, including dispute settlement mechanisms and intellectual property rights. The fourth part reviews the literature on how PTAs have affected variables other than trade flows, such as welfare and productivity. The next section reviews the literature relating PTAs to their broader policy context. The final part outlines some broad lessons for trade policy makers.

THE INCREASING COMPLEXITY OF TRADED GOODS

There are a number of explanations for the proliferation of PTAs in recent years. One explanation focuses on the changing nature of international trade, which demands more of national legal systems than was required of them in earlier years. There are a number of changes that have made legal oversight of international trade more difficult. One such change has been a shift in the nature of traded goods. Traded goods themselves have become more complex, increasing the scope for legal ambiguities to arise.

Measuring goods' complexity is not an easy thing to do, but the recent international trade literature provides some insight about how best to illustrate this trend. This section of the chapter applies the Rauch (1999) goods classification system to historical trade flows, in order to show that national export bundles are increasingly composed of 'differentiated' commodities. Because differentiated commodities are more likely than other commodities to be sold through negotiated contracts, increased trade in these goods can be taken as an indicator of increasing demands on the legal systems that oversee international trade. In this way, the increasing complexity of the goods trade can partially explain the increasing demand for comprehensive legal reforms in trade agreements.

Rauch (1999) categorizes goods according to the manner in which they are sold. 'Homogeneous goods', such as gold, are defined as those that are sold on spot markets. The characteristics of such goods can be defined so precisely that the goods producers' identity (and typically, their national origin) need not be known by the eventual end user. 'Reference priced goods' are defined as goods with prices published in public fora like trade magazines; highly specialized chemicals are an example. Like homogeneous goods, reference priced goods are typically well defined commodities. In most cases, these goods could be sold through standardized contracts that would not be especially demanding of national legal systems.

Rauch's third category of goods, 'differentiated commodities', comprises those goods that are not sold in spot markets or by posted prices. It is likely that many of these sales are accomplished with negotiated contracts. One might therefore expect that sales of differentiated commodities might require more of national legal systems in terms of enforcement. Negotiated contracts may include performance provisions such as service after the sale. Contracts may also stipulate restrictions on the purchaser's use of the product – intellectual property rights laws are an example. These complexities probably mean that the 'differentiated commodities' category of goods is more demanding of national legal systems than goods in Rauch's other two categories.

Figure 2.2 shows the share of exports that are in Rauch's differentiated commodities grouping, over time, for selected countries, and for the world as a whole. Most countries have seen relatively large increases in the share of their exports that are differentiated. As these figures are calculated for a period of greatly increased trade, growth in differentiated products' share implies even faster growth in the overall volume of trade in these products. China has seen the fastest growth in the differentiated commodities' share of exports in the group.[3]

The increased share of differentiated products in world trade coincides with the expansion of policy scope of most trade agreements. It is likely that this relationship is, in part, causal. Increased demand by exporters for government commitments in the areas of investment, services, dispute settlement procedures and intellectual property rights (IPRs) are all plausibly related to the growing share of differentiated commodities in world trade. Since these more complicated provisions are difficult to negotiate in a large multilateral forum, trade ministries may well have turned to PTAs to push forward a trade agenda that can accommodate these issues.[4]

This broader agenda is much more difficult to quantify in terms of its economic impact. One might plausibly estimate tariff equivalent effects for some policy changes, but it is far from clear that such estimates are valid treatments of the economic effects of more comprehensive reforms. The effects of many of the broader provisions are quite plausibly beyond the scope of economists' ability to quantify them. There remains considerable scope for political judgement in evaluating both the efficacy and the value of broader policy commitments.

EMPIRICAL LITERATURE ON PREFERENTIAL TRADE POLICIES AND TRADE

The most straightforward econometric exercise in evaluating a PTA is estimating its effect on trade. Data on trade flows are readily available,

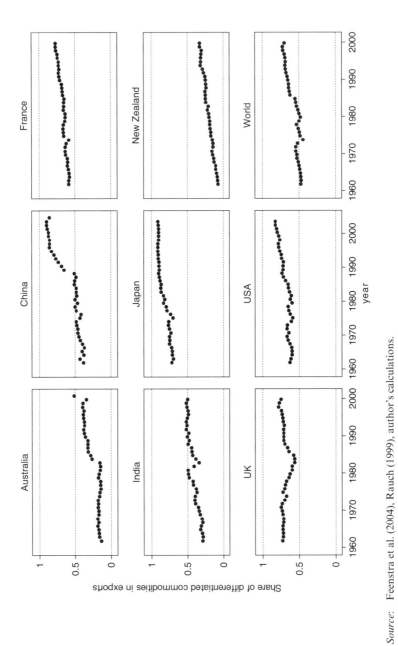

Source: Feenstra et al. (2004), Rauch (1999), author's calculations.

Figure 2.2   Differentiated commodities in exports (1962–2000)

16

the policy instruments aimed at increasing trade (i.e. tariff cuts) are also easily quantified, and theoretic predictions about the relationships between policy changes and trade flows are clear. PTAs have been especially interesting to empirical economists because (a) PTAs have ambiguous effects on economic welfare, and (b) the Vinerian framework links observable changes in the trade pattern to the unobservable variable of interest, economic welfare.

Econometric evaluation of PTAs dates from Aitken (1973), who estimated the effect of the European Economic Community and European Free Trade Area agreements on European trade. Aitken estimated an empirical gravity model, and used dummy variables to denote two countries' joint membership in a PTA. Aitken found that, in the early years of the two agreements, both agreements were trade creating, but that trade diversion occurred in later years.

Econometric specifications that identify the effects of trade policy using dummy variables, like Aitken's, are useful in that they give the analyst a framework for quantifying the total effect of the agreement, including difficult-to-quantify provisions such as commitments on investment or IPRs. In a properly specified model, a dummy variable denoting membership in the agreement would capture all of the increased trade generated by the agreement, whether it be due to tariff cuts or to other policy commitments.[5]

Unfortunately, it is impossible to know the proper econometric specification. Dummy variable approaches have a key drawback; they risk conflating the effects of the agreement with other events and policies that affect trade. For example, the North American Free Trade Agreement (NAFTA) took effect in the midst of the Mexican peso crisis. Econometric specifications that treat the agreement as a simple dummy variable will likely conflate the effects of the peso crisis with NAFTA.

A related problem with studies that employ dummy variables to identify PTA effects is that such studies frequently lack a theoretical grounding for their econometric model. Given the possibility of numerous plausible econometric specifications, it remains quite possible that analysts will report the results of specifications that confirm their prior beliefs. In an important paper, Ghosh and Yamarik (2004) investigate the effect of PTAs on trade flows, using extreme bounds analysis to test for specification uncertainty. Their estimates led them to conclude that 'the pervasive trade creation effect found in the literature reflects not the information content of the data but rather the unacknowledged beliefs of the researchers.'[6]

Few areas of study in economics have data sources as rich in variation as international trade data. Typically, there is information on bilateral trade prices and quantities, along with trade policy measures and, occasionally, freight costs. Studies that employ dummy variables to study aggregate trade flows discard much of this information. Econometric evaluations of PTAs have only recently begun to exploit the rich variation available in the data. Product-level detail is informative because (a) theoretic predictions linking tariff cuts to trade growth are most precise at the product level, and (b) additional degrees of freedom allow econometric estimates to be identified with greater precision. Economists in North America have been quick to apply such methods to trade agreements there.

Clausing (2001) exploits HS 10-digit US import data to evaluate the Canada–United States Free Trade Agreement (CUSFTA). She estimates that US imports from Canada were 26 per cent higher in 1994 than they would have been without the agreement. These estimates attribute approximately half of the growth in US imports from Canada over the period 1989–94 to tariff changes in the agreement. Clausing finds no evidence of trade diversion.

Romalis (2005) conducts a similar exercise, evaluating the effects of preferential CUSFTA and NAFTA tariffs on North American trade flows. Romalis uses EU imports to benchmark changes in trade flows, requiring him to aggregate the data somewhat, relative to Clausing.[7] On the demand side, Romalis estimates a common elasticity of substitution between import sources across commodities. In US imports, estimates of the elasticity of substitution range between 6 and 10; for Canadian imports 5–8; and for Mexican imports 0.6–2.2.[8] One explanation for the lower estimated Mexican substitution elasticity is that rules of origin requirements for final goods shipped to the US constrain Mexico's sourcing of intermediate goods.

Romalis also estimates inverse supply elasticities, using price and quantity detail from the 10-digit US import data. The estimates suggest that export supply curves into the US are price elastic. These estimates, together with the demand elasticities, are used to inform Romalis's counterfactual analysis of trade and welfare. Romalis calculates substantial trade diversion from both CUSFTA and NAFTA.[9] His welfare calculations suggest no welfare gain from the NAFTA tariff cuts, and welfare losses for Mexico.[10]

Another study that investigates NAFTA with product-level detail is USITC (2003).[11] This study also exploits time variation in the data. As in earlier studies, this one finds that preferential tariffs granted in NAFTA had a substantial effect on US–Mexico trade. USITC (2003) allows the impact of NAFTA preferences to differ from preferences in place before the agreement,[12] finding that Mexican shares of US imports were more responsive to NAFTA tariff preferences than to earlier preference arrangements. This may indicate that other features of NAFTA – including the permanence of the preferences, a dispute settlement procedure, and non-tariff provisions on related issues like investment – made US preferences in NAFTA more valuable to Mexican exporters and US importers than earlier tariff preferences.

Trade Growth via the Extensive Margin

The above studies focus primarily on the effects of PTAs on the intensive margin of trade. In other words, these studies evaluate how much preferential tariff cuts increase trade, in products that were already traded with the partner country before the agreement. A recent literature has emphasized that the extensive margin of trade (that is, trade in new goods that were not previously traded) is also important for welfare. Broda and Weinstein (2004), for example, estimate that growth in the number of imported varieties since 1972 has raised real US income by 3 per cent. These estimates are six times larger, for example, than USITC (2003) estimates of the US gains from all the trade agreements negotiated over a similar period. If Broda and Weinstein are correct, and the gains from variety growth are that large, then the effects of trade policy on the extensive margin should be a question of keen interest.[13]

Hummels and Klenow (2005) provide a decomposition framework that is useful for quantifying trade growth via the extensive margin. Hillberry and McDaniel (2002) find that most of the US trade growth with NAFTA partners occurred among already-traded goods, but that the value of US imports from Mexico included some growth along the extensive margin. Kehoe and Ruhl (2003) show that the extensive margin was important in the case of Canada–Mexico trade. More broadly, Kehoe and Ruhl point out that, across several trade liberalization episodes, there has been more trade growth in the goods that were least traded before the policy change.

None of the above papers link growth along the extensive margin directly to trade policy changes. One paper that does so is Debaere and Mostashari (2006), who estimate the contribution of tariff cuts to growth along the extensive margin of trade. Using 1989–2001 US import data, they find evidence that trade grows along the extensive margin when preferential tariff cuts are awarded, but find subsequent evidence linking this to trade diversion. There is mixed evidence that across-the-board tariff cuts generate growth in the extensive margin. Overall, Debaere and Mostashari find little evidence that tariff cuts are economically significant in inducing new trade. They do point out, however, that other policy changes frequently embedded in PTAs, such as investment guarantees, may have effects on the extensive margin that are not observed in their estimates.

PTA Effects on Trade with Excluded Countries

One of the generally overlooked outcomes of PTAs is their effects on excluded countries. If preferential access reduces third-country exporters' supply prices, then those third countries are harmed by PTAs. In a world of proliferating preferential arrangements, such effects are particularly important, as subsequent agreements by a PTA partner may dilute the effects of an existing agreement. Evidence of third-country effects can also be used to justify agreements with countries that have made agreements with other third parties.[14]

In an investigation of the effects of PTAs on third countries, Chang and Winters (2002) explore variation in Brazilian import prices following MERCOSUR. They find that prices non-MERCOSUR exporters charged in Brazil fell more in those goods where preferential tariff cuts were larger. This evidence suggests that preferential tariff cuts reduced the mark-up that non-MERCOSUR exporters receive in the Brazilian market. In the context of Chang and Winters's model, this is evidence of third-country harm.

Trade and Rules of Origin

Necessary features of PTAs are rules of origin (ROOs), which define the set of goods that can be traded under the preferential terms of the agreement. While necessary for meaningful enforcement of the agreement, such rules are problematic in that they increase firms' administrative costs, and they limit the degree to which an agreement increases trade among the parties. A recent literature has emerged that quantifies some of these effects of rules of origin.

One approach to studying these issues is to inspect the import data, and ask whether exporters are taking advantage of the preferential tariffs awarded in the PTA. If the process of establishing origin is costly, firms may choose not to do so, and to pay the most-favoured nation (MFN) tariff instead. Herin (1986) showed that around 21.5 per cent of EFTA imports from the EC, and 27.6 per cent of EC imports from EFTA paid non-preferential tariff rates.

Anson et al. (2005) calculate implied administrative costs for NAFTA rules of origin. They show that NAFTA utilization rates are well below 100 per cent on US imports from Mexico. For aggregate trade, on products for which there is a positive preference for NAFTA-qualifying imports, Anson et al. calculate a NAFTA utilization rate of 83 per cent. Utilization rates vary across sectors, and are low in some sectors (for example, textiles and apparel, leather goods) where NAFTA tariff preferences are high. Anson et al. combine information on utilization rates and tariff preferences to infer administrative costs. They estimate that the costs of meeting NAFTA ROOs are equivalent to a tariff of about 1.8 per cent. This amounts to about one-third of the preferential tariff margin that the US awards Mexican imports.

The proliferation of bilateral agreements signed by the US and the EU have produced a number of hub-and-spoke arrangements, with smaller countries entered into agreements with one or both of the larger partners. One way in which ROOs inhibit trade is that they preclude, for example, Mexico using Australian parts in products sold into the US, even though Australia and Mexico both have PTAs with the US. Faced with growing complaints from industry about the complexity of trading arrangements in Europe, the EU, EFTA, and several European countries agreed to allow 'diagonal cumulation' of ROOs across partners. This means that parts originating in a different 'spoke' of a hub-and-spoke arrangement would be able to enter under the preferential tariff.

Augier et al. (2005) argue that this change in cumulation rules in Europe is a useful natural experiment in which to evaluate the trade-reducing consequences of overlapping ROOs. The change in ROOs was not, in this case, accompanied by a change in tariffs, so that changes in the trade pattern might reasonably be linked to changes in ROOs alone. Augier et al. use a gravity framework to evaluate the impact of this rules change on intra-European trade.[15] Relatively faster spoke-to-spoke trade growth after diagonal cumulation is taken as evidence of a trade-restricting impact in the more restrictive rules. Augier et al. calculate a lower bound on the trade-restricting impact of rules of origin at 10 per cent, and an upper bound at 70 per cent.

QUANTIFIABLE EFFECTS OF POLICY COMMITMENTS OTHER THAN TARIFFS

One of the motivations for the recent spate of PTAs is the desire among many countries to undertake a more ambitious trade policy agenda. Developed country tariffs are now quite low, especially on the goods exported by other developed countries.[16] As a result, developed country trade ministries interested in removing hurdles to exporting have shifted their negotiating efforts away from tariff reduction and towards other measures. The effects of these measures can often be difficult to evaluate empirically, as – unlike tariffs and trade – neither the policy measure itself, nor the dependent variable of interest, is easily quantified. This section discusses some attempts to quantify impacts of policy changes other than tariffs.

Dispute Settlement and Administered Protection

One of Canada's primary concerns in negotiating a free trade agreement with the United States was to limit the arbitrary use of US administered protection laws. In negotiations for the CUSFTA, Canada proposed that the US and Canada eliminate anti-dumping (AD) and countervailing duty (CVD) actions against one another; the US rebuffed this suggestion. Instead, the two nations agreed to create a binational appellate panel to determine whether or not a country had made errors 'in fact or law' when reaching an AD/CVD decision. Similar language was included in NAFTA and Mexican law was also brought under the purview of a review panel.

Blonigen (2002) investigates the effects of review panels on two types of activity: the filing of AD/CVD petitions by parties in the US, and the number of affirmative decisions by US authorities. Blonigen shows that, after controlling for relatively large Mexican and Canadian shares of US imports, Mexico and Canada face relatively fewer AD/CVD actions. The calculations suggest that the two countries both experience approximately six fewer AD/CVD cases than would otherwise be expected.

Blonigen argues that the agreements could have affected US behaviour through two channels: AD/CVD activity could have increased because imports from Mexico and Canada grew after NAFTA; and/or the new appeals process could have reduced such AD/CVD activity. He finds relatively little evidence that either channel affects either measure of AD/CVD activity. Import penetration is not statistically significant in his regressions, meaning that one cannot conclude that increased imports from the NAFTA partners led to increased AD/CVD activity. His measures of panel activity appear not to affect either AD/CVD filings or affirmative determinations, with one exception.

Blonigen's empirical framework asks whether past action by the appellate panel affects either the number of filings by domestic parties in the US or affirmative determinations by US authorities. When only the previous year's activity is included in the regression, he finds no statistically significant effects between remands and either measure of AD/CVD activity. When cumulative remands are included as the independent variable, he finds generally the same pattern. The one exception is that the coefficient on the cumulative number of Canadian remands is negative and statistically significant for the affirmative determinations measure of AD/CVD activity. This is limited evidence that, in the case of Canada, the appellate panel has reduced the number of affirmative findings by US authorities. There is no such evidence for filings by US domestic petitioners.

Because the US steel industry is a frequent complainant in US administered protection hearings, Blonigen also considers the effect of the NAFTA review panels on AD/CVD activity by the steel industry. The estimates suggest that Canada and Mexico experience approximately 1.5 fewer AD/CVD cases than otherwise would be expected. As with aggregate trade, there is little evidence that NAFTA affects AD/CVD activity in the steel industry.

Blonigen concludes that the appellate panels have had relatively little impact. He argues that it would be better to pursue a broader agenda of incorporating anti-dumping and countervailing duty laws into competition policy. Because this is politically difficult, he argues that perhaps a better option would be to encourage safeguard actions as an alternative to AD/CVD cases.

Intellectual Property Rights

One of the more contentious trade policy issues in recent years has been the incorporation of commitments on intellectual property rights (IPRs) into trade agreements. The most visible and controversial of these commitments is the incorporation of an Agreement on Trade-Related Aspects of Intellectual Property Rights (TRIPS). PTAs now frequently include policy commitments in IPRs.

The inclusion of IPRs in such agreements has not yet afforded the opportunity of an investigation into the effects of specific PTA provisions on economic behaviour. There are, however, some studies that are informative about the effects of such agreements on technology transfer, investment in research and development, and income transfers between countries.

McCalman (2005) conducts a structural estimation of a dynamic model of innovation and growth. He fits the model to data on the stock of domestic and foreign patents in each country, an index measuring IP protection, other determinants of patenting behaviour (that is, distance between innovator and the country where the patent is registered). He then uses structural estimates to conduct a number of policy experiments.

McCalman first evaluates the net transfers from TRIPS under the assumption that TRIPS has no impact on the innovative activity. In this scenario, approximately half of the countries (including Australia) are net losers from TRIPS. The United States, Germany and France gain the most from the agreement, while India, Brazil and Canada lose the most.

In the second scenario, McCalman allows innovation to respond to the increased global value of patents. In this scenario, the central point estimates of the value of TRIPS to each country imply a net gain for all countries considered in the analysis.[17] While all countries are winners, the gains from TRIPS remain lopsided, with developed country innovators benefiting much more than poorer countries that are net payers of patent royalties.

In the final scenario, McCalman considers the effects of unilateral IPR reforms by each country in the sample. Approximately half of the countries show a net benefit from unilateral reform, while half show a net loss. The gains to most countries from unilateral reforms are considerably smaller than the gains from universal reform. This suggests that there are gains from coordinating IPR reforms.

Branstetter et al. (2004) conduct a somewhat different exercise. They consider the impact of IPR reforms around the world on the foreign patenting, technology transfer, and research and development activities of US multinationals. One reform episode they consider is China's IPR reforms of 1993. They find that, among firms that use patents intensively, IPR reforms have a significant and positive impact on patenting behaviour, royalty payments from affiliates (an indicator of technology transfer) and research and development spending by affiliates (such spending is often associated with technology transfer). There does not appear to be a similar increase in multinationals' arm's length licensing behaviour. Despite these reforms, multinationals prefer to keep their technologies within the firm.

Branstetter et al. also consider the effect of China's 1993 reforms alone. They find that the results from the broader sample do not generalize to China. US multinationals do not appear to have responded to Chinese reforms by increasing technology transfers. The authors argue that this is probably because Chinese enforcement of IPRs was still lacking, even after the reforms.

TRADE AGREEMENTS' ESTIMATED EFFECTS ON THE BROADER ECONOMY

This section reviews assessments of the effects of trade agreements on economic outcomes that matter: welfare, productivity and the distribution of income. Many econometric studies focus on the response of trade flows to trade policy changes, but increased trade volumes are not a meaningful end in themselves. Presumably the purpose of trade agreements is to improve economic well being, rather than simply increasing trade.

The difficulty in such assessments is that trade policy is only one of many variables that bear upon the variables we care most about. While the effect of trade policy on trade might well be observable, it is much harder to tease out effects on other variables that are only indirectly affected by trade policy. The challenge in such assessments is to avoid the *post hoc ergo propter hoc* fallacy (if an event follows A it is therefore caused by A) in making these assessments. USITC (2003) notes, for example, that some economic changes that are frequently attributed to trade agreements in the

US political debate might also be plausibly attributed to increased trade with developing countries such as India and China. This review considers only those studies that isolate the effect of specific policy changes on the variables of interest.

Welfare

The most important variable to consider in assessing trade agreements is economic welfare. But, as welfare is unobservable, assessments of welfare are also tenuous. What is typically required is a theoretical model that allows estimated changes on import prices (and/or) quantities to be translated into welfare changes. The first section above reviewed Romalis (2005), who uses models of supply and demand at the detailed product level to make inferences about the welfare consequences of tariff changes in CUSFTA and NAFTA. As noted above, he finds no welfare changes for the US and Canada in NAFTA. Mexico's estimated welfare change is −0.3 per cent of GDP, though Romalis is quick to point out that his partial equilibrium framework may miss some important aspects of welfare change.

Most welfare assessments of trade agreements are calculated ex ante in simulation analysis of applied general equilibrium (AGE) models. In its assessment of the effects of five trade agreements on the United States, USITC (2003) conducted an ex post simulation analysis in which the tariff cuts from each agreement were reimposed on the 2001 model of the US economy.[18] The estimated welfare changes from those simulations suggested that US welfare in 2001 was approximately 0.6 per cent higher than it would have been in the absence of tariff cuts embodied in these agreements.[19]

As with other AGE models, the estimates of welfare changes in these simulations are dependent on the model structure, and on the parameterization of that structure. The value of these particular simulations is that they consider the effects of five separate agreements using the same model and parameterization, allowing a transparent comparison of the relative effects of the agreements. Figure 2.3 shows the estimated welfare effects from removing each of the five agreements (that is, putting the tariffs back in place) in 2001.

These simulations are most useful in demonstrating the relative sizes of the economic impacts of the PTAs, relative to each other and relative to multilateral agreements. NAFTA and CUSFTA were significant agreements for the United States; large preferential tariff cuts were awarded to two of the US's largest trading partners. Nonetheless, these agreements appear to be substantially less significant, in terms of welfare, than multilateral rounds. The simulated gains from the Uruguay and Tokyo rounds

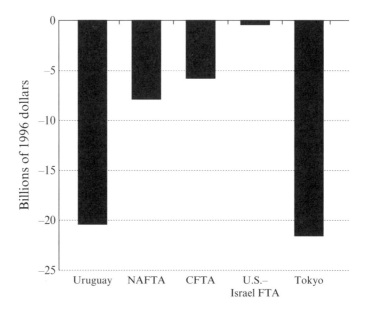

Source: USITC (2003).

*Figure 2.3   USITC ex post estimates of welfare changes in five trade
agreements*

were approximately three times as large as either of the two preferential
arrangements.

Another lesson to take from Figure 2.3 is the very small gains estimated
from the US–Israel FTA. In recent years, the US has negotiated a number
of PTAs with countries that trade even less with the US than does Israel
(for example, Bahrain, Jordan, Morocco). As these figures make clear, the
economic gains to the United States from such agreements are quite small.
These estimates help to emphasize a point discussed below, that countries
like the US frequently negotiate PTAs in which economic benefits to the
US are a secondary consideration.

Productivity

Welfare estimates like those of Romalis (2005) and USITC (2003) may
understate the gains from trade liberalization if trade liberalization
increases productivity. One motivation for Canada negotiating a PTA
with the United States was the hope that Canadian firms would be able
to increase productivity by increasing production scale. In light of this

argument, a question of interest in the empirical literature has been whether, ex post, Canadian productivity can be shown to be higher because of the agreement.

Trefler (2004) studies plant-level productivity and employment in Canadian manufacturing over a 16-year period centred around CUSFTA. He estimates separate impacts of both Canadian and US tariff changes, and combines these estimates to consider effects of the agreement on employment and labour productivity. He finds that CUSFTA reduced manufacturing employment by 5 per cent, though this number masks significant differences. Exporting industries increased employment and import-competing industries reduced employment. Given plant level output and employment levels, Trefler is able to identify effects on productivity. He finds large productivity increases in import-competing industries (where employment is falling). It appears that this productivity shift happens in large part because the least productive Canadian firms decrease their share of domestic production. On the export side, Trefler finds that CUSFTA increases productivity at the plant level; industry-level productivity is lower because less productive new firms entered the export-intensive industries.

While Bernard et al. (2006) are not looking at specific agreements, but rather changes in trade costs, their results are broadly consistent with Trefler's. Those US industries that experience the largest reductions in international trade costs experience the largest increases in productivity. It appears that the productivity change occurs in large part through the exit of less productive firms.

PTAs AND THE BROADER POLICY AGENDA

A notable contributor to worldwide growth in the number of PTAs has been the United States. Recent US bilateral arrangements would seem difficult to justify on economic grounds alone. The trading partners are distant from the US, scattered around the globe, and are generally not large US trading partners. Instead, the US trade negotiators appear to be pursuing a number of non-economic objectives such as cooperation in military matters and in drug interdiction. The US Trade Representative also argues that the negotiations are motivated by a strategy of 'competitive liberalization'. The idea is that US participation in bilateral arrangements will push forward negotiations in multilateral fora.

What recent experience with the US makes clear is that countries do not necessarily choose PTA partners with an eye toward maximizing economic welfare in the short run. In some cases, trade ministries are pursuing non-economic objectives. In others, they might be choosing partners in a manner devised to affect the negotiating environment in another forum. In any case, standard simulation analyses and measures of economic welfare do not accurately identify the full impact of the agreement.

Whalley (1996) asks the question 'Why do countries seek regional trade agreements?' Whalley notes a number of explanations for regional agreements. In addition to standard gains from trade liberalization, countries may seek (a) to strengthen domestic policy reforms by making binding international commitments, (b) to affect trade negotiations in other fora, (c) to ensure access to markets that might serve as a safe haven in a multilateral crisis, and (d) to encourage cooperation on non-economic objectives.

Two recent empirical papers consider objectives of this sort. The first paper, by Ferrantino (2006), looks at the issue of PTAs as possible anchors for domestic policy reforms, especially in developing countries. The second, by Limao (2005), considers a theoretical model of the implications of PTAs on multilateral negotiations, when non-economic objectives are taken into consideration in PTA negotiations. The implications of the theoretical model – that PTAs can undermine multilateral progress when they are negotiated with non-economic objectives in mind – are validated in the data.

Policy Anchors

Ferrantino (2006) considers the possibility that recent trade negotiations have improved governance in developing countries. One of Mexico's motivations for signing the NAFTA was to anchor the reform programme it had put in place over the previous decade. Ferrantino considers developing country partners of the US and developing countries seeking to join the WTO. He asks whether participating in negotiations has improved these countries' measures of governance. Ferrantino uses quality of governance measures taken from the Heritage Foundation's Index of Economic Freedom, and the World Bank's Governance Matters indicators.

Ferrantino notes that PTA partners of the US score better on these measures than recent applicants to join the WTO. He also notes that US PTA negotiations are considerably shorter than WTO working parties. The median US PTA negotiation takes only 2.5 years, while the median length of WTO working party negotiations is 6.8 years. This much shorter period may reflect an ability of one-on-one negotiations to deal with country specific peculiarities more quickly.

Ferrantino finds relatively little evidence that governance systematically improves, either through negotiating a PTA with the US, or through accession to the WTO. There are anecdotes of such success stories, including Mexico with NAFTA and China with the WTO.[20] However it does not appear that such negotiations can be said to improve governance as a matter of course. In fact, several measures of governance worsen across the period of negotiation. Ferrantino emphasizes that one should not jump too quickly to attribute causation to this result. It may be that a deteriorating policy environment motivated governments to enter into negotiations.

Non-economic Objectives

Whalley argues that countries may choose to enter into PTAs in order to get cooperation from their PTA partners on other issues. Limao (2005) notes that tariff preferences given on such a basis will imply a concern about preference erosion in subsequent negotiations. Reducing the trade preference by reducing the multilateral tariff in the next round may reduce the level of cooperation on the non-economic issues.

Limao (2005) investigates US tariff cuts in the Uruguay Round. He finds that US tariff cuts are systematically smaller on goods that it trades with PTA partners. Limao and Karacaovali (2005) find similar results in European Union data. This suggests that PTA preferences are reducing the degree of liberalization that large countries such as the EU and the US conduct via multilateral liberalization.

LESSONS FROM THE LITERATURE AND IMPLICATIONS FOR POLICY

A number of the studies reviewed in this chapter strengthen the argument that governments should not pursue preferential agreements if they come at the expense of progress on a multilateral agenda. Preferential agreements add complexity to the legal environment firms face. They further the need for rules of origin, which have been shown to inhibit and distort trade patterns. Preferential agreements cause harm to excluded countries. Policy commitments within the broader policy agenda, such as intellectual property or investment, are likely to be more effective when made on a multilateral basis.

Despite the limitations of PTAs, it is clear that preferential agreements will remain an important part of the policy environment. Given the evidence of harm to excluded countries, it is difficult to argue that individual governments should sit on the sidelines while other countries continue to negotiate preferential agreements. Governments might well wonder how best to engage a policy environment in which PTAs are an inescapable reality. While the broadening trade policy agenda and the rapidly changing policy environment make it difficult to be overly specific, a few broad lessons from the literature suggest themselves.

A key issue is likely to be the choice of partner countries. The welfare estimates in USITC (2003) suggest that a country is likely to do best by negotiating PTAs with its largest trading partners. In order to minimize damages from trade diversion, and from distortions associated with rules of origin, regional agreements containing multiple countries are the best alternative to unilateral/multilateral reforms. Overlapping bilateral agreements are best avoided, because they add to the policy complexity that firms face, and they compound the harm from distorting rules of origin.

Second, governments should seek to harmonize policy commitments across past, current and future PTAs. Reducing policy complexity faced by trading firms is a key point. For example, consistent rules of origin across agreements, cumulated wherever possible, can mitigate one important harm caused by proliferating PTAs.

A third lesson is that unilateral reforms should accompany preferential liberalization, in order to minimize the harm from preferential commitments. While multilateral institutions no longer enforce the most-favoured nation principle, governments are still free to employ it. In most areas of trade policy it remains the best policy.

Fourth, evidence from Canada suggests that an important source of gains from trade liberalization is productivity improvements associated with reduced market share for the least productive plants. In practice, a sizable portion of productivity growth occurs as weak firms exit; several studies have linked exits of weak plants to changes in trade policy. While governments should not encourage the exit of weak plants, neither should they protect them. It is likely that a policy aimed at reducing peak tariffs in PTA negotiations would go a long way toward forcing the least productive plants to either become more competitive or exit. A policy of peak tariff reductions would be best if phased in and accompanied by a safety net for displaced workers. In order to avoid trade diversions associated with reducing peak tariffs, it would be best if the preferential tariff reductions were accompanied by reductions in the MFN tariff.

A fifth lesson is that governments should not rely on PTAs, or any trade agreement for that matter, as anchors for domestic reforms. Ferrantino (2006) finds no apparent relationship between participation in trade negotiations and improvement in measures of governance. Some measures of governance deteriorate in the wake of trade negotiations. This may mean that governments are trying to anchor policy reforms with trade negotiations, and failing.

Sixth, Whalley (1996) suggests that one reason small countries enter preferential agreements is to guarantee access to large markets. For countries with this objective, the design of the trade agreement is likely to be a key issue. The estimates in Blonigen (2002) suggest NAFTA as a cautionary tale. The agreement included provisions that Canada intended as disciplines on certain contingent protection measures by the US. It does not appear that these disciplines were successful in substantially reducing the contingent protection claims against Canadian exports. More aggressive disciplines on these claims, like the outright prohibition on them written into Australia and New Zealand's Closer Economic Relations agreement, would likely be more successful. The difficulty, of course, is convincing a larger partner that such disciplines are mutually advantageous.

A final lesson from this review is that both the proliferation of preferential trade agreements and their broadening policy scope make it substantially more difficult for economists to quantify the economic impacts of the agreements. These areas of added uncertainty put a greater burden on policy makers' judgement, for estimates from applied general equilibrium models are becoming substantially more difficult to defend as prima facie estimates of the agreements' impact. Trade diversion versus trade creation is no longer the most important issue; Bhagwati and Panagariya's (1996) 'spaghetti bowl' of overlapping agreements is already upon us. While individual agreements may be amenable to quantitative assessment, the costs of systemic complexity associated with PTA proliferation are much harder to quantify. The costs and benefits of policy commitments in non-traditional areas such as services liberalization and investment guarantees are also exceptionally difficult to quantify in a credible fashion. Policy makers are increasingly adding non-economic objectives to the mix, and questions about the efficacy of PTAs for achieving these goals are also typically beyond the scope of applied economic theory. In short, the new environment puts an increasing burden on policy makers' judgement.

NOTES

1. Prepared for the Australia–China FTA Conference in Shenzhen, China; 28-29 June 2006. I would like to thank Witada Anukoonwattaka for valuable research assistance. Michael Ferrantino and Richard Pomfret provided helpful comments on earlier drafts.
2. The data represented in the figure only include two-way trade agreements. Accessions to existing agreements and one-way preferential programmes are also notified to the WTO, but not included in these counts. In the context of a larger review on the extent of regionalism, Pomfret (2007) argues against agreement counts as a means of quantifying this phenomenon. Many of the WTO notifications involve agreements among 'new' nation-states that were once part of larger states such as the USSR or Yugoslavia. Twenty-three of the goods trade agreements included in the figure are among states that were once members of a single state. In addition, goods and services agreements between the European Community and Bulgaria and Romania, respectively, have been superseded by the latter two countries' accession to the European Union.

3. This evidence is consistent with studies of the growing sophistication of Chinese exports. Rodrik (2006) and Schott (2006) both note that the Chinese export bundle looks increasingly similar to the export bundles of more developed countries.
4. The drawback of PTAs in this context is that they add legal complexity to international trade, on top of increasing goods complexity. It is far from obvious that the added costs of dealing with additional legal complexity necessarily compensates for better legal treatment.
5. A very common specification employing dummy variables in this manner is the empirical gravity model, which uses country sizes and bilateral distances as predictors of baseline trade. Greenaway and Milner (2002) review the literature applying the gravity model to analysis of PTAs. Baldwin and Taglioni (2006) offer a critical review of the empirical gravity literature.
6. Ghosh and Yamarik (2004, p. 72).
7. Romalis's data are at the HS 6-digit level of commodity detail.
8. These estimates differ slightly, depending on the exporter being considered. See Romalis (2005, Table 3) for more details.
9. Romalis argues that Clausing's technique treats strong growth in imports from developing countries like China as evidence against trade diversion. If Canadian import growth from these countries is attributed to other factors, as it probably should be, then Clausing's technique will miss evidence of trade diversion.
10. Romalis is quick to point out that his partial equilibrium model misses a number of possible channels of positive welfare change that might follow from such an agreement. Nonetheless, the evidence of trade diversion is troubling. Romalis argues that 'too much tariff revenue is being forgone for too small a reduction in the price index'.
11. See Chapter 6.
12. Prior to NAFTA, some Mexican imports had preferential access to the US market under the Generalized System of Preferences, which was targeted at developing countries. Certain production-sharing arrangements also allowed preferences on Mexican imports.
13. Ardelean and Lugovskyy (2007) point out that these estimates assume limited substitutability between domestic and imported varieties, a feature that will tend to exaggerate the welfare gains from additional import varieties. In a large, developed country like the United States, one might plausibly assume that reasonably close substitutes for many foreign varieties exist. If so, Broda and Weinstein's estimates would overstate the welfare gains from increased product variety.
14. For example, China's existing agreement with Chile or ASEAN might well have negative impacts on Australian export prices. These negative effects can be mitigated if Australia also signs an agreement with China.
15. This approach is sensible in this setting. However, as a dummy variable and gravity model treatment, it has some of the same weaknesses discussed above. Estimates that exploit more disaggregated data are probably warranted in future work.
16. See Gresser (2002) for anecdotal evidence that remaining US tariffs affect developing country exports more than developed country exports. For example, in 2001 the *ad valorem* equivalent of US duties collected on exports from France was 1.1 per cent; on exports from Bangladesh 14.1 per cent.
17. The 95 per cent confidence interval suggests the possibility that India may lose, even in this scenario.
18. Like the *ex ante* evaluations, this is a comparative static exercise. It has no particular advantage in being conducted after the fact.
19. One might wonder about the differences between welfare measures in this study and that of Romalis. The USITC model is working with substantially more aggregated data than the Romalis study, and so may understate the distortionary effects of large tariff preferences at the level of more disaggregated commodities. The advantage of the USITC approach is that the general equilibrium treatment of the problem allows interactions among sectors in the economy.

20. European Union agreements with various countries in Eastern Europe offer other examples of plausibly successful policy anchors.

REFERENCES

Aitken, N. (1973), 'The effect of the EEC and EFTA on European trade: a temporal cross-section analysis', *American Economic Review*, **63**, 881–92.

Anson, J., O. Cadot, A. Estevedeordal, J. de Melo, A. Suwa-Eisenmann and B. Tumurchudur (2005), 'Rules of origin in North–South preferential trading arrangements with an application to NAFTA', *Review of International Economics*, **13**, 501–17.

Ardelean, Adina and Volodymyr Lugovskyy (2007), 'When are variety gains from trade important? Domestic productivity and the cost of protectionism', mimeo, Purdue University.

Augier, P., M. Gasiorek and C. Lai-Tong (2005), 'Rules of origin', *Economic Policy*, **43**, 567–624.

Baldwin, Richard and Daria Taglioni (2006), 'Gravity for dummies and dummies for gravity equations', National Bureau for Economic Research working paper no.12516.

Bernard, A.J., B. Jensen and P. Schott (2006), 'Trade costs, firms, and productivity', *Journal of Monetary Economics*, **53**, 917–37.

Bhagwati, Jagdish and Arvind Panagariya (1996), 'Preferential trading areas and multilateralism. Strangers, friends, or foes?', in Jagdish Bhagwati and Arvind Panagariya (eds), *The Economics of Preferential Trade Agreements*, Washington, DC: American Enterprise Institute.

Blonigen, Bruce (2002), 'The effects of CUSFTA and NAFTA on antidumping and countervailing duty activity', mimeo, University of Oregon.

Branstetter, Lee, Raymond Fisman and C. Fritz Foley (2004), 'Do stronger intellectual property rights increase international technology transfer? Empirical evidence from U.S. firm-level panel data', World Bank Policy Research working paper no. 3305.

Broda, Christian and David Weinstein (2004), 'Globalization and the gains from variety', Federal Reserve Bank of New York Staff Report no. 180.

Brown, D. (1987), 'Tariffs, the terms of trade and national product differentiation', *Journal of Policy Modeling*, **9**, 503–26.

Chang, W. and A. Winters (2002), 'How regional blocs affect excluded countries: the price effects of MERCOSUR', *American Economic Review*, **92**, 889–904.

Clausing, K. (2001), 'Trade creation and trade diversion in the Canada–United States Free Trade Agreement', *Canadian Journal of Economics*, **34**, 677–96.

Debaere, Peter and Shalah Mostashari (2006), 'Do tariffs matter for the extensive margin of international trade? An empirical analysis', mimeo, University of Texas.

Feenstra, Robert C., Robert E. Lipsey, Haiyan Deng, Alyson C. Ma and Hengyong Mo (2004), 'World trade flows: 1962–2000', National Bureau for Economic Research working paper no. 11040.

Ferrantino, Michael (2006), 'Policy anchors: do free trade agreements and WTO accessions serve as vehicles for developing-country policy reform?', US International Trade Commission working paper no. 2006-04-A.

Ghosh, S. and S. Yamarik (2004), 'Are regional trading arrangements trade creating? An application of extreme bounds analysis', *Journal of International Economics*, **63**, 369–95.

Greenaway, D. and C. Milner (2002), 'Regionalism and gravity', *Scottish Journal of Political Economy*, **49**, 574–85.

Gresser, E. (2002), 'Toughest on the poor', *Foreign Affairs*, **81**, 9–14.

Herin, J. (1986), 'Rules of origin and differences between tariff levels in EFTA and the EC', European Free Trade Association occasional paper no. 13.

Hillberry, Russell and Christine McDaniel (2002), 'A decomposition of North American trade growth since NAFTA', US International Trade Commission working paper no. 02-12-A.

Hummels, D. and P. Klenow (2005), 'The variety and quality of a nation's exports', *American Economic Review*, **95**, 704–23.

Kehoe, Timothy and Kim Ruhl (2003), 'How important is the new goods margin in international trade?', Federal Reserve Bank of Minneapolis staff report no. 324.

Limao, Nuno (2005), 'Preferential trade agreements as stumbling blocks for multilateral trade liberalization: Evidence for the U.S.', Centre for Economic Policy Research working paper no. 4884.

Limao, Nuno and Baybars Karacaovali (2005), 'The clash of liberalizations: preferential vs. multilateral trade liberalization in the European Union', World Bank Policy Research working paper no. 3493.

McCalman, P. (2005), 'Who enjoys "TRIPs" abroad? An empirical analysis of intellectual property rights in the Uruguay Round', *Canadian Journal of Economics*, **38**, 574–603.

Pomfret, R. (2007), 'Is regionalism an increasing feature of the world economy?', *World Economy*, **30**, 923–47.

Rauch, J. (1999), 'Networks vs markets in international trade', *Journal of International Economics*, **48**, 7–35.

Rodrik, Dani (2006), 'What's so special about China's exports?', National Bureau for Economic Research working paper no. 11947.

Romalis, John (2005), 'NAFTA's and CUSFTA's impact on international trade', National Bureau for Economic Research working paper no. 11059.

Schott, Peter (2006), 'The relative sophistication of Chinese exports', National Bureau for Economic Research working paper no. 12173.

Trefler, D. (2004), 'The long and the short of the U.S.–Canada Free Trade Agreement', *American Economic Review*, **94**, 870–95.

US International Trade Commission (USITC) (2003), 'The impact of trade agreements: effect of the Tokyo Round, U.S.–Israel FTA, U.S.–Canada FTA, NAFTA, and the Uruguay Round on the U.S. economy', publication no. 3621.

Whalley, John (1996), 'Why do countries seek regional trade agreements?', National Bureau for Economic Research working paper no. 5552.

3. Multilateralism and FTAs: a Chinese perspective on an Australia–China FTA

Dashu Wang

INTRODUCTION

The World Trade Organization (WTO) reports that as of the end of 2005, there existed 300 regional trading agreements between WTO members, up from 130 at the end of 1994. There have been many excellent surveys of regional economic integration in Asia (e.g. Kawai 2005, Naya 2002, Asian Development Bank 2002). Nevertheless, it is much harder to find a good synthesis of the broader literature, in part because the literature is evolving so rapidly in response to the radical developments the world has seen in the past years.

The main issues involved in the multilateralization of free trade agreements (FTAs) turn on rules of origin, rules of cumulation and the economic spillovers on third nations. These are immensely complex and involve a very subtle economic and legal logic (Baldwin 2006). A related point was underscored analytically in Wonnecott and Wonnecott (1981) in terms of tariff liberalization. Bilateral liberalization is an attempt to achieve deeper integration with their trading partners on a formal basis, going beyond reductions in border restrictions. Early advocates of a purely non-discriminatory approach to tariff liberalization maintained that such a strategy was always superior to a regional approach. Lloyd (2002) argues that bilateralism/ FTA will likely lead toward, not impede, multilateralism, while Brown et al. (2003) believe in the superiority of multilateralism. Baldwin (2006) suggests that, while rules of origin for FTAs in some sensitive sectors are political landmines, it would seem possible to develop global standards for preferential rules of origin in less sensitive sectors. Every country has the ability to liberalize its commercial policy regime unilaterally, and if this is done on a non-discriminatory basis there will be only trade creation and no trade diversion. Hence, unilateral trade liberalization 'dominates' FTAs and customs unions as the latter generate trade diversion as well as trade creation. Wonnecott and Wonnecott (1981) pointed out that these 'unilateralists' missed the obvious point that countries engage in regional trade negotiations in order to open up the market of their partner(s), rather than merely to extract gains through greater domestic liberalization. Thus, while trade diversion is eliminated under a non-discriminatory approach, the fact that foreign markets are left untouched without negotiation would suggest that the welfare gains would be limited. An FTA could be superior to unilateral liberalization if the gains in terms of increased national welfare due to foreign reductions in tariff barriers were greater than the losses due to trade diversion (Plummer 2006).

Chinese experts have also contributed in the area of FTA research. For example, Fang Hua (2005) suggests that it is the existence of countries and transaction costs that leads to the formation of FTAs. Teng Ying (2004) states that the advantages of FTAs are as follows: (1) there are fewer obstacles to the establishment of FTAs; (2) FTAs encourage competition and adjustment of industrial structure; (3) FTAs can advance multilateral negotiations under the WTO framework.

China has experienced rapid economic and trade growth over the past two decades or so. From 1979 to 2000, the average annual growth rate of China's GDP reached 9.5 per cent, and during the same period its average annual growth rate of total trade was 17 per cent. Both growth rates were considerably higher than the world average economic and trade growth over the same period. China's accession to the WTO in 2001 has given China another impetus to its external trade. In 2003, China's foreign trade reached 851.2 billion US dollars, an increase of 37.1 per cent from 2002, which was the first year of China's membership of the WTO. On that year, with the total imports reaching 412.8 billion US dollars, China surpassed Japan to become the largest import market in Asia, contributing to about 10 per cent of the growth of world trade. With its external trade surpassing 1000 billion US dollars in 2004, China exceeded Japan and became the world's third largest trading nation after the United States and Germany. In fact, the expansion of trade has become the engine of economic growth and development in China.

At the November 2000 China–ASEAN Summit, the Chinese then prime minister, Mr Zhu Rongji suggested an FTA between China and ASEAN. The idea, which came as a surprise, led to the 2003 ASEAN–China Free Trade Agreement (ACFTA), which is scheduled to eliminate tariffs on almost all bilateral trade between China and the ASEANs by the year 2010.

In addition to the ACFTA, China established an FTA with Chile, and the China–Pakistan FTA was signed. As far as China's FTAs are concerned, there are some key features. First, China's FTA partners are small economies. An FTA with a small economy does not have a significant effect on domestic industries. It is easy for negotiators to take a flexible strategy because they are not under heavy pressures. Second, China's FTA trade involved mainly goods; services are excluded. Because Chinese service industries are more advanced than theirs, the developing countries in Asia are protectionist and reluctant to open up the service sector. In fact, China's FTA with ASEAN and Pakistan are only in the areas of trade in goods; the liberalization in services and investment is still under negotiation. Third, the FTA partners' resources complement China's, for example, woods in the ASEAN and copper in Chile. This reflects China's strategy for FTAs: to relieve the shortage in resource supply in the process of rapid economic growth.

MULTILATERALISM AND THE WTO

Global governance in a rapidly integrating world economy has become increasingly important, as policies can have large and immediate detrimental effects on trade. There is a growing need for more formal institutional mechanisms for trade and investment facilitation, harmonization of rules, standards and procedures, and dispute settlement. Because there is no central authority in international relations, political scientists have developed the concept of a regime, defined as sets of principles, norms, rules and decision-making procedures around which actors' expectations converge in a given area of international relations (Krasner 1983). Although the institutional mechanisms and regimes are arrangements motivated by self-interest, they reflect patterns of cooperation among members based on shared interests. As a major building block of the multilateral trade regime, the WTO establishes the system of rules and disciplines and allows the system to be enforced more rigorously than in the past by the use of impartial judgement from an independent third party as a mechanism for solving disputes.

The WTO contains a set of specific legal obligations regulating the trade policies of member countries. It embodies a rule-oriented approach to multilateral cooperation. Indeed, this approach focuses not on results or outcomes, but on the rules of the game, and involves agreements on the level of trade barriers that are permitted as well as attempts to establish the general conditions of competition facing foreign producers in export markets.

Some viewpoints are important to understand the role of the WTO. The first is to see the institute as a code of conduct; the second is to regard it as a market. The WTO is probably the only international organization that is well-placed to help tame the tangle of free trade deals at the global level; it is probably the only international organization that has a clear incentive to do so (Baldwin 2006).

These days, nations find it useful to switch from special deals to a non-discriminatory lowering of the applied most-favoured nation (MFN) tariff. Some East Asian countries have always had low tariffs and some still have high tariffs (India and Vietnam), but the major East Asian developing nations cut tariffs unilaterally in an impressive way in the last 15 years, especially in the 1990s (Baldwin 2006). This implication of the juggernaut effect, that small nations are now seeking global networks of FTAs, has made the three classic trade blocs, the Big-3 – Europe, North American and East Asia – into what might be called fuzzy, leaky trade blocs (Baldwin 2006); 'fuzzy' since the proliferation of bilateral agreements among countries which previously had preferential links with only one of the major blocs make it difficult to determine the boundaries of the Big-3, and 'leaky' because some countries have FTAs with more than one of the Big-3 trade blocs.

Prior to accession to the WTO, China had one of the highest rates of protection in the world. For example, tariffs averaged over 40 per cent in 1992 and were complemented by an array of non-tariff measures such as quotas, licences and state trading (Ianchovichina and Martin 2004). Afterwards, China undertook a liberalization of trade in the course of its accession to the WTO, and this generated substantial welfare gains. Earlier analyses of the potential for multilateral reform have typically identified China as a major gainer from the reform (Ianchovichina and Martin 2004). In fact, these gains were a consequence of China's high initial levels of protection and of the relatively high barriers facing China in some product areas. However, a World Bank analysis by Anderson, Martin and van der Mensbrugghe (2005) finds China's potential gains to be relatively modest. Still, as pointed out by Zhai (2006), these gains are larger than anything potentially available from participation in Asian regional arrangements because only multilateral reforms can liberalize barriers against China's largest export flows to developed countries such as the United States and the European Union.

One of the WTO's great assets is its role as a convenor (Baldwin 2006). Among other things, one of China's strategic goals in joining the WTO was to provide a neutral forum for the resolution of the trade disputes that are inevitable given the rapidity of China's expansion as a trading power, and to ensure a predictable trading environment and thus a more viable business environment. China's accession commitments to the WTO involved substantial reductions in tariffs in virtually all areas as well as reductions in non-tariff barriers.

TRADE BETWEEN CHINA AND AUSTRALIA

From the mid 1980s Australia undertook a major redirection of economic policy – from protection of domestic industries and regulated financial structure to a position of lower protection and more openness – in an attempt to improve competitiveness and export performance. Australia diversified its external trade in the late 1990s, lowering the relative importance of Japanese markets for many key commodity exports, though Japan remains a very important customer.

Table 3.1 shows fundamental shifts in the direction of Australian exports. Since 1991–2, the US, EU and Japan have bought less than half of Australia's exports. There are many medium-sized buyers sucfh as South Korea, Hong Kong, Taiwan and China, and Australia's exports face increasing competition in the market, which generates many changes. Australian exports have improved their penetration of Asian markets, to the extent that about 60 per cent of current exports are destined for East Asia. More importantly, while all the shares of exports are steady or declining, the exports to China are dramatically increasing, from 2.8 per cent in 1988–9 to 11.9 per cent in 2005–6.

Table 3.2 shows that the shares of imports from the US, Japan and EU have declined. Australia has imported more goods from Asia, China in particular is the largest import source, and its share has increased from 2.4 per cent in 1989–90 to 13.8 per cent in 2005–6.

Table 3.1   Merchandise export shares by selected countries

Period	EU	US	Japan	NZ	S Korea	HK	Taiwan	China	ASEAN
1988–9	13.9	10.2	27.1	5.1	5.0	4.3	3.6	2.8	8.8
1989–90	14.0	11.1	26.0	5.3	5.5	2.7	3.7	2.4	10.4
1990–1	12.6	11.0	27.4	4.9	6.2	3.0	3.7	2.6	12.2
1991–2	13.0	9.5	26.5	5.1	6.1	3.8	4.6	2.7	13.3
1992–3	12.1	8.1	25.1	5.5	6.5	4.3	4.4	3.7	14.5
1993–4	11.8	7.9	24.7	6.2	7.3	4.3	4.3	4.0	14.0
1994–5	11.2	6.9	24.3	7.1	7.8	3.9	4.6	4.4	15.6
1995–6	11.1	6.1	21.6	7.4	8.7	4.0	4.5	5.0	15.4
1996–7	10.4	7.0	19.5	7.9	9.0	3.9	4.6	4.5	15.5
1997–8	11.7	8.8	20.0	6.4	7.3	4.7	4.8	4.4	13.1
2003–4	11.9	8.7	18.2	7.4	7.8	2.5	3.4	9.1	11.3
2004–5	10.9	7.5	19.7	7.2	7.7	2.1	3.9	10.3	11.8
2005–6	12.2	6.4	20.4	5.7	7.7	1.9	3.9	11.9	11.1

Sources: ABS (various issues).

Table 3.2   Merchandise import shares by selected countries

Period	UK	US	Japan	NZ	S Korea	HK	Taiwan	China	ASEAN
1989–90	6.5	24.1	19.2	4.2	2.4	1.6	3.8	2.4	5.8
1990–1	6.7	23.5	18.1	4.4	2.6	1.5	3.6	3.1	7.1
1991–2	6.1	23.0	18.2	4.7	2.4	1.6	3.9	3.9	8.1
1992–3	5.7	21.8	18.7	4.7	2.8	1.3	3.7	4.3	8.4
1993–4	5.7	21.7	18.1	5.0	2.9	1.2	3.7	4.8	8.2
1994–5	5.9	21.5	17.1	4.8	2.7	1.2	3.4	4.9	8.6
1995–6	6.3	22.6	13.9	4.6	2.9	1.2	3.3	5.2	9.5
1996–7	6.6	22.3	13.0	4.7	3.2	1.1	3.2	5.3	10.5
1997–8	6.2	21.9	14.0	4.1	4.1	1.1	3.1	5.8	11.6
2003–4	4.2	15.2	12.3	3.9	3.7	0.9	2.6	11.7	15.7
2004–5	4.0	14.2	11.5	3.6	3.3	0.8	2.4	13.3	16.8
2005–6	3.6	13.6	10.3	3.3	3.9	1.0	2.3	13.8	19.9

Sources: ABS (various issues).

Over the past decades, the Australian economy has gone through the most dramatic globalization in its history. Australia has substantially broadened its trade profile and export base. Financial deregulation, the removal of controls over capital flow, the floating of the Australian dollar, and reductions in industry protection and assistance have increased Australia's vulnerability to the fluctuations of the world economy, forced all sectors of the economy to become more internationally competitive and dynamic. It is assumed that Australian's comparative advantage in agricultural and mineral production can be maximized by ensuring that Asia's markets are open to it.

According to the statistics from the Ministry of Commerce, China (2006), the two-way trade volume between China and Australia surged to 34.6 billion US dollars in 2006, pushing the trade to the highest level in history. Exports from Australia to China were valued at 15.4 billion US dollars, and China became the second largest exporting market; imports from China were valued at 19.2 billion US dollars, with China the largest import source. Currently China is the second largest trade partner for Australia, and in the foreseeable future will become the first. An FTA between China and Australia is highly desirable in promoting trade.

AN FTA BETWEEN AUSTRALIA AND CHINA

It is accepted that as a code of conduct for trade policy, the WTO involves four principles: non-discrimination, reciprocity, market access and fair competition. It should be noted, however, that these principles are not always consistent with – or complementary to – each other. For example, there is a tension between non-discrimination and reciprocity on the one hand, and between market access and the notion of fair competition on the other. In fact, foreign trade sometimes, if not often, involves preferential treatment to specific countries. The MFNs can be regarded as an example. Indeed, preferential trading arrangements, such as FTAs and customs unions, are by their very nature discriminatory (Plummer 2006). The principle of reciprocity is based on a balance of rights and obligations, achieved through the reciprocal exchange of market-access commitments. In practice, a balanced exchange of concessions is necessary for agreement to be possible. Usually the concessions that are offered would benefit the nations involved even if implemented unilaterally. Thus, trade liberalization occurs on a quid pro quo basis. In fact, by requiring reciprocity, nations attempt to minimize free-riding, and are generally successful in doing so.

The WTO is a major building block of the multilateral trade regime, and it allows the system of rules and disciplines to be enforced more rigorously than in the past. However, it should be noted that the mechanism of the WTO is more effective for global and general questions. There are many individual or specific issues which cannot be governed by a universal rule and discipline. In this area, FTAs can play an important role. Although a proposal for a China–Australia FTA is quite new, in China it has received much attention, from perspectives of complementarity, consumer surplus, economies of scale and politics.

Complementarity

An element in the trade relationship is the elevated importance of both countries in the eyes of the other and a better appreciation of the benefits of partnership. This can never be a partnership of equals given the obvious disparities in population, strategic weight and economic muscle. But there is a far greater appreciation in China and Australia of their natural economic complementarities. It is well known that Australia is a fortunate country. Casual observation suggests, among other things, that Australia has a relative abundance of land, energy, mineral deposits, highly educated labour, natural beauty and fine weather.

Complementarity can be generated from diversity and heterogeneity in economic, financial and social development between trading partners in areas such as per capita incomes, industrial and financial structures, trade openness and patterns, scope and extent of exchange and capital controls, institutional and human capacities, and various social conditions. For example, Terada (2003) argues that diversity of membership enhances the

Table 3.3   Top ten exports from Australia to China (2006)

	US$ million	%
Iron ore and concentrated iron ore	5 797.0	37.6
Uncombed wool	1 039.0	6.7
Copper ore and concentrated ore	911.7	5.9
Coal and similar solid fuel	450.6	2.9
Uncombed cotton	281.6	1.8
Nickel	267.7	1.7
Manganese ore and concentrated ore	222.7	1.5
Sheep or lamb rawhide	196.0	1.3
Lead ore and concentrated ore	181.4	1.2
Crude oil	167.9	1.1

Source: Ministry of Commerce, China (2006).

potential for cooperation in East Asia. The more different two countries are in their developing stages, the more complementary they are, the more benefit they can get if an FTA is established.

The two economies are highly complementary with Australia having advantages in raw material, agriculture and services, while China has advantages in manufacturing, human resources and market size. The proposed China–Australia FTA will be good for the two sides to exploit these advantages and further promote the constructive and win–win cooperation. Table 3.3 shows that Australian exports to China are mainly resources, while Table 3.4 shows that Australian imports from China are mainly manufactured goods.

Take energy as an example. Energy security has become a critical factor in China's international strategy, and China's increasing dependence on energy imports is producing a new set of strategic vulnerabilities tied to the possible disruption of oil and gas supplies. China was forced to turn to foreign suppliers in 1993 and will probably have to import 40 per cent of its estimated needs by 2010. About half of this is expected to come from Chinese-owned oil fields overseas. Imports of gas are set to double as China attempts to diversify away from coal, which currently provides over 70 per cent of its energy needs. Australia's significance as a stable, long-term supplier of energy, particularly gas, has risen in concert with China's need for imported energy.

Consumer Surplus

The most fundamental driving force behind the move to the formation of FTAs is the deepening of economic interdependence. As presented above,

Table 3.4   Top ten imports from China to Australia (2006)

	US$ million	%
Automatic data processing equipment and its parts	1 949.0	10.1
Mobile, telegram, TV transmitters and video cameras	913.3	4.8
TVs including monitors and projectors	489.0	2.5
Women clothes	431.7	2.2
Office equipment (mainly for word processing) and its parts	427.3	2.2
Other furniture and components	414.2	2.2
Other toys; intelligence toys	351.4	1.8
Seats, chairs and their components	349.0	1.8
Shoes and boots	329.9	1.7
Games and toys for entertainment	308.7	1.6

Source: Ministry of Commerce, China (2006).

the interdependence between China and Australia is increasing. The growing macroeconomic and financial interdependence suggests a need for concerted efforts to internalize externalities and spillover effects, because macroeconomic/financial developments and policies of one country can easily affect other countries' performance and developments.

An FTA between two countries is a market in the sense that they come together to exchange market-access commitments on a reciprocal basis. As stated by Winters (1987), reciprocity in trade negotiations comes in many guises. It may be expressed in quantitative or qualitative terms, and may apply to different levels or to changes in protection. Preferential trading arrangements are by their nature selective.

It is well accepted that the international market is a buyers' market, and that buyers enjoy consumer sovereignty. The world market has only a few buyers but competitive on the selling side. In a competitive market, prices are determined by the free play of market demand and supply forces, and consumer surplus is generated. Consumer surplus is defined as the extra satisfaction or utility gained by consumers from paying an actual price for a good which is lower than the price which they would have been prepared to pay. As far as China and Australia are concerned in this area, one consumer surplus can be compensated by another due to complementarities between the two countries. China will enjoy consumer surplus from the purchase of energy and resources, while Australia can ensure consumer surplus from the purchase of some manufacturing goods. Another related point is that sellers can offer better terms to larger buyers and long-term customers.

Economies of Scale

Attitudes towards environmental quality or product safety differ across countries, and this is reflected in differences in environmental or product standards. It is accepted that an FTA between two countries generates economies of scale, because governments can employ well-deliberated support policy and meet certain quality, legal and quarantine requirements. Kemp and Wan (1976) were the first to show that a customs union could be made Pareto optimal, i.e. first best, focusing on tariff adjustments. Indeed, by choosing one or several like-minded partners, countries are able to make more progress in terms of deep integration than they could in the extremely diverse WTO context (Plummer 2006). Of course, the FTA should have transparent, simple rules with regard to external tariffs, exclusion lists, rules of origin and harmonization of standards, procedures and regulations.

Agriculture

Oversimplifying for the purposes of this discussion, interest groups in a country can be divided into two categories: those with an interest in maintaining domestic trade barriers and those with an interest in greater access to foreign markets. In practice, the costs of liberalization are usually concentrated in specific industries, and they will often be well organized in terms of generating political opposition to a reduction in protection. On the other hand, benefits, while in the aggregate usually greater than costs, accrue to a much larger group of people, but those people do not have a great individual incentive to organize themselves politically (Tumlir 1985). In such a setting, policy makers need to point to reciprocal, sector-specific export gains to be able to sell the liberalization politically. Losers can obtain some automatic compensation through access to cheaper imports.

The agricultural sector is probably the last sector for China to open. Chinese people are worried about their farmers, and think if the FTA is implemented, agricultural products from Australia will be flooding into China. In reality, this worry is unnecessary. In 2006 I was invited by the Australian government to inspect its agriculture for FTA purposes, and my feeling is that the supply of agricultural products from Australia cannot be increased dramatically due to the shortage of water. More importantly, China is located in the north, while Australia is in the south, and agriculture in the two countries is counter-seasonal. To put it another way, another complementarity between China and Australia is seasonal complementarity in their agricultural sectors.

Political Considerations

An FTA is not merely an economic issue; sometimes international politics is involved. The politically optimal structure of a given bilateral FTA depends upon the comparative advantages of the two nations and the particular political strengths of various interest groups at the time the deal is signed (Baldwin 2006).

Australia has demonstrated it is a good-faith trading partner for the supply of raw materials to China, most notably natural gas and iron ore. Australia has also given China market-economy status, giving its manufacturers advantages through access to the Australian market. It should not be forgotten that China's push for an FTA with Australia is one of several that China is pursuing with other regional states. These can be seen as a form of confidence building by China but they also have an overt political purpose which is to challenge US supremacy in Asia and Japan's position as the dominant economic power.

At the Sino-Japanese summit in 2002, Chinese prime minister, Mr Wen Jiabao suggested an FTA between China and Japan, but the Japanese government has been very cautious about such an arrangement. Their official view is that, before negotiating an FTA, China must comply with all the commitments undertaken in WTO accession negotiations. They think China is at least a potential competitor for Japan (Yu 2006).

China and ASEAN established a relationship as strategic partners and agreed that an FTA will be implemented in 2010. However, Japan acted more quickly and chose Korea, Singapore, the Philippines and Thailand to negotiate. Japan and Singapore concluded an economic partnership agreement (EPA)[1] in 2002. Japan has put into effect its EPA with the Philippines and Thailand. The Japan–Korea FTA has been implemented. Moreover, official negotiations for an EPA have been speeded up between Japan and Indonesia, and Vietnam has shown interest in an EPA with Japan. Recently, Taiwan has been seeking to establish an FTA with Japan, Korea, ASEAN and the United States. It is only a slight exaggeration to say that China is now surrounded by Japanese EPA strategy (Liu 2005). In this situation an FTA with Australia is highly desirable for China to bypass the Japanese FTAs.

NOTE

1. As explained by the Ministry of Foreign Affairs of Japan, an EPA goes beyond an FTA, including the cooperation in investment, finance, enterprise management, property rights and professional training.

REFERENCES

Anderson, K., W. Martin and D. van der Mensbrugghe (2006), 'Doha merchandise trade reform: what's at stake for developing countries?', *World Bank Economic Review*, **20**(2), 169–96.

Asian Development Bank (2002), *Asian Development Outlook 2002*, Manila: Asian Development Bank.

Australian Bureau of Statistics (ABS), (various issues), Australian Economic Indicators, http://www.abs.gov.au/.

Baldwin, Richard E. (2006), 'Multilateralising regionalism', paper presented at the 2006 World Economy Annual Lecture, Nottingham, UK.

Brown, Drusilla, Alan Deardorff and Robert Stern (2003), 'Multilateralism, regional and bilateral trade-policy options for the United States and Japan', *World Economy*, **26**(6), 803–28

Fang, Hua (2005), 'An explanation of FTAs from institutional economics point of view', *Journal of the Business College of Lanzhou*, **21**(5), 20–2.

Francois, J. and W. Martin (2006), 'Great expectations: ex ante assessment of the welfare impacts of trade reforms', paper presented to the 9th Annual Conference on Global Economic Analysis, Addis Ababa, 15-17 June 2006.

Ianchovichina, E. and W. Martin (2004), 'Economic impacts of China's accession to the World Trade Organization', *World Bank Economic Review*, **18**(1), 3–28.

Kawai, Masahiro (2005), 'East Asian economic regionalism: progress and challenges', *Journal of Asian Economics*, **16**(1), 19–55.

Kemp, Murray C. and Henry Wan, Jr (1976), 'An elementary proposition concerning the formation of customs union', *Journal of International Economics*, **6**(1), 95–7.

Krasner, S. (1983), 'Structural causes and regime consequences: regimes as intervening variables', in S. Krasner (ed.), *International Regimes*, Ithaca, NY: Cornell University Press, pp. 1–21.

Liu, Changli (2005), 'Reasons and features of development in bilateral free trade in the world and China's countermeasures', *Research on World Economics*, **4**, 40–47.

Lloyd, Peter (2002), 'New bilateralism in the Asia Pacific', *World Economy*, **25**(9), 1279–96.

Ministry of Commerce, China (2006), 'Country report, Australia', http://countryreport.mofcom.gov.cn/.

Naya, Seiji F. (2002), *The Asian Development Experience*, Manila: Asian Development Bank.

Plummer, Michael G. (2006), '"Best practices" in regional trading agreements: an application to Asia', paper presented at an Office of Regional Economic Integration conference, 'Brainstorming on Asian FTAs', held at the Asian Development Bank, 20 March 2006.

Terada, T. (2003), 'Constructing an East Asian concept and growing regional identity: from EAEC to ASEAN+3', *Pacific Review*, (2), 251–77.

Teng, Ying (2004), 'FTA: the regionalism that is popular in the world', *Journal of Zhejiang College of Industrial and Commercial Skills*, **3**(2), 40–42.

Tumlir, J. (1985), *Protectionism: Trade Policy in Democratic Societies*, Washington, DC: American Enterprise Institute.

Winters, L.A. (1987), 'Reciprocity', in J. Finger and A. Olechowski (eds), *The Uruguay Round: A Handbook for the Multilateral Trade Negotiations*, Washington, DC: World Bank.

Wonnecott, P. and R. Wonnecott (1981), 'Is unilateral tariff reduction preferable to a customs union?', *American Economic Review*, **71**(4), 704–14.

WTO website, http://www.wto.org/english/tratop_e/region_e/region_e.htm, accessed 11 September 2005.

Yu, Xiao (2006), 'The Sino-Japan competition in the process of FTA in East Asia', *Modern Japanese Economy*, **4**, 37–46.

Zhai, Fan (2006), 'Preferential trade agreements in Asia: alternative scenarios of "hub and spoke"', paper presented to the 9th Annual Conference on Global Economic Analysis, Addis Ababa, 15-17 June 2006.

PART II

Sector-specific issues

4. Manufacturing products and related issues in a free trade agreement between China and Australia[1]

Neville Norman

This chapter addresses the most important issues effects and policy options arising from a China–Australia Free Trade Agreement (CAFTA) involving manufacturing industry. To perform this task requires some background appreciation of the developments in and setting of manufacturing industry in both countries, of existing trade and related barriers that might be removed and some important pointers from economic analysis. We bring all three things together in this chapter. We also incorporate some recent findings from other situations of adjustment to significant trade policy changes to assist in predicting economic consequences and business and political sensitivities. The purpose is also to identify some tensions and negotiation issues that are specific to manufacturing in the context of the proposed CAFTA.

We show that the product, industry and business setting for manufacturing is in many ways distinctly different from the agricultural, resources and services sectors, which are treated separately in this volume. Moreover, some recent trends in manufacturing trade policy issues have not been captured in the standard trade theory that is the usual framework for conducting exercises of this kind. We outline those trends and features as important ingredients for assessing and shaping the CAFTA and similar future free trade agreements (FTAs).

The context for this study is a global scene for trade policy dominated by the emergence and execution of many FTAs, including Australia's long-established FTA with New Zealand and the implementation of its FTA with the United States. Equally, China has invoked and is in the course of negotiating several FTAs with a wide range of other countries. Perhaps of even greater significance, China has effected from about 1990 some spectacular reductions in import duty rates, largely but not entirely as part of its commitment to enter the World Trade Organization (WTO) in 2001. This fact establishes at once that the effects and issues arising from

CAFTA must be seen in a genuinely dynamic and multi-causal setting. The multi-causal aspect is that a wide range of change drivers affecting the same industries and economic variables will be in operation at the same time as the CAFTA is implemented. Here we embrace at once a potential conflict with the mainstream of the economic theory of standard tariff and preferential trading arrangements, which have been structured for a static setting examining a one-off policy change in isolation from other events. In addition, some particular characteristics of manufacturing industry – especially product differentiation and the central role of multinational firms – mean that some amended form of trade and tariff theory will be needed to secure the insights we need for this task.

THE BOUNDARIES OF THE MANUFACTURING SECTOR

The manufacturing sector is best defined by what it excludes. Plainly, all primary or agricultural and raw material products are excluded, as are government and all other (tertiary) services, including finance and banking. The convention in most statistical classifications is that processed agricultural, mineral and resource materials are then deemed to be, entirely, manufactured items. Thus, refined copper, alumina, pig iron, canned meat and fruits are deemed to be manufacturing. It is arguable that the sales value of these products should be broken down on a value-added basis, so that the manufacturing component is confined to value added in the physical transformation or processing stage. Whatever the case for this partitioning, it does not normally happen in the recording of traded goods – exports and imports – which are normally deemed to be 'manufacturing' if *any* processing takes place. Equally, import duties tend to follow the state of processing in their descriptions and applications. We are thus forced to follow convention here, so some overlap will occur with other sectors and treatments in this volume. Products that have most of their values added attributed to the primary and mineral activities will be wholly classified in trade data as manufacturing.

THE MANUFACTURING SCENE IN AUSTRALIA AND CHINA

There are a number of relevant trends established for the manufacturing sector in general, and some specific forces at work in both China and Australia. In general, manufacturing tends to absorb a falling proportion of final national expenditures and of resources, as consumer expenditures focus on services in the course of long-term economic development. The long-term relative decline of the manufacturing sector in Australia has been evident for over 30 years. This so-called Fisher–Clark thesis contains both a demand-side and supply-side explanation: consumers seek luxury goods as real incomes (per head) rise with economic development;[2] on the supply side, faster productivity growth in the non-services sector releases resources for tertiary activities, even if the demand composition does not change.

The Fisher–Clark thesis predicts that an increasing share of tertiary activities accompanies economic development, and it is almost universally observed that this happens. The position of manufacturing is more complex. In the early stages of development, the manufacturing share will tend to rise, especially if explicit government policies supporting domestic and foreign investment in industries are offered. This is exactly the case of China in the period 1988–2000, and perhaps of Australia in the period 1920–60. Thereafter, the sophistication of tastes, perhaps combined with rising import competition, leads to a decline in the manufacturing share – a feature that started in Australia from about 1960 and in China from about 2000.

In 2005, Australia's manufacturing sector contributed just 12 per cent to Australia's national income (national value added); it provided 10.8 per cent of Australian employment and generated 21 per cent of Australia's exports. Some 60 per cent of Australia's manufactured exports are elaborately transformed, rather than simply transformed.[3] While this distinction between simply and elaborately transformed product categories within manufacturing has taken hold in recent discussions of manufacturing, further distinctions and classification bases are needed to give effective insights and predictions of the types needed here. In particular such broad groupings are demonstrably inadequate as a basis for trade policy negotiations, such as in relation to the proposed CAFTA.

By contrast to the Australian experience, manufacturing in China has taken a much more prominent and enduring role. The simple ratios of manufacturing value added to national income (aggregate value added) show the striking contrast: China's secondary industry share has hovered around 50 per cent of Chinese GDP and has been rising from 1990 to about 2000.[4] These events are not unrelated, as the rise of China and of other developing manufacturing bases have brought about some part of the decline in Australian manufacturing, in conjunction with the lowering of trade barriers imposed in imports entering Australia.

There has been much research into the degree of development, complexity and sophistication of the product structure in manufacturing operations around the world. Basic manufacturing operations are labour intensive, with limited mechanization, supporting a product range that concentrates on agricultural and mineral product transformations, with limited style, fashion and technological complexity. As manufacturing operations mature with economic development, the technology and product range assume characteristics more akin to those in advanced economies such as Germany, Canada and the United States. Economists have produced formal measures of this degree of sophistication in the manufacturing operations of many countries. Not least because the rapid pace of direct foreign investment into Chinese manufacturing has enabled it to mature remarkably rapidly, Chinese manufacturing will have reached a degree of complexity and sophistication reasonably close to that of Australia's when any agreed CAFTA begins to take effect. Some specific examples of the sophistication of Chinese manufacturing production are documented in consultant reports covering both broad sectors and specific product concentrations.[5]

Along the same theme, Rodrik (2006) shows that China's export composition is demonstrably more sophisticated than would normally be expected for a country at its (still low) income level. Specifically, Rodrik's analysis is that China's export bundle 'is that of a country with an income-per-capita three times higher than China's' (Rodrik 2006, p. 4). A completely different research method gives similar conclusions (Schott 2006). The significant presence of sophisticated electronics in the Chinese export bundle is an outstanding example of this feature. The product categories identified as absolute outliers in the export structure for a country with such a low national income per head as China has are electric accumulators, telegraphy, video recording equipment, electronic printed circuits and integrated circuits and micro assemblies. Foreign direct investment has enabled China to implement manufacturing production strategies that went well beyond the capacities expected from the capital market and the expertise of a low-income country. Plainly, China jumped some stages in manufacturing development that dependence on its own resources would have taken 30 to 50 years longer to achieve.[6] The message for trade policy analysis is that trade competition in future is unlikely to be confined to the basic manufacturing products which featured in documented accounts of Chinese trade competition in the 1960–90 period, when Chinese-produced basic clothing and footwear epitomized the likely threats to Australian industry.

Some well-known examples of sophisticated Chinese production, and export, arising from joint-venture foreign investment cooperation with foreign firms include: mobile phones (Motorola, Nokia, Siemens and Samsung); personal computers (IBM, HP, Dell, Epson), brown household goods (Sony, Philips, Toshiba) and white household goods (Samsung, LG, Mitsubishi, Sanyo and Toshiba). While colour television production faced difficult times in China in the 1980s, the more recent productivity or relatively fault-free performance of the auto-part supply chain in China has confounded potential critics with examples to cite from early Japanese and other Asian developing country experience in this area. (Rodrik 2006, pp. 22–4 gives fuller details). Again, it is evident that China seemed to skip the teething stages of industrial development in many ways and is already placed to exhibit industrial prowess to match that of nations with many times its overall economic development. This is relevant to CAFTA because the image of China marketing only basic, labour-intensive industrial goods is already outmoded and will be more so when CAFTA takes effect.

China's development has hardly been a one-way success story. It is shown (Rodrik 2006, p. 2) that China's share of world exports actually lapsed from 2 per cent in 1960 to below 1 per cent for the entire decade 1970–80, before surging from 2 per cent in 1991 to 4 per cent in 1996 to 8 per cent by 2003. It is not clear that high tariffs retarded Chinese export development as very little tariff liberalization took place until the later 1990s, when export development surged. Two aspects of the high Chinese tariff policy might actually have assisted export development: (1) an aggressive system of export tariff relief (drawbacks) removed cost-inflating effects from the imported components of exported goods; and (2) the 'tariff factory' effect provided incentives for foreign firms to set up behind the high-tariff walls. With punitive import barriers at rates such as 100 per cent *ad valorem* or more for some categories of motor vehicles, combined with the open-door foreign investment policy from about 1988, there is significant support for a tariff-factory argument.

Australian manufacturing came under threat in the 1970s, since when its GDP share has been declining persistently. While federal and many state governments explicitly supported Australian manufacturing during and after World War II, the tide turned in the 1960s. The high degree of government support, especially from state governments, led to the proliferation of plants in industries such as chemicals and motor vehicle production. From 1973, tariffs were cut radically, specific protection arrangements were reduced, the currency was uplifted and import competition from low-valued goods especially rose sharply. This sparked many adjustment assistance debates and inquiries during the 1970s, the most notable being the Crawford Report of 1978. Crawford proposed a variety of adjustment assistance measures and recommended that no tariff should be further reduced while unemployment rates exceed 5 per cent. In more recent times, basic footwear, clothing and textiles operations have ceased; film and photographic production has ended and a range of manufacturing supply operations (to the vehicles sector especially) have been closed.

THE PRESENT SITUATION OF TRADE BETWEEN CHINA AND AUSTRALIA

The emphasis we place in this chapter on dynamic shifts in manufacturing product specifications is evident from trade data involving Australian manufacturing exports to China. DFAT (2006) comments that the value of Australia's manufacturing exports to China rose by 18 per cent in 2005. However, simply transformed manufactured (STM) exports declined by 3 per cent, while elaborately transformed manufactured (ETM) exports rose by an impressive 29 per cent. A spectacular increase in ETM exports occurred in relation to passenger motor vehicles which increased from A$6 million in 2004 to A$153 million in 2005. The intensity and the increase of this export component are undoubtedly associated with the development of automotive production in China by the same multinational firms, an indispensable part of the manufacturing story in judging probable impacts of the FTA. DFAT (2006, p. 5) opines that by 2010 China will have the world's second-largest automotive market, with substantial opportunities for both manufacturers of vehicles and those providing after-market services.

Manufacturing in Australia has been much affected by unilateral, multilateral and FTA components of tariff reduction, by the emergence of global supply chains and by the trend to increasing product differentiation. Most import duties that had been applied by Australia to trade in manufactures with New Zealand, the United States, Singapore and Thailand have been eliminated or are being phased out. While emphasis in this chapter is upon the China–Australia FTA, this FTA (CAFTA) is being negotiated concurrently with FTAs involving Australia with ASEAN and Malaysia.

The main manufactured imports of Australia from China in 2005–6 were clothing (A$3.24 billion); computers (A$2.48 billion), telecommunications equipment (A$1.29 billion) and toys, games and sporting goods (A$1.20 billion) (Australian Bureau of Statistics – ABS), with total imports from China being A$21.3 billion. The main manufactured exports from Australia to China are iron ore (A$6.88 billion), wool (A$1.31 billion), copper ores (A$1.01 billion) and lead, manganese and other ores (A$0.76 billion), total Australian exports to China being around A$14 billion in 2005–6.[7] The rapidly growing Chinese middle class is already opening up opportunities for Australian processed food exports (especially organics, wine and dairy products) and some consumer products such as jewellery, cosmetics, giftware and pet care products.

Some impressive individual Australian industry export commercial successes in China have already been recorded, in advance of the FTA. BlueScope Steel (known previously as BHP Steel) provided decking for China's largest building, the Jinmao Tower, and the World Financial Centre in Shanghai. BlueScope provided roofing for the Beijing International Airport, the Guangzhou Olympic Centre and for 11 metro train stations in Beijing. Perth-based Medic Vision has made substantial exports to China of medical simulation devices. Some other examples of Australia ETM exports include bionic ears, antennas, microwave radio equipment, automotive parts and scientific and laboratory equipment and instruments.[8]

We turn now to the trade policy setting, which must also be seen as a fast-moving feast, with further changes predictable before a CAFTA is likely to take effect.

MAJOR TRADE POLICY LIBERALIZATION BEFORE CAFTA

Both Australia and China have made significant reductions in the rates of import barrier protection. The reasons have been different, though the world trend to general tariff barrier reduction has motivated both countries. Equally, the current and prospective round of FTAs has occasioned further rate reductions in the weighted average of imported goods entering each country.

The marked reduction in nominal tariffs in Australia since 1990 followed a decade when most non-tariff barriers were reduced or removed. The main non-tariff barriers of the 1980s were quotas on imported textiles, steel products, textiles, clothing and footwear. Since 1990, motor vehicle tariffs in Australia have been reduced from 40 per cent to 25 per cent in 1996 and after controversy and some delay to just 10 per cent by 2005, with a 5 per cent rate scheduled for 2010, which is the general duty rate for manufactured products, which would by then have applied if CAFTA were not negotiated. In other words, the duty rates yet to be eliminated by Australia as part of a CAFTA are very small indeed. In other product classes, in the Australian customs tariff schedule, apparel and other finished textiles incurred a dramatic rate reduction from 55 per cent in 1990 to 17.5 per cent today, making this sector a prime product class of interest under CAFTA, if only because of the extent of duty reductions likely under CAFTA. We shall argue on the basis of our economic analysis that these are not the only considerations. However, when only very low duty rates are left to remove in an FTA, there is not much scope for any other factor to cause significant adjustment burdens.

Australian footwear tariffs fell from 45 per cent in 1990 to just 10 per cent from 2005, with similar reductions for carpet and woven fabrics. The only other notable category within manufacturing that does not presently bear the general 5 per cent duty rate is sleeping bags, which remains at 7.5 per cent. The forces behind these significant reductions in tariff and no-tariff barriers are both domestic and international. By the time Australia starts to implement any agreed CAFTA, import duty rates will be even lower, especially for any nation with whom an FTA is concluded.

The picture in relation to China's reductions in import barrier protection is even more spectacular, coming from many higher import-duty rates at around 1990 to rates quite similar to, or just above, those currently applying in Australia.[9] Tariffs imposed by China against imports remained quite high and variable as recently as in 2000.[10]

The impact of these huge tariff reductions in China has not been entirely positive for Chinese firms. Some economic studies are already available on the impacts. A penetrating analysis by Liu (2001) contrasts the effects of Chinese trade liberalization on an open sector (shipbuilding) with the effects on a protected light industry sector (bicycles and home appliances) and on automotive operations. In relation to shipbuilding, the dominant state-owned enterprise (SOE) operated in a competitive environment with the tariffs on imported products already as low as just 8 per cent in 1998. The main rivals in this market were from South Korea and Japan. China's light industry sector contained over 16 000 firms in 1998, of which nearly 6000 were SOEs (Liu 2001, p. 19). The domestic market share eroded from 96 per cent in 1990 to 74 per cent in 1998 (Liu 2001, p. 20). By contrast Chinese colour TV manufacturers raised their China market share from 15 per cent in 1983 to 81 per cent in 1997 (Liu 2001, p. 23). The number of firms in bicycle production (tariff 25 per cent in the late 1990s) was reduced by three-quarters between 1990 and 1998.

Motor vehicle tariffs in the late 1990s were levied at exceptionally high *ad valorem* rates of either 80 per cent or 100 per cent. At that time, the top three firms had 18 per cent, 15 per cent and 12 per cent of the national market, respectively. These major firms then in response to the tariff reductions lowered their prices and cut their costs radically to deter foreign entry that was emerging both by direct foreign investment and by market entry (imports).

A central message from our analysis is that the impact of CAFTA on Australian, Chinese, and other producers must be seen in the context of considerable liberalization in China's protective regime. The scope for further liberalization after all other initiatives have been taken into account in significantly less than it would have been ten years ago, before the unilateral, WTO- and FTA-based tariff reductions had a radical impact on Chinese tariff rates.

SOME POINTERS FROM ECONOMIC ANALYSIS

We focus on a liberated trade policy scene under CAFTA. However, this is not to ignore other policy aspects of the CAFTA. It is difficult to believe that foreign investment regulations can be much further changed by CAFTA to liberalize China's already relatively open direct foreign investment regime.[11] It is also difficult to predict precise directions for competition policy and intellectual property laws that might be affected by CAFTA. We thus focus on actions arising from trade barrier/border protection liberalization under CAFTA.

Economic theory provides a useful framework for analysis and also some indications of areas for closer investigation. There is a classical approach to trade policy found in undergraduate textbooks in international economics which gives us a starting point. It will need to be amended in significant ways to gain the insights we need for the circumstances of CAFTA.

In the classic conception, trade barriers are simply tariffs or tariff equivalent of quotas and other restrictions, and a close relationship between tariffs and prices exists. We shall presently review the basis for this close link, as it holds the clue to differential effects of trade policy options that are particularly important in relation to manufactured products.

There are other important features and assumptions of the basic FTA theory that have to be identified and questioned to give us further insights relevant to our stated tasks. The classical FTA theory presupposed that identical (homogeneous) products are the subject of all relevant trade and trade policy activity. This premise clearly derives from the nature of traded products observed in the eighteenth and nineteenth centuries when trade theory was devised. Accordingly textbook treatments even now illustrate the theory with sample products such as wheat, cotton and other agricultural and mineral products. When trade barriers are reduced as part of the FTA, the close movement of tariffs and prices remains the key to predicting price movements and welfare measures associated with them. A corollary of this classical set-up is that the firms are all small-scale perfect competitors. This implies that the scale and multi-country reach of multinational corporations is excluded as well as significant product differentiation or variety differences within markets.

As a matter of common observation upon manufacturing operations today, it is easy to contradict these central promises of the classical theory. Product categories are severely segmented and multinational firms dominate the manufacturing landscape in general and in Australia and China in particular. The significance of this point is not specifically that some assumptions are severely violated; it is more that vital pointers to our research task will be overlooked if we accept the classical theory uncritically, and price and other predictions of the FTA will be astray.

There is also some direct theory written for FTAs specifically. Much of the literature and debates about it are found in Bhagwati and Panagariya (1996). The focus of this treatment is on the welfare effects of partners and third parties. The models are almost entirely static[12] and the industrial economic assumptions are of fixed (usually homogeneous) product selections.

The limitations of classical tariff theory for modern applications to trade policy issues have been recognized by many authorities, such as Helpmann and Krugman (1982, 1989), who provided a wider range of theories to overcome them, and by Dornbusch (1987), who predicted and encouraged modern industrial organization concepts to be integrated.[13] The result has been a flood of literature attesting to imperfect competition, product differentiation and scale economies as the modern core of empirical results and modelling.[14] The significance of substituting more relevant product concepts into the framework used for trade policy analysis is that both quantity and price effects will be affected significantly.[15] Possible product assumptions in trade theory fit into four categories: the first two are common in the literature; the last two are vital for understanding effects of modern FTA in manufacturing and have been little developed. They are: (1) homogeneous products; (2) differentiated products; (3) dynamically differentiated products; and (4) endogenously differentiated products.

Lloyd and MacLaren (2004, p. 450) describe the first two of these product postulates as first and second generation computable general equilibrium (CGE) models, respectively. We say that the third and fourth generation postulates need also to be incorporated, because they significantly change the picture of economic effects. The point made plain by this schema is that most models of product differentiation as such are defined for unchanged degrees of product differentiation over time. The (static) product substitutability (between home and foreign goods) is reflected in demand substitution parameters which are constants both over time and in relation to changing circumstances such as trade policy. That is, they do not embrace generations three and four. While the prices of (home and foreign) products may then differ, the general consequences of these models are that upon solution the relative prices (of home and foreign products, in theory) remain fixed. The proposition is challenged by modern independent econometric studies (such as Coutts and Norman 2007) and leads to serious questioning as to whether simple static product differentiation is all that is at work. Thus our third and fourth (more realistic and more relevant) conceptions of the product assumption are entered above.

Besedes and Prusa (2004, p. 19) find that about 80 per cent of the internationally traded products they studied are differentiated rather than homogeneous. With particular emphasis on manufacturing, as in this chapter, this is strong support for moving beyond the homogeneous product assumptions of classical trade theory in making a contemporary application such as we do here to the CAFTA exercise. The literature also emphasizes that the quality and specification of the products subject to international competition are themselves subject to change, often in response to changes in trade policy and the dynamics of foreign competition. This aspect has been emphasized in Aw (1991), Aw and Roberts (1986) and Das and Donnenfeld (1987). It is the dominant empirical finding in Coutts and Norman (2007). The message for trade negotiators in terms of FTA design is that sectors which are not able to make product quality adjustments, over time or in response to trade policy and other events, are more prone to adjustment difficulties and thus subject to greater sensitivities.[16]

The blunt reality of modern markets for manufactures is that price relativities swing significantly, often in response to competitive pressures, technology and trade policy, and price dispersion is the standard feature of most markets.[17] There is already an established proposition that productive differentiation models perform in different ways to the conventional homogeneous product models of classical trade and tariff theory.[18]

This short survey of theory enables us to identify some of the major issues and pointers to pursue in our review of the CAFTA affecting manufacturing products, especially:

1. The height of existing tariffs and trade barriers likely to be reduced or removed by the CAFTA. While this is the obvious and dominating pointer from standard trade theory, it will form only a starting point for all that follows.
2. The nature of products and extent of market segmentation. Contrary to the premises of classical theory, severe market segmentation might imply in some areas a very limited change or threat to local producers where, for instance, Chinese producers have at the start of the CAFTA already dominated the basic product areas of clothing and shoes, for instance, while Australian and other producers are focused on the high-value/fashion end. We begin and proceed with a suspicion that trade and industry classifications will not be wide enough here: clothes aren't just clothes!
3. The presence and role of multinational companies. Contrary to standard trade theory, some firms have a presence in both (and other) countries and have already at the start of any FTA made decisions on the global allocation of production which may influence the scope for future changes and significantly influence the analysis of FTA impacts and sensitivities. As in the UK car industry, decisions to cease, expand

and vary productive operations are taken strategically (Coutts and Norman 2007). The future course of vehicle production in China, Australia and in trade between them may be largely determined in Detroit, USA – or in Tokyo.

4. Dynamic and investment considerations. This factor, completely omitted from static classical FTA theory, is important, not only because investment and multinational company decisions are involved, especially in both China and Australia, but also because FTAs tends to embrace the liberalization of any arrangements impeding foreign investment and expansion of firms already operating through acquisition and physical investment activity. There is some interaction here between dynamic and product considerations. Indeed, we shall argue that circumstances differ markedly between products that can be changed, refined and further differentiated, either over time or in response to trade pressures themselves.

There are two related aspects here: (1) the products traded in international commerce are increasingly *not* the homogeneous commodity-style products of classical economic theory; and (2) partly reflecting point (1), the extent of price changes that supervene upon tariff changes tends to be considerably less than the one-for-one price responses that are built in to standard tariff theory. This is important because, at least in the manufacturing sector, politicians and trade negotiators cannot expect significant consumer benefits from price reductions associated with the elimination of tariff duties that accompany an FTA in today's circumstances. These are the main messages from empirical analysis, even though the core of trade policy theory has not yet caught up with the evidence. There are some further findings about both traded product structures and pricing responses that are again interrelated and have a more dynamic flavour: (1a) traded manufactured products are being dynamically differentiated and are evolving and changing rapidly over time, generally and in response to international and competitive pressures; and (2a) the price responses arising from trade policy changes tend to differ markedly between product categories, within manufacturing.

It will be important to document these findings, because in the manufacturing area we say that these results are relevant and realistic economic conditions conducive to deriving results from a China–Australia FTA in the circumstances likely to develop around 2010 and beyond. The supporting product evidence has already been provided above, including the trend to a significant increase in the sophistication of Chinese manufactured exports, and in the shift to elaborately transformed products in Australia's export structure.

The recent evidence on industrial product pricing responses has most lately been summarized and extended in Coutts and Norman (2007).[19] In many ways the findings are eminently transportable to the product structures associated with the China–Australia trade pattern.

A most pertinent aspect of this study is the classification of price responses, according to how domestic prices changed in relation to costs and import prices after 1996. These results affirm the emerging dominating modern pattern of considerable heterogeneity in price responses to global competition between sectors, within manufacturing itself. Prediction, trade policy and model specification needs to be sensitive to this finding. The study identified three broad categories of price adjustment:

1. Sectors that produce mainly homogeneous products traded at international prices. The chemicals and base metals sectors largely belong to this group. In both sectors, the sterling price of imported goods fell in line with exchange rate appreciation between 1996 and 2000, and domestic prices fell substantially.
2. Sectors in which international competitor prices fell in line with the exchange rate rise, but in which domestic prices increased, or fell by modest amounts.
3. Sectors whose competitor prices fell by only about 8 per cent or less, while domestic prices increased, or fell by only modest amounts.

The message of these findings is that price effects of global competition (including changes arising from the spate of FTAs) on domestic markets are normally *not* dominant; they are often delayed and differ between products, in each case in contrast to the core postulates of standard trade and tariff theory. The message for judging the effects of a China–Australia FTA is that, with tariffs being reduced as far as they already have been, and with products becoming so sophisticated and differentiated as they have been, the price and welfare effects of an FTA should not be overstated and also they will differ somewhat between sectors. When we come to predict and focus on the most sensitive areas likely to be most affected by such agreements, these considerations will be important.

We now seek guidance from some further economic analysis that takes a very different approach.

POINTERS FROM COMPUTABLE GENERAL EQUILIBRIUM MODELS

There are many linkages by which a policy event such as CAFTA will intersect with and affect the economies involved, and potentially affect other economies as well. Accordingly, there has been the emergence of and rapid growth in computable general equilibrium (CGE) models to handle these issues. Such models provide a mathematical facsimile of the relevant economies, including a breakdown of their main producing sectors by broad industry class. They are capable in most cases of handling macroeconomic effects as well as intersectoral linkages and impacts. Such models began to appear in the 1970s. Their growth was stimulated by the need for guidance on the effects of NAFTA in particular.

Some of the claimed advantages of these models are that they are numerical, explicit and based on time-specific (dynamic) responses or policy descriptions. The numerical advantage is plain enough: quantitative and comparable assessments are made of macro effects and specific industry adjustment factors, which can be converted into dollar values or ratios, to illustrate orders of magnitude. This enables us to get the overall thrust of the policy event into context and to debate it. That said, there is an obligation on all debaters (and, perhaps, negotiators) to learn the properties of the CGE models and to take issue with any specific model procedures, parameters or closure conditions that might be arguable and different. Lloyd and MacLaren (2004) posit some of the cautionary tales in their review of CGE models applied to assessing FTAs, which they describe as 'useful, but incomplete tools . . .'

The claim that CGE models are explicit is, in practice, only partly correct, as it is unusual to have the entire workings bared for public consumption. Indeed, the procedure is so complex that it can be impossible to unveil the entire apparatus. Nevertheless, the description of procedures and main generating parameters are usually disclosed. The dynamic property of CGE models is important for policy events that are phased in or have impacts of growth rates of national aggregates and industry output.

There are a number of cautionary procedures that should be adopted before the messages of these CGE approaches should be taken as gospel. In particular, it is possible that some of the claimed macroeconomics and industry spillover benefits from policy initiatives such as FTAs derive from efficiency effects and externality built into the models or inserted extraneously. As long as this process is explicit and documented through research-based findings, it is acceptable procedure. Another issue is that parameters may be inserted that are not computed by acceptable research means, or which are applied at a common value across a range of industry sectors, for want of specific information. At the least, the complete research procedures need to be documented openly here to permit independent assessment.

The CGE approach to the proposed CAFTA has been studied by Mai et al. (2005) using the Monash multi-country model. The report was commissioned by DFAT to conduct the analysis. The general approach is to construct a set of baseline scenarios that portray the economy and producing sectors as they would have evolved in the period 2006–15 in the absence of CAFTA. Three aspects of the proposed CAFTA are then imposed on the model as from 2006. The differences as compared with the baseline scenarios are the computed net differences that CAFTA is judged to have made.

In the Monash approach, three experiments are conducted: (1) the removal of border protection between China and Australia; (2) enhanced direct foreign investment; and (3) trade liberalization in services. We can effectively bypass item (3) as being of only indirect relevant to our focus on manufacturing industry effects.

There needs to be fuller consideration of (2): enhanced direct foreign investment opportunities. In Mai et al. (2005) the authors argue that CAFTA would, by assumption, 'enhance the understanding of Chinese investment rules and regulations by Australian investors and vice versa' (Mai et al. 2005, Section 5, p. 15). The present writer cautions here on the extent to which CAFTA is likely to foster any further understanding, appreciation or facilitation of direct foreign investment among potential foreign investors in China and Australia that is not already present. There is a very high level of understanding of foreign investment rules and procedures by both Chinese and Australian foreign investors. More recently, indeed since 2005, full ownership options have been fostered and information services are widely available.[20] This is not to say that there are not limitations, barriers and obstacles, especially in reaction to the Chinese requirements to impose conditions and to mandate joint-venture requirements in relation to most proposals. It is to question that the research procedures of reducing investment hurdle rates and injecting significant real investment and productivity effects by assumption is a realistic expectation.

There is very little scope for further liberalization in relation to direct foreign investment in China or productivity/growth consequences therefrom. Accordingly, in this appreciation and advice we propose largely to ignore the likely potential for further stimulation of foreign investment, on the grounds that CAFTA is unlikely to achieve much more here. Instead we recommend that the main areas of realistic impact concerning manufacturing sectors in both China and Australia will be derived from the joint elimination of border protection in each country.

Further, the Monash study seems to overlook the prospect that direct foreign investment might actually be reduced by the adoption of CAFTA. This is because some part of the incentive to engage in direct foreign investment is to jump the tariff wall and become a domestic producer. We thus focus on the impact of mutual border barrier reductions in our appraisal of manufacturing industry effects in the Monash study. We briefly summarize the results in Mai et al. (2005), which can be divided into economy-wide effects and specific industry effects.

Mai (2005, Section 4.1) finds that removal of border protection under CAFTA would uplift the baseline path of real GDP by small fractions of one percentage point. The welfare impact is measured as an increase of 0.2 of 1 per cent in real GNP (Section 4.3). The sources of the gain are efficiency effects, improved terms of trade and greater capital supplies induced by the FTA. The results are significantly influenced by the incorporation of productivity growth effects of CAFTA, which the authors explain is based on empirical data from a 1998 study.

In Section 4.4 of Mai et al. (2005) the sectoral effects of CAFTA are recorded. This is particularly germane to our task. The impacts are a reflection of macro feedback effects and specific sectoral impacts, reflecting in part the height of trade barriers being removed under the executed CAFTA. The results are expressed, as for the macro results, as percentage deviations relative to baseline values.

For China, no industrial sector experiences a decline in real output. For Australia there are some real output declines in wearing apparel (clothing and footwear) and automotive products and parts. These results are similar to the employment effects, in which net job losses are experienced relative to baseline in Australian sectors of wearing apparel, motor vehicles and miscellaneous manufactures (Mai et al. 2005, Section 4.4). Chinese textile, wearing apparel, chemicals, metals and motor vehicle industries experience employment gains.[21]

It is notable that the same sectors of greatest adjustment coincide with those identified in our own analysis – wearing apparel and motor vehicles – except that we place great concentration upon the parts sector of motor vehicles, for reasons associated with greater product homogeneity and the ability of multinational companies to adapt faster by changing the international balance of their operations.

We thus affirm and are in agreement with the Monash modellers that, among the Australian manufacturing sectors, those with the largest potential negative adjustment are wearing apparel and within the motor vehicles sector. Suitably, Mai et al. (2005) devote a short specific section of commentary on both these sectors (in Sections 7.3.1. and 7.3.2, respectively). Each of these sectors has incurred significant long-term reductions in Australian employment and prospective further reduction in the period to 2015 in the absence of any CAFTA effects. In this sense, CAFTA is most likely to be a relatively small part of the adjustment pressures that are in force in any event.[22]

The employment scene in motor vehicles and parts is relatively much smaller – from 78 200 in 2004 to near 70 000 in 2015, with a percentage of baseline effects from CAFTA of 0.6 per cent or 400 jobs. Our own analysis based on a tighter focus on decision making at the industry-specific level suggests that the relative output and employment losses in auto parts especially may be larger than this.

In our view a finer breakdown of some of the sectors is necessary, and this point is nowhere more evident than in relation to motor vehicles and parts. The major producers of motor vehicles in both Australia and China are multinational companies with ready-made experience and options to shift the location of production between countries, and if necessary third countries, if the FTA or other influences cause any adverse appraisal of manufacturing prospects in either China or Australia. While some parts manufacturers are also multinationals, the vast proportion of vehicle parts manufactures are nationally based, with less flexibility in location than vehicle producers. Of great importance is that the specification of parts required by vehicle builders is to rigid engineering specifications. This means that the prospect to deal with trade-policy-induced pressures on profits by dynamic, or any, product differentiation is exceptionally limited in the case of parts suppliers. Almost by definition, the product specification of pistons, cylinders, electrical componentry, rear axles, gearboxes, trans-mission systems, glassware and trim are predetermined by manufacturer.

There is no special commentary in relation to the computed adverse effects of CAFTA on any specific Chinese manufacturing industries because the competition produces no specific adverse effects on any Chinese manufacturing industry, according to the Monash findings. From a negotiation viewpoint, the notable point is the predicted large negative effects on Chinese agricultural employment and activity. While that is the subject of a separate consideration in this volume, it becomes relevant as a potential bargaining point if sensitivities to likely output and employment losses in Australian manufacturing industry are traded at the political level with any adjustment assistance or delay in implementing CAFTA in specific areas.

There is a real chance for Australian firms who are not regionally specific to seek specific encouragement for setting up in the western regions of China. Chinese material support for the promotion of FDI tends emphatically to encourage western region involvement.[23]

ADJUSTMENT COST ISSUES SPECIFIC TO MANUFACTURING

There has been much research into adjustment costs associated with trade policies, and directly into those arising from FTAs in particular. A good

account of findings and messages is found in Wonnacott and Hill (1987).
The authors show that adjustment assistance is widely, but not always
wisely, granted. Most industrial countries practise it. In some ways, it is
better to delay and schedule reductions than to grant it (p. 51). To grant it
creates complications in distinguishing workers displaced for trade policy
and other reasons. Most programmes are justified according to equity
arguments. The case for supporting firms rather than workers is difficult to
make out (p. 63). In general, temporary protection and delayed reduction
in protection may be better than granting adjustment assistance, especially
to firms (pp. 92–3). The writers show theoretically that adjustment issues
are far easier in a high-growth context, like China has, than in a low or
no-growth setting, more akin to Australia's situation.

TIPS AND POINTERS FOR TRADE NEGOTIATORS – LOOKING TO 2010 AND BEYOND

We take 2010 as the first effective year, realistically, for the frontal operation of a CAFTA. By that time, at current rates of nominal economic
growth, the Chinese economy will have GDP of around US$4000 billion
and Australia's GDP will be around US$800 billion – the Chinese economy
will be nearly five times Australia's size.[24] If manufacturing remains near
50 per cent of the Chinese GDP and Australia's hovers near 10 per cent,
the manufacturing sectors will exhibit values added of US$1900 billion and
US$80 billion, respectively, with China's manufacturing sector some 24
times larger than that of Australia. We think this a salutary starting point
to discuss impacts and sensitivities.

By 2010, tariff rates will most likely be further reduced in both countries,
as compared with those operating today, and China will have implemented
a number of FTAs. The sophistication of Chinese manufactured products,
including those exported, will have advanced much further, and more
Australian manufacturing operations will have closed or be under threat.
We think this the relevant scene that will apply as any negotiated CAFTA
starts to take effect.

Competition from Chinese imports will intensify and move higher up
the product range (of transformation, elaboration and sophistication),
and the impact of Chinese import competition will probably be exagger-
ated by Australian import-competing interests. However, we see greater
real threats and less offsets from providential direct foreign investment
opportunities for Australian firms in China than the cited Monash study
has stated. Within specific manufacturing sectors we identity two product
areas that are likely to incur intense competitive effects under the CAFTA:

clothing products (including increasingly more fashion-oriented products) and motor vehicle parts. This identification comes directly from the economic analysis we have used: the former from analysis of the sophistication of Chinese exports in the spirit of Rodrik (2006); the latter from the relative homogeneity of products in car parts driven by vehicle-builder specifications permitting little or no scope for branding and strategic pricing.

Trade negotiators will need to be aware of sensitive areas like this and take stands based not simply on the politics of appeasing affected sectors, but on the economic consequences of doing or not doing so. The main strategy will be to build in delays in moving to tariff-rate elimination, perhaps by claiming that the alternative is the imposition of anti-dumping or other protective duties on Chinese manufactured imports to Australia, if the adjustment burdens became too intense – as the USA has recently threatened and adopted in relation to certain categories of Chinese imports.

There is also need for action, education and adjustment assistance in some areas. It is likely that CAFTA will be a major political event; we do not see it as being a trend-changing economic event, except for the few sensitive areas we have identified. We are thus at issue in some ways with the unswervingly enthusiastic message of notable, positive economic results arising from the Monash study.

NOTES

1. The author acknowledges discussions with many academic colleagues and the comments of an independent reader.
2. This can be expressed as seeking products with income elasticities of demand above unity.
3. The data are from Australian Bureau of Statistics, Catalogues 5206, 6203, 5676 and 5625.
4. Some useful data and descriptions of these trends for China are found in Chapter 7 of Garnaut and Song (2005). A good recent account of China's development and emphasis on industry as a growth and productivity driver is given in Garnaut and Song (2002). They emphasize the role of Mr Deng and specific pro-industry-development initiatives, especially the ongoing encouragement to direct foreign investment, albeit with joint-venture requirements in most cases.
5. An example of the latter is the range of consultant reports by the Li and Fung Research Centre based in Hong Kong, especially those concerning electronics, fashion goods and cosmetic products (See Li and Fung (2006)).
6. An excellent account of China's spectacular development under Mr Deng is found in Ash and Kueh (1996).
7. Source: Department of Foreign Affairs and Trade, country economic fact sheet.
8. Fuller information is given in the DFAT fact sheets on China.
9. Drysdale and Song (2000, p. 55) show that China's mean *ad valorem* tariff rate fell from 47.2 per cent in 1992 to 23 per cent by 1996. Findlay (2001) shows that China's unweighted average tariff fell from 40.1 per cent in 1992 to 16.5 per cent in 2005.

10. Some samples of duty rates at that time are as follows; colour television receivers: 35 per cent; electric fans: 15 per cent; air conditioners: 25 per cent; refrigerators: 18 to 30 per cent; most domestic electrical appliances: 35 per cent; bicycles: 25 per cent; computers: 9–15 per cent; motor cars up to engine capacity 2500cc: 80 per cent; cars of engine capacity over 2500cc: 100 per cent; trucks: 40 to 50 per cent; buses: 50 to 70 per cent; and toys: 10 per cent.

11. The account in Wu and Ye (1998) is instructive here.

12. There is a single diagram on p. 45 of Bhagwati and Panagariya (1996) and brief accompanying text covering alternative time paths but there is no real analysis to support it.

13. Dornbusch (1987) shows that in more general models of the firm, those which incorporate involving imperfect competition and strategic behaviour, that the price effects from trade liberalization will be much smaller than in models of perfect competition. The consequences predicted will depend on the characteristics of the specific industry.

14. Leading examples include: Armington (1969a, 1969b), Benson and Hartigan (1983), Cheng (1988), Christodoulakis and Weale (1992), Devarajan and Rodrik (1992), Dixit (1984), Flam and Helpman (1987), Harris (1984), Helpman and Krugman (1985, 1989), Hocking (1980), Isard (1977), Krugman (1979, 1982, 1990a, 1990b), Lancaster (1980), Lyons (1981), Melvyn and Markusen (1981), Negishi (1961), N. Norman (1975, 1996), V. Norman (1989), Pettengill (1979), Staelin (1976), Thomas (1988) and Venables (1982).

15. Helpman and Krugman (1985) show that some slight twists in the underlying assumptions can turn price predictions on their heads: the imposition of tariffs can actually reduce prices. Dornbusch (1987) argues that theory is not catching up with the world.

16. In the classic survey of the so-called economics of preferential trade agreements (Bhagwati and Panagariya 1996), all the models explained there are homogeneous product models and the only dynamics is given in a short section (at pp. 43–9) relating to phasing-in FTAs; there is no consideration of delayed and sequenced industrial responses to the FTA or any other trade policy initiative.

17. A comprehensive study for the European car market is performed by Goldberg and Verboven (1998).

18. Besedes and Prusa (2004) show that episodes for product market penetration from foreign producers last significantly longer when products are differentiated: 'the median survival time for trade relationships involving differentiated products is five years as compared to two years for homogeneous products' (p. 18).

19. Coutts and Norman use time-series econometrics applied to a unique data set incorporating matched series of imported and locally produced industrial products, relating the domestic price to unit costs and the competing import price and separating unit costs into labour and materials. Auto-regressive distributed lag (ARDL) equations were estimated, combining unit labour costs with material prices, using weights derived from input–output tables. From the preferred ARDL models, long-run values of the relationship between domestic prices, domestic costs and import prices were obtained. The sector-specific results of UK manufacturing tend to confirm that the main influence on specific-sector UK industrial prices is the movement of domestic unit costs. Only in chemicals and base metals are dominating import price effects found. Most products therein are relatively homogeneous. One would therefore expect these two sectors to behave more like the commodity markets of classical trade theory than the 'customer' markets that typify modern differentiated products. We could add motor vehicles, where import price effects are almost significant. These three sectors comprise about one-third of the whole manufacturing sector. One of the fascinating features evident in the data produced for this study was the divergent movement between domestic and international prices that opened up from 1996 with the appreciation of sterling which was sustained for some years thereafter. As the import price in sterling fell, the domestic price continued to increase, or fell at a much slower rate.

20. Li and Fung (2006) report that 625 out of the 1027 newly established industrial enterprises in China in 2005 and early 2006 were commenced as wholly foreign owned.

21. We have sought independently to relate the import duty rates to the real output effects for each industry and each country. There is no simple correspondence, as one would expect with differential feedback effects through the model solution.
22. To get some order of magnitude, the Monash model cites employment in Australian wearing apparel as 52 000 persons in 1997, falling to 22 300 by 2004 and by projection to just 13 000 by 2015. Applying the computed solution of a 12 per cent reduction compared with baseline at 2015, a net further reduction of 1500 jobs is in prospect due to CAFTA, which is about one-third of the employment reduction that actually took place between 1997 and 2004.
23. Only a small fraction of accumulated FDI has gone west – just over 3 per cent, according to computations made in Garnaut and Song (2002, p. 133).
24. The data begin at 2006 at US$2512 billion and US$645 billion, respectively, and are extrapolated at rates of 12 per cent and 5.5 per cent, respectively, for China and Australia.

REFERENCES

Armington, P. (1969a), 'A theory of demand for products distinguished by place of production', *International Monetary Fund Staff Papers*, **16**, 159–78.
Armington, P. (1969b), 'The geographic pattern of trade and the effect of price changes', *International Monetary Fund Staff Papers*, **16**, 179–201.
Ash, Robert and Y.Y. Kueh (1996), *The Chinese Economy Under Deng Xiaoping*, Oxford: Clarendon Press.
Aw, Bee-Yan (1991), 'Estimating the effects of quantitative restrictions in imperfectly competitive markets: the footwear case', in Robert E. Baldwin (ed.), *Empirical Studies of Commercial Policy*, Chicago: Chicago University Press, pp. 201–13.
Aw, Bee-Yan and M. Roberts (1986), 'Measuring quality change in quota-constrained import markets. The case of U.S. footwear', *Journal of International Economics*, **21**(1), 45–60.
Benson, B. and J. Hartigan (1983), 'Tariffs which lower price in the restricting country', *Journal of International Economics*, **15**, 117–33.
Besedes, Tibor and Thomas Prusa (2004), 'Surviving the U.S. import market: the role of production differentiation', New York: National Bureau for Economic Research working paper no. 10319.
Bhagwati, Jagdish and A. Panagariya (1996), *The Economics of Preferential Trade Agreements*, Washington, DC: AEI Press.
Cheng, L. (1988), 'Assisting domestic industries under international oligopoly: the relevance of the nature of competition to optimal policies', *American Economic Review*, **78**(4), 746–58.
Christodoulakis, N. and M. Weale (1992), 'Imperfect competition in an open economy', *Journal of Policy Modelling*, **14**(5), 599–629.
Coutts, K. and N. Norman (2007), 'Global influences on UK manufacturing prices: 1970–2000', *European Economic Review*, **51**, 1205–21.
Das, S. and S. Donnenfeld (1987), 'Trade policy and its impact on quality of imports', *Journal of International Economics*, **23**, 77–95.
Devarajan, S. and D. Rodrik (1992), 'Trade liberalisation in developing countries: do imperfect competition and scale economies matter?', *American Economic Review Papers and Proceedings*, **79**, 283–7.

DFAT (Department of Foreign Affairs and Trade) (2006), *Australia's Exports to China, 2005*, Canberra: Department of Foreign Affairs and Trade, Trade and Economic Analysis Branch.

Dixit, A. (1984), 'International trade policy for oligopolistic industries', *Economic Journal Supplement*, **94**, 1–16.

Dornbusch, Rudiger (1987), 'Open economy macroeconomics: new directions', New York: National Bureau for Economic Research working paper no. 2372.

Drysdale, Peter and Ligang Song (eds) (2000), *China's Entry to the WTO*, London: Routledge.

Findlay, C. (2001), 'China's admittance to the WTO and industrial structural adjustment in the world economy', Canberra Pacific Economic Papers, no. 315, May.

Flam, H. and E. Helpman (1987), 'Industrial policy under monopolistic competition', *Journal of International Economics*, **22**(1), 79–102.

Garnaut, Ross and Ligang Song (eds) (2002), *China 2002: WTO Entry and World Recession*, Canberra: ANU Press.

Garnaut, Ross and Ligang Song (eds) (2005), *The China Boom and its Discontents*, Canberra: Asia Pacific Press.

Goldberg, Peter and F. Verboven (1998), 'The evolution of price dispersion in the European car market', New York: National Bureau for Economic Research working paper no. 6818.

Harris, R. (1984), 'Applied general equilibrium analysis of small open economies with scale economies and imperfect competition', *American Economic Review*, **74**(5), 1016–32.

Helpman, Elphanan and Paul Krugman (1985), *Market Structure and Foreign Trade. Increasing Returns, Imperfect Competition and the International Economy*, Brighton: Wheatsheaf.

Helpman, Elphanan and Paul R. Krugman (1989), *Trade Policy and Market Structure*, Cambridge, MA: MIT Press.

Hocking, R. (1980), 'Trade in motor cars between the major European producers', *Economic Journal*, **90**, 504–19.

Isard, P. (1977), 'How far can we push the "Law of One Price"?', *American Economic Review*, **67**(5), 942–8.

Krugman, P. (1979), 'Increasing returns, monopolistic competition, and international trade', *Journal of International Economics*, **9**(4), 469–79.

Krugman, Paul (1982), 'Trade in differentiated products and the political economy of trade liberalization', in Jagdish Bhagwati (ed.), *Import Competition and Response*, Chicago: National Bureau for Economic Research, pp. 197–208.

Krugman, Paul (1990a), 'Industrial organization and international trade', in Richard Schmalensee and Robert D. Willig (eds), *Handbook of Industrial Organization*, Volume II, Amsterdam: North-Holland, pp. 1179–223.

Krugman, Paul (1990b), *Rethinking International Trade*, Cambridge, MA: MIT Press.

Lancaster, K. (1980), 'Intra-industry trade under perfect monopolistic competition', *Journal of International Economics*, **10**(2), 151–75.

Li and Fung (2006), 'What do experts say?: the ten highlights of China's commercial sector 2006–2007', Hong Kong: Li and Fung Research Centre, available at http://www.lifunggroup.com/research/pdf/china_special_061005.pdf.

Liu, G. (2001), *China's WTO Accession and the Impact on its Large Manufacturing Enterprises*, Singapore: Singapore University Press.

Lloyd, P. and D. MacLaren (2004), 'Gains and losses from regional trading agreements: a survey', *Economic Record*, **80**(251), 445–67.

Lyons, Bruce (1981), 'Price–cost margins, market structure and international trade', in David Currie, D. Peel and W. Peters (eds), *Microeconomic Analysis: Essays in Microeconomics and Economic Development*, London: Croom Helm, pp. 276–95.

Mai, Y., P. Adams, M. Fan, R. Li and Z. Zheng (2005), 'Modelling the potential benefits of an Australia–China Free Trade Agreement', Monash University Centre of Policy Studies working paper no. G-153, available at www.monash.edu.au/policy/.

Martin, C. (1997), 'Price formation in an open economy: theory and evidence for the United Kingdom, 1951–1991', *Economic Journal*, **107**, 1391–404.

Martin, S. (2002), *Advanced Industrial Economics*, Oxford: Blackwell.

Melvin, J. and J. Markusen (1981), 'Trade and the gains from trade with imperfect competition', *Journal of International Economics*, **11**(4), 531–51.

Mutti, J. (1978), 'Aspects of unilateral trade policy and factor adjustment costs', *Review of Economics and Statistics*, **60**(1), 102–10.

Negishi, T. (1961), 'Monopolistic competition and general equilibrium', *Review of Economic Studies*, **27**, 196–201.

Norman, N. (1975), 'On the relationship between prices of home-produced and foreign commodities', *Oxford Economic Papers*, **27**, 426–39.

Norman, N. (1996), 'A general post Keynesian theory of protection', *Journal of Post Keynesian Economics*, **18**(4), 509–31.

Norman, V. (1989), 'Trade policy under imperfect competition', *European Economic Review*, **33**, 473–9.

Pettengill, J. (1979), 'Monopolistic competition and optimum product diversity: comment', *American Economic Review*, **69**(5), 957–60.

Rodrik, D. (2006), 'What's so special about China's exports?', New York: National Bureau for Economic Research working paper no. 11947.

Schott, P. (2006), 'The relative sophistication of Chinese exports', New York: National Bureau for Economic Research working paper no. 12173.

Shy, Oz (2000), *The Theory of Industrial Economics*, Cambridge, MA: MIT Press.

Staelin, C. (1976), 'A general-equilibrium model of tariffs in a noncompetitive economy', *Journal of International Economics*, **6**(1), 39–63.

Suzuki, Katsuhiko (1991), 'Choice between free trade and controlled trade under economy of scale', in Akira Takayama (ed.), *Trade Policy and International Adjustments*, San Diego: Academic Press, pp. 173–92.

Thomas, W. (1988), 'Movements towards free trade and domestic market performance with imperfect competition', *Canadian Journal of Economics*, **21**(3), 507–24.

Venables, A. (1982), 'Optimal tariffs for trade in monopolistically competitive commodities', *Journal of International Economics*, **12**(4), 225–41.

Wonnacott, Robert and Ronald Hill, (1987), *Canadian and U.S. Adjustment Policies in a Bilateral Trade Agreement*, Washington, DC: Canadian–American Committee.

Wu, Yanrui and Qiang Ye (eds) (1998), *China's Reform and Economic Growth: Problems and Prospects*, Canberra: Asia Pacific Press.

5. Agriculture

Donald MacLaren

An FTA has the potential to place Australian farmers ahead of their competitors in the Chinese market.[1]

INTRODUCTION

The liberalization of international trade in agricultural products has proved to be difficult to achieve in bilateral, regional and multilateral trade negotiations. These difficulties stem from the role of agriculture in the economy, from the political economy of the agricultural sector and from the belief in some societies that agriculture is in some way 'special'. It is well known that the relative position of agriculture in the economy declines with economic growth and yet the sector seems able to maintain a substantial political influence despite its declining relative economic importance.[2] It is also well known that agriculture remained largely outside the trade rules of the General Agreement on Tariffs and Trade 1947 (GATT), that the sector has its own Agreement in the World Trade Organization (WTO) and that specific commodities are frequently excluded from bilateral trade agreements in possible violation of Article XXIV of GATT 1994 or, if included, the transition periods are well in excess of the 10-year period allowed in the Understanding.[3] In some developed economies, support by farmers for government intervention in their own sector is reinforced by society's apparent belief in the agrarian myth.[4] This belief provides part of the underpinning for the so-called multifunctionality of agriculture.[5] In developing countries and especially in the least-developed countries, a large part of economic activity is generated by the poor in rural communities and the dynamics that play out in relation to the agricultural sector are quite different in these countries. In particular, the sector is often taxed rather than subsidized.

The question to be investigated in this chapter is: will agriculture prove to be a sensitive sector in the negotiation of a free trade agreement between Australia and China as it has been in most recently negotiated bilateral FTAs?[6] In exploring this question and in providing a possible answer, the material is structured as follows. First, the typical objectives and instruments of agricultural policy are summarized. Second, in considering the issues faced by the negotiators in the Australia–China FTA and the impediments to agricultural trade liberalization, a brief description is provided of the policy objectives and instruments in each country. Third, the trends in bilateral agricultural commodity trade for Australia and China are studied through time series data. Fourth, for a number of reasons on each side of the negotiations, some commodities, and the issues associated with them, will be sensitive and these potential impediments to a comprehensive negotiation on agriculture are identified.[7] In the final section some conclusions are drawn.

GOVERNMENT AND AGRICULTURE

The objectives of government intervention are many and the weight given to each tends to vary across countries and over time within countries. In broad terms and traditionally, they include *inter alia*: the level and stability of the incomes of farm households; the moderation of price risk to achieve market stability; the security of food supply; the maintenance of livelihood security; the raising of productivity in the sector, especially that of labour; the maintenance of employment in rural areas; and the efficient marketing of agricultural products.[8] In more recent times, these objectives have been augmented by objectives such as the conservation of biodiverse habitats and the provision of safe food.[9]

In order to achieve these objectives, governments employ a wide variety of policy instruments. The choices made often do not satisfy any rational choice based upon economic criteria such as the targeting principle of welfare economics, but seem to be selected on the basis of considerations of political economy. Given the wide variety of instruments used and the need to make some sense of their economic effects, these tools are often categorized as those which affect: the prices received or paid by farmers (for example, subsidies on outputs and inputs, tariffs on imports and subsidies on exports); the size distribution of farms (for example, adjustment assistance programmes and, to induce earlier retirement, pensions for older farmers); the distribution of farm products (for example, statutory marketing authorities, public stock-holding and inspection services); incomes (for example, tax averaging and special depreciation allowances); and the capacity of farmers to adopt new technologies (for example, publicly funded research and development, and extension services).[10]

In the developed economies in general, the agricultural sector is subsidized in order to achieve several of the objectives listed above. The origin of this intervention is based largely on the consequences for the sector as the economy experiences economic growth and, today, those consequences have largely been forgotten as the *raison d'être* for intervention. In these countries, the agricultural sector contributes in the region of 2 per cent to GDP and perhaps 3 per cent to employment. Nevertheless, its political importance is substantially greater than these figures might suggest.[11] With a structure for the sector which may be characterized as one of atomistic producers in an industry with freedom of entry and exit, and one in which technological change constantly puts downward pressure on product prices and profits (the 'treadmill' effect), there is always the need for farmers either to increase the size of their business through improved productivity and investment in order to generate sufficient business and household income, or to leave the industry. For mixed reasons of equity, political economy and support by society in general, governments intervene to influence the extent to which these economic forces operate.

The consequences are several. First, there is a loss of static economic efficiency as farmers respond to corrupted price signals and misallocate resources both within the sector and across the economy. Second, there is moral hazard as risk-averse farmers face distorted income (wealth) security and alter their production decisions. Third, there is a loss of innovation in the long run as intervention slows the treadmill, although higher farm-gate prices and lower prices for variable inputs increase short-run profits and provide opportunities for increased investment. Fourth, these short-term gains become dissipated in the long run through their capitalization in higher land prices. Fifth, as large developed countries employ agricultural policy instruments which affect domestic production and consumption decisions, these countries affect and distort international markets for agricultural products by lowering international prices, to the benefit of third-country importers and to the detriment of third-country exporters. And sixth, the players in the political economy of the agricultural sector include not only politicians and farmers but also firms that are upstream and downstream of production agriculture, consumer welfare groups and the bureaucrats who administer the policies. Their interactions render policy reform extremely difficult even on a unilateral basis, let alone a bilateral, regional or multilateral basis.[12]

On the consumption side of the markets for agricultural products, there are four important characteristics. The first is that the price elasticities of demand for individual food products tend to be in the inelastic range and this attribute creates the volatility of prices at the farm gate when accompanied by unplanned variations in production and, for storable commodities, storage capacity that is inadequate to smooth quantities through time. The second is that income elasticities of demand for individual foods also tend to be low. This characteristic causes the Engel effect, that is, that households with higher incomes spend a lower proportion of their household budgets on food and in richer countries a smaller proportion of total expenditure goes on food. The third is that the composition of the diet changes as per capita incomes rise. Relatively more meat and dairy products are consumed and relatively smaller quantities of staples are consumed, although it is important to note that total cereal consumption continues to increase through the use of cereals as livestock feed. The fourth is that preferences are changing as globalization in general is increasingly being reflected in the globalization of diets (Lang 1999).

In an open economy, the pressure on farmers to expand or to exit is exacerbated by competition from imported substitutes. At the same time, openness to international trade tends to reduce the importance of the demand-side effects for an exporting country because both the price and the income elasticities of the export demand function may be very large. Therefore, there is an important asymmetry: farmers who compete with imported products suffer from both the 'treadmill' effect and the demand-side effect; those who export suffer less from the 'treadmill' effect than farmers producing import-competing commodities, although they remain in competition with farmers in other exporting countries, and they also gain from a larger and possibly growing export market. This asymmetry may help to explain why the forces of political economy are more difficult for governments to resist in countries that are predominantly importing countries for specific commodities than in those which export.

In developing economies and in the least-developed countries, the role of agriculture in economic development plays a part in determining agricultural policy but sensitivities about the livelihood security of the large, rural population and the political instability caused by high food prices for the urban population tend to dominate as reasons for government intervention. Thus, just as in developed economies, stability of markets is an important objective of agricultural and rural policy in developing economies. In the absence of market mechanisms – for example, futures markets – to offset the instability, government intervention may be the only feasible mechanism to help producers and consumers of food to accommodate risk. In addition, because of the limited opportunities for governments to raise tax revenue through domestic labour and product markets, tariffs on imports are important as a source of tax revenue. For this reason alone, there remains a reluctance on the part of governments in developing and especially the least-developed countries to liberalize their import regimes. But there are also other reasons. These governments have become captured by the political economy of the sector, although the details may differ from developed country cases because of the different political structures in place, especially in countries which do not have democratic governments. Thus, just as agricultural markets in developed countries are distorted by government intervention, so too are those in the developing and least-developed countries through inappropriate manipulation of prices.

Import demand functions and export supply functions reflect not only the underlying domestic demand and supply functions but also the effects of the domestic and trade instruments in place. The consequence of these distorted, domestic commodity markets is the distortion of international markets. Thus the trade flows and the prices that are observed reflect government action as well as the decisions made by economic agents. In addition, observed prices in international markets may also reflect the extent of imperfect competition that exists in international supply chains with the consequence that price transmission from international to domestic markets is less than perfect. Therefore, any attempt to measure the welfare gains from a reduction in barriers to imports needs to be conducted with care.

Against the background of agricultural policy described above, which has been presented in order to understand why agriculture is often a difficult sector over which to negotiate in any trade agreement, it is necessary now to become more specific. To achieve this outcome, a summary of the current objectives and instruments of agricultural policy in Australia and China is presented. Also of importance are quantitative measures of the extent to which the individual commodities within the agricultural sector in each economy are supported. By identifying those commodities which are now subject to high levels of support, it is possible to identify for each country those commodities which have the potential to be sensitive in a bilateral trade negotiation.

AGRICULTURAL POLICY IN AUSTRALIA AND CHINA

Australia

In 2005–6, the agricultural sector contributed 2.6 per cent to GDP, 3.1 per cent to employment and 18 per cent to merchandise exports (ABARE 2006b, Tables 1, 3 and 5, respectively). Two decades earlier, the corresponding figures had been 6.3 per cent, 5.6 per cent and 19.5 per cent, respectively. The current objectives of Australian agricultural policy are: to help individual farm businesses to profit from change; to ensure that the farm sector has access to an adequate welfare safety net; to provide positive incentives for ongoing farm adjustment; and to encourage social and economic development in rural areas (Commonwealth Government 1997).[13] Assistance to exports through explicit export subsidies does not exist.[14] However, it is not obvious whether products such as wheat, rice and sugar which are exported through a single export desk, receive implicit export subsidies through the ability of the export desk to price discriminate between the domestic and export market while pursuing an objective other than the maximization of profit.[15] On the import side, Australia has a tariff quota in place for cheese (which had an out-of-quota *ad valorem* tariff equivalent of approximately 40 per cent when introduced in the mid-1990s (MacLaren 2001)). Otherwise, tariffs are essentially zero.

Of considerably more importance for all potential exporters of agricultural products to Australia is the extensive range of quarantine measures that exist. These regulations exist largely to protect the life and health of plants and animals and to a lesser extent the life and health of humans. The measures have been challenged in recent years on a direct bilateral basis between governments, in the Sanitary and Phytosanitary (SPS) Committee in the WTO and formally through the Dispute Settlement Body in the WTO. Examples include the long-standing claim by New Zealand that its apples are safe to be imported by Australia, a claim which has been the subject of several import risk assessments in Australia and which remains unresolved. There is the claim by the Philippines that its exports of pineapples and bananas are safe to be imported by Australia but such imports are currently banned. There is also the concern expressed by the European Union and the United States about the perceived severity of Australia's import risk assessments and the strict quarantine regulations which derive from them.[16] Therefore, in the context of an FTA, any exports of agricultural products by China to Australia will face quarantine measures rather than tariffs or tariff quotas. However, it has been agreed that these measures are not on the agenda of the negotiations.

Domestic support which, formerly, took the form of product and input price manipulation has almost entirely ceased and domestic producer prices are now aligned with world prices. For example, the nominal rates of protection (NPCs) for some of the major products of Australian agriculture, namely, wheat, rice, sugar, cotton, beef and veal, mutton and lamb, milk and wool, are 1.0 (OECD 2006b). Even for imported commodities such as soybeans, the NPC is 1.0. Thus Australian domestic prices and world market prices (both measured at the farm gate) for each of these commodities are equal.

It is important to appreciate the significance of the current situation in Australia with respect to assistance to exports, import protection and domestic support. Until the 1970s, Australian agriculture was supported by government intervention but the manufacturing sector was even more

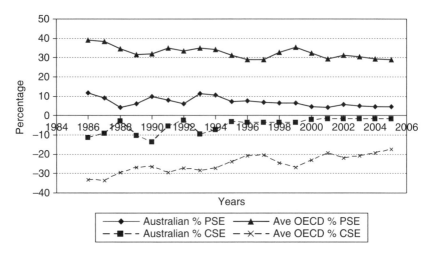

Notes:
Producer Support Estimate (PSE): an indicator of the annual monetary value of gross transfers from consumers and taxpayers to agricultural producers, measured at the farm-gate level, arising from policy measures that support agriculture, regardless of their nature, objectives or impacts on farm production or income. It includes market price support and budgetary payments, i.e. gross transfers from taxpayers to agricultural producers arising from policy measures based on: current output, area planted/animal numbers, historical entitlements, input use, input constraints, and overall farming income. The %PSE measures the transfers as a share of gross farm receipts.
Consumer Support Estimate (CSE): an indicator of the annual monetary value of gross transfers to (from) consumers of agricultural commodities, measured at the farm-gate level, arising from policy measures that support agriculture, regardless of their nature, objectives or impacts on consumption of farm products. If negative, the CSE measures the burden on consumers by agricultural policies, from higher prices and consumer charges or subsidies that lower prices to consumers. The %CSE measures the implicit tax (or subsidy, if CSE is positive) on consumers as a share of consumption expenditure at the farm gate (OECD 2006a, pp. 39–40).
N.B. Consumers in this context are the buyers of farm products at the first stage beyond the farm gate and are not final consumers of food products as usually described.

Source: OECD (2006b) PSE/CSE Database, Paris.

Figure 5.1   Percentage PSE and CSE, 1986–2005

heavily supported. This meant that agriculture, relative to manufacturing, was actually implicitly taxed, as remains typical in developing countries, with the attendant static misallocation of resources and loss of economic efficiency.[17] Since that time, the Commonwealth and the state governments in Australia have largely withdrawn from agricultural policy and the consequences of these withdrawals are shown in Figure 5.1.[18] The downward trend in the overall level of support to farmers, as measured

Table 5.1   *Nominal rates of assistance (NRA in percentage) for selected agricultural commodities, Australia, 1985–9 to 2000–3*

Fiscal year (starting 1 July)	1985–9	1990–4	1995–9	2000–3
Wheat	3.8	2.1	1.1	0.0
Rice	10.6	2.5	2.3	1.7
Sugar	12.4	5.8	1.7	0.0
Cotton	2.0	0.0	0.0	0.0
Beef and veal	1.2	0.3	0.0	0.0
Mutton and lamb	1.8	0.9	0.0	0.0
Milk	39.6	23.8	19.3	0.0
Wool	1.0	5.4	0.7	0.0
Maize	0.0	0.0	0.0	0.0
Tobacco	37.6	48.5	19.8	0.0

Source: Anderson et al. (2007), Table 2.

by the percentage producer support estimate (%PSE), is remarkable, especially when put in the context of other OECD countries/regions as represented by the average for the 30 OECD countries.[19] In 2005, the %PSE for Australia was 5 and the average for the OECD countries was 29.[20] Australian consumers of commodities face lower prices than do those in the average OECD country because, in most other OECD countries, farm prices are supported in part through instruments which also raise prices to consumers. What is also different about the Australian situation today is that the percentage of the overall support that comes from market price manipulation of both output and input prices is practically zero. The support that remains comes through so-called 'green box' instruments which are thought not to distort domestic and, hence, international markets.[21]

The data in Figure 5.1 mask the variation in support that existed on a commodity-by-commodity basis and the timing of the subsequent changes in that support. This detail is provided for two decades in Table 5.1. Of particular note is support for milk, which was a factor of approximately 10 higher than support for the other commodities listed. However, the domestic milk market was totally deregulated in 2000 when the political economy allowed, and the effect can be seen to have been a substantial reduction in the nominal rate of assistance (NRA) from 19.3 per cent to 0.0 per cent.[22] There are two importable commodities in the table, namely, maize and tobacco. In the case of maize, there was no support during the period shown and in the case of tobacco, which was heavily supported in

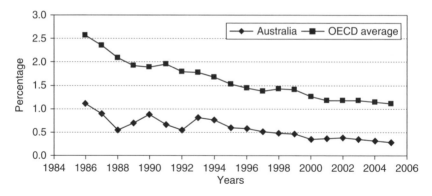

Source: OECD (2006b) PSE/CSE Database, Paris.

*Figure 5.2   Total support estimate as a percentage of GDP (%TSE),
                 1986–2005*

the past, there is no longer support. Both examples again contrast with the
situation on other OECD countries, with the exception of New Zealand
(see Anderson et al. 2007), in which the NRAs have fallen to a much
smaller extent.

The total support provided to the agricultural sector by taxpayers and
consumers is computed by the OECD as the total support estimate (TSE
– see OECD 2006a, p. 40). This total is then expressed as a percentage of
GDP to enable cross-country comparisons to be made.[23] For Australia
and for the average of OECD countries, there has been a downward
trend in that percentage since the mid-1980s (Figure 5.2). In addition, the
support in Australia compared with that for the OECD is considerably
lower. This difference largely, but not totally, reflects the withdrawal of
government from agricultural sector support in Australia when compared
with the behaviour of governments in other OECD countries, countries in
which the percentage of GDP generated in the sector is comparable with
Australia's.

The agricultural sector in Australia today operates with little assistance
from government as shown in Table 5.1 and, in comparison with other
OECD countries the support is negligible, as shown in Figures 5.1 and
5.2. However, to the extent that quarantine regulations are unnecessarily
import restrictive in order to achieve the acceptable level of protection from
risk, as claimed by some countries that would wish to export to Australia,
the industry is also supported by these regulations, especially in the
horticultural sector, a sector which may have a comparative disadvantage
with respect to China's horticultural sector in any preferential trade

agreement. From this summary of Australian agricultural policy, it is clear that Australian negotiators have very little, if anything, to offer Chinese negotiators on agricultural sector negotiations, it having been agreed by both sides that Sanitary and Phytosanitary (SPS) measures are not on the negotiating table.

China

The agricultural and rural policy reforms that began in China in 1979 with the demise of the commune system and its replacement with the household responsibility system continued to evolve through the 1980s and 1990s and they culminated in the changes that were required to be made as part of China's accession to the WTO in 2001.[24] The final steps in the process of reform were completed in 2004 at the conclusion of the transition period. The Chinese government's level of support for the agricultural sector is much lower than that provided in most of the OECD countries and much of it comes through barriers to imports in the form of tariffs, tariff quotas and state trading enterprises. Today, farmers face fewer constraints in the form of government procurement on their production and marketing decisions than they did in earlier times; domestic markets are less distorted, for example, producers of wheat and rice are no longer being implicitly taxed through low government procurement prices; and domestic and international prices are more closely aligned, especially for wheat and rice.

International trade in agricultural products was used formerly as a balancing item between domestic consumption and planned production. Any deviation between planned and actual production was neutralized by net trade flows controlled by state trading enterprises and by changes in stocks. However, long before membership of the WTO was realized, China had begun to be more open to trade (Huang et al. 2007). Today, the foreign exchange rate regime has been modernized but still controlled, international trade is now determined more by market forces than by bureaucratic decision, and the impediments to imports caused by import quotas, licensing and tariffs have been reduced but not removed (Huang et al. 2007). At the time of China's accession to the WTO, the average bound tariff rate on agricultural products was 22 per cent. At the end of the transition period in 2004, this figure was to be 17 per cent (WTO 2001). However, there remain many non-tariff barriers and these are a source of concern to Australian firms exporting agricultural products to China.[25]

The overall effect of these changes in policy has been to allow the agricultural sector to grow over the past two decades by around 3.6 per cent per annum compared with an annual growth rate during the period 1970–8 of 2.7 per cent (Huang et al. 2007, Table 1). For the economy as a whole, the corresponding figures for GDP were 8.9 per cent and 4.9 per cent. Because of the relatively slower rate of increase in agricultural output, the share of the sector in GDP fell from 40 per cent in 1970 to less than 13 per cent in 2005 (Huang et al. 2007, p. 12). Over the same period, the agricultural sector's contribution to employment fell from 81 per cent to 45 per cent. Within the agricultural sector (defined here as crops, livestock, fishery and forestry) the composition of products has changed between 1980 and 2005: the share of crops has fallen from 80 per cent to 51 per cent, the share of fisheries has grown from 2 per cent to 10 per cent and that of livestock products from 18 per cent to 35 per cent, with forestry unchanged (Huang et al. 2007, Table 2). These changes in the composition of production reflect the changes in the composition of diets as economic development and growth have proceeded in an environment of partially managed international trade.

The changes in diet have been significant. For example, between 1981 and 2004, per capita annual grain consumption fell from 145 kilos to 78 kilos while per capita consumption of meat, eggs and aquatic products increased over the same period from 20, 5 and 7 kilos respectively, to 29, 10 and 12 kilos (Dong and Fuller 2006). Such changes could have been due to changes in relative prices, to increased per capita incomes and to changes in preferences. Dong and Fuller concluded that all three explanations are necessary to account for changes in the composition of food consumed in urban areas but they found that changes in preferences which have been brought about by changing lifestyles and changes in the marketing of food products (including the increasing importance of supermarkets) were more important for some products than for others. For example, changes in the consumption of grains, pork and vegetables could be explained by price and income effects whereas changes for fruits, fish and beef were explained by a shift in preferences. With the increased openness of the Chinese economy to international trade, these changes on the consumption side will be translated into changes in import demand or export supply for different commodities with attendant implications for Australian exports of agricultural and food commodities to, and imports from, China.

As part of the terms of accession, China introduced tariff quotas on a number of commodities while others were to be protected only by tariffs. Tariff quotas (TQs) were introduced *inter alia* for wheat, rice, canola, sugar, wool (raw and tops) and cotton. In 2001, the bound percentage tariff rates for out-of-quota imports were 74, 74, 63, 71.6, 38 and 61.6 respectively, while by 2005 they were 65, 65, 9, 50, 38 and 40 (ABARE 2006a, Table 1.6). In 2005, the bound, in-quota rates for wheat, rice, raw wool and cotton were 1 per cent, for sugar the rate was 15 per cent, for canola 9 per cent and for wool tops 3 per cent. Which of these tariff rates applies in any year (that is, the in-quota or out-of-quota) depends upon whether or not the quota is binding.

In general, an import regime which involves TQs has three possible outcomes: first, the quota is not binding and the domestic market is protected by the in-quota tariff only; second, the quota binds and the domestic market is protected by the quota only; and third, imports exceed the quota and the domestic market reflects both the quota and the out-of-quota tariff.[26] In the first of these three situations, the fill rate can be measured, that is, actual imports as a percentage of the quota, and it is usually found to be less then 100 per cent. The evidence for China in 2003 was that the fill rate for wheat and for rice was 5 per cent, for sugar 42 per cent, for canola 14.9 per cent, for raw wool 40 per cent and for wool tops 36 per cent (ABARE 2006a, Table 1.8). The reasons for this outcome include the position of the import demand function relative to the quota and the way in which the quota is allocated to importing firms. In China, the state trading enterprises retain a guaranteed share of the quotas for several commodities and as these enterprises do not necessarily act on the basis of profit maximization and their purchasing decisions are opaque, there remains the suspicion that they restrict imports to ensure a greater share of the domestic market for domestic producers (Carter and Li 2005). The guaranteed access to the quotas for the state trading enterprises are 90 per cent for wheat, 50 per cent for rice, 70 per cent for sugar, and for wool the corresponding figure is 0 per cent (ABARE 2006a). However, whether the fill rates can be explained by the maladministration of the quotas by the state trading enterprises or because domestic production is higher than normal or domestic consumption is lower than normal, is not pursued here.

Not all imports of agricultural products are subject to a regime of tariff quotas. Most face a regime of only tariffs. For these products, the bound rates as of 2005 are, generally, reasonably low by the standards of OECD countries. For example, for feed grains (including barley) the rates average around 3 per cent, for vegetables around 10 per cent, for fruits around 11 per cent and for dairy products around 10 per cent. For meat products, the bound rates are somewhat higher, being between 12 per cent and 20 per cent for beef and for pig meat, and 15 per cent for lamb (ABARE 2006a). The values of the most-favoured nation (MFN) rates are important because they partly determine the extent to which trade within an FTA occurs at preferential rates.[27]

In its accession commitments to the WTO, China agreed to undertake reforms of its agricultural policy to an extent which the major OECD countries have been unwilling for years to undertake for themselves.[28] First, the period of transition was only three years compared with the six (ten) years that the developed (developing) countries were allowed in the WTO Agreement on Agriculture to introduce the reforms which had been mandated. Second, all tariffs are *ad valorem*, while both the European Union and the United States, in particular among other OECD countries, make considerable use of specific tariffs. These have the effect of obscuring the protection provided, of providing greater protection when world prices are low and, thereby, reducing the extent of down-side price risk for their domestic producers.[29]

In addition to tariffs and tariff quotas, exports of agricultural products to China face SPS measures. These measures should be applied in a manner which is consistent with the SPS Agreement. It is well known that developing countries experience difficulties when attempting to apply these measures in conformity with the Agreement because of lack of technical, testing and scientific resources.[30] While this situation may explain the problems which exporters face, some of the inconsistencies in applying SPS standards appear to lie with the different behaviour of the provincial and the central governments (ABARE 2006a). However, the problems are more varied than differences between levels of government. They include: the non-adoption of international standards;[31] the use of different standards for different sources of imports; differences in the standards applied to domestic and import product; and lack of transparency (ABARE 2006a, p. 48).

The producer nominal protection coefficient for the average of the OECD countries in 2003–5 was estimated to be 1.27, ranging from a low of 1.00 for Australia, to 1.07 for the USA, to 1.29 for the EU, to a high of 2.53 for Korea (OECD 2006a, Table I.1.3).[32] These figures are not directly comparable with the figure of the average tariff of 17 per cent on China's imports of agricultural products, because the OECD statistics include the effects of non-tariff measures, but they do suggest that protection from imports for Chinese domestic agriculture is considerably less than that for the OECD countries on average, as well as that for the important agricultural traders within that group, namely, the EU, Japan and Korea. Unlike the situation in Australia where the overall assistance to farmers, as measured by the %PSE, has been falling steadily (see Figure 5.1), in China support for agriculture has fluctuated. In particular, in 1993 and again in 1999, the sector was taxed and not subsidized as it was in the years in between, as well as between 2000 and 2003 (Table 5.2). What is also noticeable from Table 5.2 is that the %PSE was increasing during the transition period. It should be noted that these numbers, nevertheless, compare very favourably with the average for the OECD countries in 2003 of 30 per cent (Figure 5.1).

The form in which the support was provided in 2000–3 was approximately

Table 5.2   %PSE for China, 1993–2003

	1993	1994	1995	1996	1997	1998	1999	2000	2001	2002	2003
%PSE	−14	1	6	1	1	1	−3	3	5	7	8

Source: OECD 2006a, Table I.2.1.

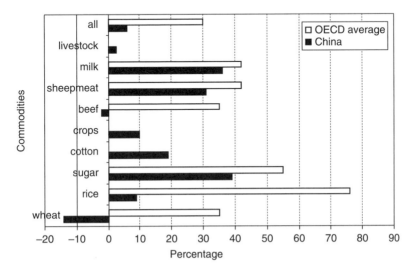

Note: For China, the data are estimated from Figure 3 in OECD (2005a) and are the average for the period 2000–3. For the OECD average, the data are the average for 2002–4 and are exact, from OECD (2005b).

Source: OECD (2005a, Figure 3) and OECD (2005b, Table 1.6).

Figure 5.3   %PSE for selected commodities, China and OECD

60 per cent through product price supports, 20 per cent through support on output and input use and 20 per cent through other means (OECD 2006a, Figure I.2.1). Between 1995–7 and 2000–3, the support provided through market price support had increased by some 20 percentage points with a corresponding decrease in the percentage provided through output and input use. This is not a trend that would be supported by economists.

Within the overall %PSE for China, there is substantial variation with some commodities being heavily supported, for example, sugar, and others – for example, wheat – being heavily taxed (Figure 5.3). The pattern of commodity support that is evident in OECD countries on average differs somewhat from that which is evident in China. In particular, while milk and sugar are heavily supported in each, there are substantial differences for beef and for wheat: both are taxed in China but subsidized in the OECD countries. Support for import-competing commodities (for example, sugar, milk, sheep meat) comes through state trading enterprises (OECD 2005a).

The total cost of agricultural support in China to its economy can be measured as the %TSE. For the period 2000–3, the %TSE was 3.3 per cent (OECD 2005a). This compares with the average for the OECD countries of 1.2 for 2002–4 (OECD 2005b). However, for China, 56 per cent of the total TSE comes largely from budgetary expenditures (the general services support estimate in OECD language) which are not commodity specific but sector-wide. This relatively high %TSE reflects two characteristics of the situation in China: the absolute size of the budgetary expenditures, and the relatively large contribution of the agricultural sector to GDP (approximately 13 per cent in 2005 (OECD 2006a, p. 36)). The first of these characteristics suggests that the Chinese government is investing in long-run productivity improvements in the sector and this emphasis is a positive sign for the long-run economic health of the sector.[33] As also noted by the OECD (2005a), increasing productivity will increase farmers' incomes.

Bilateral Trade in Agricultural Products

The share of Australian exports of agricultural products destined for China in total exports of agricultural products has almost doubled from 6 per cent in 1989–99 to 11 per cent in 2005–6 (computed from ABARE 2006b, Table 21). The share for cotton has increased from 1 per cent to 11 per cent, for grains from 2 per cent to 5 per cent, for dairy products from 1 per cent to 3 per cent and for sugar from 2 per cent to 4 per cent. The only product for which China is a relatively very important destination is wool, the share having grown over the same period from 48 per cent to 58 per cent (computed from ABARE 2006a, Table 1.9, and ABARE 2006b, Table 20). China is now the second most important destination for exports of Australian barley, having overtaken Japan. Over the past decade China's share of the Australian market for imports of agricultural products has increased from 3 per cent to 5 per cent. However, the most important source is the European Union (EU25) at 31 per cent thus putting in perspective the position with respect to China. However, agricultural products (food and live animals) remain unimportant in total imports from China − the share being 1.7 per cent in 2003–4 in a total of $15,339 million (ABARE 2006a, Table 1.9).

SENSITIVE PRODUCTS IN THE FTA

According to the Hecksher–Ohlin theory of comparative advantage, bilateral trade is explained by differences in relative factor endowments. It is often suggested on this basis that, in the context of a bilateral free trade agreement between Australia and China, Australia would export to China land-intensive and capital-intensive products such as grains, dairy products, meats and wine, and China would export to Australia labour-intensive products such as fruits and vegetables. In principle, it would be possible to investigate this conjecture by calculating an index of revealed comparative advantage.[34]

However, as discussed above, Australian imports of agricultural products are strictly controlled through SPS measures and to the extent that they protect the incomes of Australian producers of import-competing products as well as protecting the health and life of Australian plants, animals and humans as intended, trade flows will not truly reveal comparative disadvantage. China's imports and exports of agricultural products also reflect government intervention both at the border and behind the border (see above) as well as any comparative advantage. Thus, no attempt has been made in this chapter to compute indexes of revealed comparative advantage as a means of determining the possible pattern of agricultural commodity trade that might exist after an FTA were implemented because the resulting indexes could not be interpreted as revealing comparative advantage; instead they would partially reflect government intervention.

Instead, all that can be accomplished is a review of the trade barriers which are currently faced by Australian exports to China and an identification of those which provide grounds for negotiation. It was noted in a previous section that the Chinese government restricts import market access through a combination of tariffs, tariff quotas, SPS measures and state trading enterprises. It has already been noted that China's tariff rates on imports of agricultural products are low by OECD standards and it may be difficult for the Chinese government now to concede on a preferential basis more than it has already done multilaterally in its accession to the WTO.

However, tariff quotas are a different matter: there is lack of transparency in the administration of the quotas; there is involvement of state trading enterprises in their allocation and there are high out-of quota tariff rates. Here there is scope for some downward adjustment on a preferential basis of the in-quota and out-of-quota tariff rates, as well as of preferential allocation of the quota. For commodities such as wheat and rice, state trading enterprises are guaranteed a 90 per cent share of the quota and, given their objectives and the opportunity for political influence, the volume of imports may not duplicate the volumes that would be imported by private traders in a deregulated market. While it would be straightforward for some countries to seek the deregulation of state trading enterprises as a means of improving import market access in general, this item for negotiation is difficult for Australian negotiators given the continued existence of exporting state trading enterprises in Australia for wheat, rice and sugar.

A lack of transparency in the allocation of tariff quotas is only one manifestation of the way in which officialdom can increase the costs for exporters and provide domestic producers with subtle and opaque additions to their levels of protection. In a recent study, the Australian Bureau of Agriculture and Resource Economics (ABARE 2006a, Chapter 2) presented some evidence of the difficulties faced by exporters of agricultural products to China. These difficulties were classified as non-tariff barriers, some of which are tariff quotas, some of which are SPS and food-safety measures, some of which are state trading enterprises and some of which are bureaucratic, perhaps the most difficult for exporters to counter. Although SPS measures per se are not on the negotiating table, the way in which these and associated measures are applied could be a very important component of the negotiations on agriculture.

In summary, the evidence presented by ABARE (2006a, Chapter 2) is as follows. There is duplication of the inspection processes for imported commodities which have already been inspected prior to export. This is an issue for wool, genetic material and cotton. The application of SPS measures through inspection and testing is an issue for grains, meat and other animal products, and horticultural products. Apart from lack of transparency, there is also the claim made that agreed standards are inconsistently applied in different ports and for imports from different export sources. Food safety standards for imports of raw meat have been set at tolerances which are impossible to achieve. There is a lack of legal enforcement of contracts especially for imports of cotton, a commodity which has been imported by mills and then not paid for. Labelling is an issue for imported dairy products and wine, products which Australia would be anxious to export to China in increasing volumes. For dairy products the issue is that the standards for storage are such that butter could only be imported in frozen form. In the case of wine, the packaging must have labels in Chinese and these must be approved by Chinese authorities, leading to delays and added costs to exporters. Lastly, there is evidence that value added tax is applied differentially between products sourced domestically and imported which, if true, might be in violation of GATT Article III (see WTO 1995, p. 490).

CONCLUSIONS

The deregulation of agricultural commodity markets both at the border and behind the border continues to be difficult. This reality is present in unilateral, bilateral and multilateral situations. Australia is almost alone in successfully achieving a high degree of deregulation in its domestic and trade policies with respect to agricultural products. The agricultural sector receives relatively little support behind the border (with the exception of under-priced irrigation water) or at the border through government activity; the only outstanding trade issue as far as its trading partners are concerned is the existence of very strict quarantine regulations. Thus, in any bilateral trade negotiation, such as the one with China, Australia has little, if anything, to offer on agriculture in exchange for gains for her exporters of agricultural products. Hence, any claims for preferential access to a bilateral partner will require some accommodation in other sectors of the Australian economy such as manufactures and services and there may be little to offer there either.

For almost three decades China has undertaken a series of economic reforms in its agricultural sector. These have occurred both domestically and at the border. Nevertheless, there is scope for further deregulation and scope for preferential gains for Australia. In domestic markets for agricultural products, there remains some market intervention by governments which distorts production decisions and, therefore, international trade. At the border, there remain *ad valorem* tariffs and non-tariff measures such as tariff quotas, SPS regulations and state trading enterprises. Each of these non-tariff measures provides scope for the bureaucracy to impose itself in the form of opaque and lengthy processes which increase the costs for exporters, discourage exports and ultimately, provide a larger market for domestically produced import-competing products. This scope exists in the allocation of the quota for each product among potential exporters, in the interaction of state trading enterprises with the quota regime, and in the application of SPS measures to individual shipments of products.

By their very nature, these administrative barriers to trade exist essentially behind the border and they are difficult to deal with in a bilateral trade negotiation. Moreover, it is unlikely that they could be made more efficient on a preferential basis. Whilst it is relatively straightforward to alter tariff rates on a preferential basis, bureaucracy is more difficult to deal with. In any case, there is bound to be tension for the exporting country in trying to benefit in practice from administrative favour, while in principle decrying in the WTO such lack of transparency and arbitrariness in bureaucratic processes.

The political emphasis in bilateral FTAs, just as in the WTO, is on the mercantilist position – it is all about increasing the gains to exporting firms with some regard paid to the losses of import-competing firms and little, if any, mention made of domestic consumers. In this chapter, the focus has been on the economics of agriculture in the context of the FTA being negotiated between Australia and China. It is concluded that it will be difficult for Australia to gain much because of the nature of the administered protection in place in China.

NOTES

1. http://www.dfat.gov.au/geo/china/fta/facts/agriculture.pdf.
2. Agriculture's contribution to global production and trade is approximately 7 per cent (Martin and Anderson 2006, p. 1211) and yet failure to conclude the multilateral negotiations on agriculture was largely responsible for the suspension of the Doha Round in the World Trade Organization in July 2006, although negotiations were resumed in early 2007.
3. The 'Understanding' refers to the Understanding on the Interpretation of Article XXIV of GATT 1994 (see WTO 1995, pp. 31–4). For a history of agriculture in the GATT, see Josling et al. (1996). In the FTA between Australia and the USA, the latter refused to allow sugar to be on the negotiating table. This outcome arose despite sugar being one of five commodities on which the Australian government was keen to achieve preferential access. As a consequence of the failure to achieve this outcome, Australian sugar producers received compensation amounting to A$440 million for promised benefits which had not been realized (see Dee 2005). The fact that such unusual compensation was thought necessary by the Commonwealth government in the face of refusal by the USA to negotiate illustrates the strength of the political economy of the sugar lobby in both countries.
4. This myth amounts to a strongly-held belief in the virtues of rural life and of the risks attendant upon low self-sufficiency in food; see Galbraith (1987, p. 52) for an account of the historical setting.
5. The term multifunctionality is ill-defined but it refers to the public goods produced by agricultural production in addition to the private goods of food and fibre. For an economic analysis of multifunctionality, see OECD (2001).
6. In the recently concluded negotiations for an FTA involving Korea and the USA, agriculture proved to be a difficult sector for the negotiators: Korea refused to allow rice to be on the negotiating table while agreeing that beef would be allowed a long transition period. In the FTA between Australia and the USA, the USA agreed to preferential access for beef and for dairy products with implementation periods of 18 years and 17 years, respectively (DFAT 2004). In the case of beef, as well as of some horticultural products, safeguard mechanisms were also insisted upon which will diminish the extent of preferential access if an import surge occurs. For a detailed account of the Australia–USA FTA, see Mitchell and Voon (2007).
7. It would have been useful to present results for agriculture obtained *ex ante* from quantitative economic modelling of an Australia–China FTA. However, the study by Mai et al. (2005) is too aggregated and it does not provide welfare results.
8. Sometimes these objectives are referred to as non-economic objectives in the sense that they are not designed to achieve economic efficiency. For a discussion of this view, see Winters (1990).
9. Supply chains in the food industry have been lengthening and with that lengthening there has been increased recognition of additional sources of risks to the provision of safe food. In order to prevent excessive and unwarranted use of import barriers to moderate these risks, Members of the WTO are required to abide by their obligations as

specified in the Agreement on the Application of Sanitary and Phytosanitary Measures (see WTO 1995).

10. This classification is not the only one available. For example, the OECD uses a more comprehensive classification in calculating the components of the total support estimate (see note 23).

11. The history of agriculture in the GATT 1947 and its more recent history in the Doha Development Round in the WTO illustrates clearly the political muscle of farmers in the OECD countries. For an account of the political economy of agriculture, see Swinnen and van der Zee (1993) and Brooks (1996); for a more wide-ranging account of the economics of agricultural policy, see Anderson and Josling (2005), especially Volume I, parts 1 and 2.

12. For a discussion of the role of the bureaucracy in the maintenance and continuation of agricultural policy, see Harvey (2004).

13. To put these objectives in context, they should be compared with those of 20 years ago. At that time there was much more emphasis on expanding production and on stabilizing incomes. The instruments chosen by the Commonwealth government and by state governments to achieve these goals included institutionally influenced product and variable input prices, quotas and statutory marketing arrangements for many commodities.

14. Until the mid-1990s, there was a levy on milk producers. The levy was rebated on sales of dairy products for exports and this rebate had the effect of providing an implicit export subsidy through reducing sales of dairy products to the domestic market and thereby increasing them on export markets.

15. The trade effects of a state trading enterprise depend on the interaction of the nature of the exclusive rights given to it by government and the objective function which it pursues. McCorriston and MacLaren (2007) have shown that the trade effects of the Australian Wheat Board have changed over the years as the nature of its exclusive rights and objectives have changed from having exclusive rights in both the domestic and export markets to having exclusive rights in only the export market and as its objective has changed from maximizing returns to wheat growers to a mixture of maximizing these returns together with maximizing returns to its shareholders.

16. Under Article 7.4 of the AUSFTA, a Committee on Sanitary and Phytosanitary (SPS) matters was established with the aim of enhancing each country's implementation of the WTO SPS Agreement.

17. For an account of this economic history, see Anderson et al. (2007).

18. For an account of the political economy of agricultural policy in Australia during the 1980s, see Martin (1990).

19. For a definition, see the note attached to Figure 5.1.

20. Given the current concerns in many countries, including Australia and China, about the misallocation of water used in agriculture, it is important to note the following statement from the OECD: '[s]ubject to data availability, the amount of support resulting from reduced water prices for farmers is included in the PSE as payments based on the use of variable inputs. Government support for the operation and maintenance of water infrastructure is included in the General Services Support Estimate, but initial investments for building the infrastructure are not taken into account' (OECD 2006a, p. 27).

21. The term 'green box' originated in the Uruguay Round negotiations and refers to those agricultural policy instruments which are deemed to be minimally trade distorting and which are funded solely through the national budget. These instruments include items such as payments for drought relief, pensions for farmers to encourage early retirement and payments for the environmental services provided by farmers. There continues to be a debate about whether these 'decoupled' payments are minimally trade distorting in practice given the acknowledged risk-averse behaviour by farmers. To the extent that farmers are risk averse, such payments will alter their production decisions, *ceteris paribus*, and cause production of risky commodities to increase. This outcome will affect trade flows.

22. As part of this deregulation, consumers of liquid milk pay a levy at retail of 11 cents per litre until 2008 in order to compensate milk producers for lower farm-gate prices and to provide adjustment assistance where requested.
23. The support to producers (PSE) and to consumers (CSE) are terms which have been defined already – see the notes attached to Figure 5.1. The general services support estimate (GSSE) is a component of the total support estimate (TSE) and is defined as 'an indicator of the annual monetary value of gross transfers to general services provided to agriculture collectively, arising from policy measures that support agriculture regardless of their nature, objectives and impacts on farm production, income, or consumption' (OECD 2006a, p. 40). The TSE is 'an indicator of the annual monetary value of all gross transfers from taxpayers and consumers arising from policy measures that support agriculture, net of the associated budgetary receipts, regardless of their objectives and impacts on farm production and income, or consumption of farm products. The %TSE measures the overall transfers from agricultural policy as a percentage of GDP' (OECD 2006a, p. 40).
24. For an analysis of the effects of the household responsibility system, see Lin (1992). The details of China's accession protocol is available in WTO (2001).
25. For an account, see DFAT (2005).
26. For an economic analysis of tariff quotas, see de Gorter (2004).
27. It has been found (see, for example Augier et al. 2005) that a margin of at least four percentage points between the MFN and preferential rates is required to enable preferential trade to take place. Moreover, rules of origin may be sufficiently onerous to fulfil that, again, trade within the FTA may not occur at the preferential rates.
28. The current negotiations on agriculture taking place in the WTO began in 2000 (see WTO 2004b for details). Thereafter, they became part of the Doha Round. In comparing the stage that they had reached in July 2004 (see WTO 2004a) and July 2006 (see WTO 2006), it is clear that almost no progress had been made on the substantive issue of modalities.
29. For an analysis of the insulating effect of different import barriers, see Lloyd and Falvey (1985). These countries were resistant in the Doha Round negotiations to converting their specific tariffs to *ad valorem* form for the purposes of defining the modalities for tariff reform, partly because such conversions would reveal the true extent of the protection being provided.
30. For analysis and discussion, see Athukorala and Jayasuriya (2003).
31. Departures from international standards are permitted in the SPS Agreement but they need to be justified on the basis of a properly conducted import risk assessment (see Annex A:5 of the SPS Agreement (WTO 1995)).
32. The producer nominal protection coefficient is defined as 'the ratio between the average price received by producers (at farm gate), including payments per tonne of current output, and the border price (measured at farm gate)' (OECD 2006a, p. 40).
33. Huang et al. (2007) note that agricultural research and plant breeding is 'almost completely organized by the government' (p. 19) and that plant breeding programmes going back to the 1960s were successful in producing semi-dwarf, high-yielding varieties of rice 'several years before the Green Revolution began in other parts of Asia' (p. 8).
34. RCA is defined as $RCA_{ij} = (X_{ij}/\Sigma_i X_{ij}) \div (\Sigma_j X_{ij}/\Sigma_i\Sigma_j X_{ij})$, where: X_{ij} are the exports of sector i from country j; $\Sigma_i X_{ij}$ are country j's total exports; $\Sigma_j X_{ij}$ are total exports of sector i across all countries; and $\Sigma_i\Sigma_j X_{ij}$ are total exports across all sectors and all countries.

REFERENCES

ABARE (Australian Bureau of Agricultural and Resource Economics) (2006a), 'Agriculture in China: Developments and Significance for Australia', research report 06.2, March, Canberra.

ABARE (Australian Bureau of Agricultural and Resource Economics) (2006b), *Australian Commodity Statistics 2006*, Canberra: ABARE.

Anderson, K. and T.E. Josling (eds) (2005), *The WTO and Agriculture*, Cheltenham, UK and Northampton, MA, USA: Edward Elgar.

Anderson, K., R. Lattimore, P.J. Lloyd and D. MacLaren (2007), 'Distortions to agricultural incentives in Australia and New Zealand', World Bank Agricultural Distortions working paper 09, August, Washington, DC.

Athukorala, P.-C. and S. Jayasuriya (2003), 'Food safety issues, trade and WTO rules: a developing country perspective', *The World Economy*, **26**, 1395–416.

Augier, P., M. Gasiorek and C.L. Tong (2005), 'The impact of rules of origin on trade flows', *Economic Policy*, **20**(43), 567–624.

Brooks, J. (1996), 'Agricultural policies in OECD countries: what can we learn from political economy models?', *Journal of Agricultural Economics*, **47**(3), 366–89.

Carter, C. and X. Li (2005), 'Agricultural tariff rate quotas: impacts on market access', paper presented at the American Agricultural Economics Association Annual Meeting, Providence, Rhode Island, 24-7 July.

Commonwealth Government (1997), *Agriculture – Advancing Australia*, Canberra, available at www.daff.gov.av/agriculture-food/aac.

de Gorter, H. (2004), 'Market access, export subsidies, and domestic support: developing new rules', in M.D. Ingco and A.L. Winters (eds), *Agriculture and the New Trade Agenda: Creating a Global Trading Environment for Development*, Cambridge: Cambridge University Press, pp. 151–75.

DFAT (Department of Foreign Affairs and Trade) (2004), *Australia–United States Free Trade Agreement*, Canberra: Department of Foreign Affairs and Trade, Annex 2-B Schedule of the United States, General Notes: Tariff Schedule of the United States.

DFAT (Department of Foreign Affairs and Trade) (2005), 'Australia–China FTA negotiations: Interest and concerns of the Australian agriculture sector', available at www.dfat.gov.au/geo/china/fta/facts/agriculture_2.html.

Dee, P. (2005), 'The Australia–US Free Trade Agreement: an assessment', Pacific economic paper no. 345, Canberra: Australian National University.

Dong, F. and F.H. Fuller (2006), 'Changing diets in China's cities: Empirical fact or urban legend?', Ames: Center for Agricultural and Rural Development, Iowa State University working paper no. 06-WP 437, November.

Galbraith, J.K. (1987), *The History of Economics: the Past as the Present*, London: Hamish Hamilton.

Harvey, D.R. (2004), 'Policy dependency and reform: economic gains versus political pains', *Agricultural Economics*, **31**, 265–75.

Huang, J., S. Rozelle, W. Martin and Y. Liu (2007), 'Distortions to agricultural incentives in China', agricultural distortions working paper, February, Washington, DC: The World Bank.

Josling, T.E. and K. Anderson (2005), *The WTO and Agriculture*, Cheltenham, UK and Northampton, MA, USA: Edward Elgar.

Josling, T.E., S. Tangermann and T.K. Warley (1996), *Agriculture in the GATT*, Basingstoke: Macmillan Press.

Lang, T. (1999), 'Diet, health and globalization: five key questions', *Proceedings of the Nutrition Society*, **58**, 335–43.

Lin, J. (1992), 'Rural reforms and agricultural growth in China', *American Economic Review*, **82**(1), 34–51.

Lloyd, P.J. and R.E. Falvey (1985), 'The choice of instrument for industry protection', in R.H. Snape (ed.), *Issues in World Trade Policy: GATT at the Crossroads*, London: Macmillan Press, chapter 2.

MacLaren, D. (2001), 'The case of Australia and New Zealand facing TRQs', in H. de Gorter and I. Sheldon (eds), *Issues in the Administration of Tariff-Rate Import Quotas in the Agreement on Agriculture in the WTO*, International Agricultural Trade Research Consortium commissioned paper no. 13, University of Minnesota, St Paul: Department of Applied Economics, pp. 142–51.

Mai, Y., P. Adams, M. Fan, R. Li and Z. Zheng (2005), 'Modelling the potential benefits of an Australia–China free trade agreement', an independent report prepared for the Australia–China FTA Feasibility Study by the Centre of Policy Studies, Monash University, March.

Martin, W. (1990), 'Public choice theory and Australian agricultural policy reform', *Australian Journal of Agricultural Economics*, **34**, 189–211.

Martin, W. and K. Anderson (2006), 'The Doha Agenda negotiations on agriculture: what could they deliver?', *American Journal of Agricultural Economics*, **88**, 1211–18.

McCorriston, S. and D. MacLaren (2007), 'Deregulation as (welfare reducing) trade reform: the case of the Australian Wheat Board', *American Journal of Agricultural Economics*, **89**(3), 637–50.

Mitchell, A.D. and T. Voon (2007), 'Australia–United States Free Trade Agreement', in S. Lester and B. Mercurio (eds), *Bilateral and Regional Trade Agreements: Case Studies*, Cambridge: Cambridge University Press, pp. 6–43.

OECD (2001), *Multifunctionality: Towards an Analytical Framework*, Paris: OECD.

OECD (2005a), 'Agricultural policy Reform in China', policy brief, October, Paris.

OECD (2005b), *Agricultural Policies in OECD Countries: Monitoring and Evaluation 2005: Highlights*, Paris: OECD.

OECD (2006a), *Agricultural Policies in OECD Countries: at a Glance*, Paris: OECD.

OECD (2006b), *PSE/CSE Database*, Paris: OECD.

Swinnen, J. and F.A. van der Zee (1993), 'The political economy of agricultural policies: a survey', *European Review of Agricultural Economics*, **20**(3), 261–90.

Winters, L.A. (1990), 'The so-called "non-economic" objectives of agricultural support', *OECD Economic Studies*, **13**, 237–66.

WTO (1995), *The Results of the Uruguay Round of Multilateral Trade Negotiations: the Legal Texts*, Geneva: WTO.

WTO (2001), 'Accession of the People's Republic of China', WT/L/432, available at http://docsonline.wto.org/DDFDocuments/t/WT/L/432.doc and www.wto.org/english/thewto_e/acc_e/china_schedule.zip.

WTO (2004a), 'Doha Work Programme', decisions adopted by the General Council on 1 August 2004, WT/L/579, Geneva.

WTO (2004b), 'Agriculture negotiations: backgrounder, the issues, and where we are now', updated 1 December, available at www.wto.org/english/tratop_e/agric_e/negs_bkgrnd00_contents_e.htm.

WTO (2006), 'Draft possible modalities on agriculture', Committee on Agriculture Special Session, TN/AG/W/3, 12 July, Geneva.

6. Services in PTAs – donuts or holes?[1]

Philippa Dee and Christopher Findlay

INTRODUCTION

There are at least four ways of assessing the services provisions of preferential trade agreements (PTAs):

- evaluating the rules;
- evaluating the commitments made under those rules;
- evaluating the extent to which the commitments constrain or change the status quo, given that there can be large gaps between bound and applied protection in the areas of both services and investment;
- evaluating whether any change to the status quo has economic significance.

Those who have evaluated the services provisions of preferential trade agreements according to the first two criteria have tended to see 'donuts'. Those who have evaluated them according to the second two criteria have tended to see 'holes'. The purpose of this chapter is to outline some of the evidence according to the four methods of evaluation, and to spell out the implications for the likely effects of an Australia–China preferential trade agreement.

EVALUATING THE RULES

The standard way of evaluating the trading rules established by the services provisions of preferential trade agreements (PTAs) is to compare them to the rules established by the General Agreement on Trade in Services (GATS) under the WTO.

The GATS imposes one key discipline on all services trade – the most-favoured nation obligation. This requires a country to treat the services suppliers of all other countries equally. There is to be no discrimination among the various different foreign sources of services. Beyond that, there are two other key disciplines that apply on a positive list basis, that is, they only apply to selected services sectors that a country chooses to subject to those disciplines. The first is a national treatment obligation. This requires a country to treat the services suppliers of all other countries the same as its domestic suppliers. There is to be no discrimination between domestic and foreign suppliers. The second is a market access obligation. This requires a country to refrain from applying six specific types of quantitative restrictions on services suppliers, be they domestic or foreign suppliers. For example, there is to be no limit on the number of services suppliers, or on the value of services transactions.

A country may choose to 'schedule' a particular services sector, thus subjecting it to both these disciplines, but it is also allowed to list any 'limitations' on the application of the disciplines, reflecting restrictive policy measures that it wishes to retain. Countries can also be selective in which modes of service delivery they will subject to these disciplines. A country can selectively 'schedule', or refrain from 'scheduling', any of the four recognized modes of delivery:

- mode 1 – 'cross-border trade' – where both the producer and consumer stay in their home countries, and the services are typically delivered electronically;
- mode 2 – 'consumption abroad' – where the consumer moves temporarily to the country of the producer;
- mode 3 – 'commercial presence' – where the producer establishes a permanent commercial presence in the country of the consumer;
- mode 4 – 'the movement of natural persons' – where the producer moves temporarily to the country of the consumer.

By recognizing all these modes of services delivery, the GATS recognizes that services transactions typically occur face to face, behind the border of the producing or consuming country. But under the positive list approach, countries have a great deal of discretion in whether to subject their services sectors to the disciplines of national treatment and market access in practice.

The GATS also recognizes that services are an area where market failures can occur. For example, there is a legitimate role for regulation of natural monopoly in some network industries, for regulation to protect against information asymmetries in the professions, for prudential regulation of financial services to ensure systemic stability and for safety regulation in air passenger transport.

The GATS recognizes the right of individual governments to regulate. Non-economic objectives can be pursued, for example, through universal service obligations. Services provided by governments are quarantined. But GATS also requires that domestic regulatory regimes be the 'least burdensome' necessary to achieve their objectives. This provides a further WTO discipline on non-discriminatory measures that fall outside of the narrow scope of GATS 'market access' commitments, although the discipline is rather loose, especially since the definition of 'least burdensome' has yet to be decided by WTO members.

There is a presumption that the services provisions of PTAs will be GATS-plus. That is, they will impose rules at least as liberal as the GATS, and impose them on at least as many sectors. In part, this presumption is written into the GATS itself. For the services provisions of PTAs to be WTO-consistent, they need to have 'substantial sectoral coverage', and provide for the absence or elimination of 'substantially all discrimination', in the sense of the national treatment obligation. But note that there is no WTO requirement for PTAs to address non-discriminatory market access limitations, or to address domestic regulation. And enforcing WTO consistency has proved no easier in services than it has in goods.

In practice, when PTAs have included services provisions, they have tended to be of two types. GATS-style agreements have included national treatment and market access obligations for services on a positive list basis. They have included investment provisions only via the treatment of commercial presence in the services sector. By contrast, North American Free Trade Agreement (NAFTA) style agreements have included national treatment and market access obligations for services on a negative list basis. That is, the obligations apply to all services sectors, except those nominated for exclusion in an annex of reservations and exceptions. And they have typically included a separate chapter on investment that imposes most-favoured nation and national treatment obligations on investment in all sectors (again, subject to reservations and exceptions), not just in services.

Both types of agreements cover obligations to facilitate the temporary movement of individual services suppliers, since this is one of the modes by which services are delivered. Some agreements of either type may also include a separate chapter on the movement of business persons. Such chapters may outline obligations such as limits on the use of economic needs tests for immigration purposes. These obligations typically apply to all business persons, not just services suppliers.

There are many more aspects to the rules governing services in the GATS and in PTAs. Good detailed discussion of all aspects is contained in three OECD documents (OECD 2002a, 2002b, 2002c) that examine the relationship between PTAs and the multilateral trading system for services, investment and labour mobility.

The discussion in those papers has been used to devise a template for scoring the services, investment and labour mobility provisions of PTAs. The purpose is to compare PTAs with each other and with multilateral disciplines under the WTO (not just the GATS, but other relevant agreements such as the WTO Agreement on Trade Related Investment Measures).

The templates for evaluating these dimensions of PTAs are shown in Tables 6.1, 6.2 and 6.3 at the end of this chapter. The top section of each template has been designed to compare agreements at the rule-making stage. Thus the top section of each template contains categories and scores for ranking the *form* of the agreement, as indicated in the relevant chapters. The templates also contain a few broad summary measures to compare the levels of commitments contained in each agreement. Thus the bottom section of each template contains categories and scores for ranking the *content* of the agreement, as indicated in the relevant annexes of commitments, reservations or exceptions. However, the measures of content are relatively crude.

The first template deals with cross-border trade (defined as modes 1 and 2), but also picks up some of the more general features that appear in services chapters, such as provisions to deal with domestic regulation and monopolies. This template refers primarily to the services chapters of the agreements.

The second template deals with investment (defined as mode 3 plus portfolio investment). It notes whether agreements deal with investment in services only, or more generally. It also covers some of the issues such as investment protection that are peculiar to investment. This template captures the content of the services, investment, and possibly the dispute settlement chapters of the agreements.

The third template deals with the movement of people (defined as mode 4), but also picks up whether there are additional measures in the agreements to facilitate labour mobility, either for service providers, investors or more generally. This template captures the content of the services, investment and labour mobility chapters of the agreements.

These templates have been used to score all of the major agreements involving a preselected list of 73 countries in the years up to 2004. The 66 agreements, and their country membership, are shown in Table 6.4. Most of these agreements have been notified to the WTO, but some have not. The templates have also been used to score comparable WTO disciplines, where they exist. It was not possible to give a general score for the content dimension of the WTO agreements, as this depends on the commitments of each individual member country. Each agreement, whether a PTA or a WTO agreement, is given a score between 0 and 1 against each characteristic where 0 is most restrictive and 1 most liberal. Summaries of the scoring exercise are shown in Tables 6.5 to 6.7. The scoring shows that in virtually all dimensions, PTAs have become more liberal over time, and with fewer exclusions. This is shown by the average scores across PTAs being higher for later subgroups of agreements than they are for the sample as a whole.

In many dimensions, PTAs are not as liberal on average as WTO agreements. This is only in part because the sample of PTAs includes agreements that have no substantive services provisions at all (note that it would involve selection bias to exclude such agreements from the sample). It is also because many PTAs are silent on issues such as domestic regulation, monopolies, private business practices, safeguards and subsidies. These are not areas where PTAs have forged ahead of WTO disciplines. But on the two core issues of market access and national treatment, PTAs are now more liberal on average than the WTO. This is largely because of the growing list of agreements that include these disciplines on a negative list rather than positive list basis.

Other writers have suggested that on core rules, at least, PTAs are generally GATS-plus. Stephenson (2002) has argued that the NAFTA-style agreements that characterize PTAs in the western hemisphere outperform the GATS in three key respects. First, the negative list approach promotes transparency. Second, she argues that it precludes the possibility of making binding commitments that lag actual practice (an assessment that will be further examined in a later section), and hence promote stability. Finally, she argues that they promote more liberal commitments than the GATS, an assessment that is now examined in more detail.

EVALUATING THE COMMITMENTS

Again, the standard way of evaluating the trade commitments made under the services provisions of preferential trade agreements is to compare them to commitments made under the GATS.

It is often simply asserted that because negative list PTAs commit to market access and national treatment in all services sectors and modes of delivery except those specifically excluded, they must be more liberalizing than GATS schedules or positive list PTAs, which only commit to market access and national treatment in specifically nominated sectors. In principle, however, it is possible for a negative list agreement to be no more liberalizing than a positive list one, if the annexes of reservations and exceptions are sufficiently long. And some lists are quite long – Singapore's lists of reservations and exceptions in its negative list agreement with the United States run to 71 pages.

Accordingly, a definitive assessment requires a careful sector-by-sector and mode-by-mode comparison of the commitments actually made in PTAs, both positive and negative list, against the commitments made in GATS schedules. An early comparison along these lines was made by Dee (2005), who compared the negative list commitments made by Australia and the United States in the Australia–United Stats Free Trade Agreement (AUSFTA) with their positive list commitments under the GATS. The assessment concluded that the areas of overlap were considerable. AUSFTA did go further than GATS commitments, but the areas of additional market opening were relatively minor, and not generally in areas where there were significant barriers to begin with. This was consistent with the claim by the Australian government that the major achievement of AUSFTA in the areas of services and investment was to prevent the introduction of any new discriminatory measures, rather than to roll back any existing ones.

A more widespread comparison along these lines has been done by Roy et al. (2006). The authors compared the commitments undertaken by 29 WTO members (counting the EC as one) under mode 1 (cross-border supply) and mode 3 (commercial presence) in 28 PTAs negotiated since 2000, and compared these with both the prevailing GATS commitments and recent Doha Round offers of these countries. Roy et al. (2006) agree with the above assessment that PTAs appear to offer limited value added over GATS disciplines in the areas of rules governing safeguard mechanisms, subsidies, domestic regulation and the like. Their main contribution appears to be in their levels of commitments.

On commitments, the authors find that PTAs tend to go significantly beyond GATS offers in terms of improved and new bindings. Further, the proportion of new/improved commitments is generally much greater in PTAs (compared to GATS offers) than in GATS offers (when compared to existing GATS commitments). Some countries are described as showing spectacular improvements in their PTA commitments. Among them are countries that have signed a PTA with the United States. On average, these now have mode 1 and mode 3 commitments in more than 80 per cent of services subsectors, compared to commitments in less than half of services subsectors in their GATS schedules/offers.

In most cases where PTA commitments improve on WTO commitments, it is primarily through new bindings rather than through improvements on existing bindings. Arguably, though, the commitments are more likely to imply real liberalization in the latter case than in the former. Exceptions to the general trend include China and India, whose PTA commitments (China's with Hong Kong and Macao, India's with Singapore) tend to take the form of improvements to sectors already committed under

GATS schedules/offers rather than new bindings, and are mostly limited to mode 3.

Roy et al. (2006) find that the countries that have a smaller proportion of new/improved commitments in PTAs have all used the positive list scheduling approach. This is not to say that all positive list agreements have led to lesser commitments than negative list ones. China's agreements with Hong Kong and Macao were positive list agreements that nevertheless provided significant new commercial opportunities. But those countries such as Australia and Singapore that have signed agreements of both types have made greater commitments in their negative list ones.

Finally, the authors note that PTAs have provided for advances both for sectors that have tended to attract fewer offers in the GATS (for example, audiovisual, road, rail, postal, courier), as well as for sectors that were already popular targets for GATS offers (for example, professional, financial services). One exception was health services, where PTA commitments did not appear to go significantly beyond GATS offers. Overall, the authors conclude (Roy et al. 2006, p. 33) that 'PTAs generally have provided for significant improvements over GATS commitments, sometimes even leading to real liberalization of the market.'

EVALUATING THE EXTENT OF REAL LIBERALIZATION

Comparing PTA commitments to actual regulatory policies to evaluate the extent of real liberalization is even more labour intensive than comparing positive and negative list agreements. And it generally cannot be done in a mechanical fashion, because information about regulatory policies and the reasons for regulatory changes is spread unevenly around different sources. The sources need to be read and interpreted carefully, and there is still a danger that the results of any comparison will reflect paucity of information rather than anything else.

One recent such comparison has capitalized on a pre-existing database of actual regulatory practice that was complied for a different purpose. Barth et al. (2006) make use of a database on actual regulatory practice in banking as it stood around 2000, as reported in responses to a detailed World Bank survey. The database had been used previously to assess the impact of that regulation on banking performance (for example, Barth et al. 2004). In the more recent exercise, Barth et al. (2006) compare regulatory practice with actual WTO commitments in the financial sector for 123 WTO members.

The authors find significant differences between commitments and actual practice. Some of their examples are as follows.

- More than 30 WTO members that prohibit foreign firms from entering through acquisitions, subsidiaries or branches in their WTO
  schedules allow such entry in practice.
- Six WTO members do not allow foreign entry through subsidiaries or branches even though in their schedules they indicated
  they do. This anomaly may reflect the 'prudential carveout' in the
  GATS, whereby members are not required to schedule limitations
  maintained for prudential purposes. However, it is highly questionable whether bans on foreign entry could be defended as purely
  prudential measures.
- A large number of WTO members prohibit banks from engaging in
  insurance or securities activities in their schedules, but allow such
  activities in practice.
- Twenty-six WTO members in practice set the same minimal capital
  entry requirements for domestic and foreign banks, even though
  in their schedules they do not commit to such non-discriminatory
  treatment.

The authors also look for evidence of statistically significant correlations
between WTO commitments and regulatory practice. Even if the two do
not match exactly, they expect the correlation to be positive. However,
their finding does not bear this out.

> The results . . . indicate that on average countries are more open based on actual
> practice than their WTO commitments. The difference in means between actual
> practice and commitments, moreover, is statistically significant. Also, there
> is no significant correlation between actual practice and commitments. These
> results hold for developing countries and countries with more than two million
> people, but not for the developed countries. The latter group of countries is on
> average less open based upon actual practice than commitments (Barth et al.
> 2006, p. 25).

This last, rather explosive finding passes without further comment! The
authors also try to explain the gap between commitments and actual practice. One of their findings is that countries with greater foreign ownership of
total bank assets also tend to have the biggest divergence between the indices
for commitments and actual practice. Countries with greater foreign ownership also tend to display less actual discrimination against foreign banks,
but tend to display more discrimination based on commitments. Lastly,
developed countries that made commitments earlier tend to display less discrimination, while the opposite is the case for developing countries.

In general, therefore, the authors find many instances where WTO
commitments are significantly less liberal than actual practice. They also

find instances where WTO commitments are more liberal than actual practice, particularly in developed countries. As evidence about whether PTAs promote real liberalization, the findings are merely circumstantial. However, if WTO commitments lag behind actual practice by a significant margin, then even if PTAs improve significantly on WTO commitments, they may still themselves lack actual practice.

Furthermore, if actual practice lags behind WTO commitments, as it appears to in a few cases, then there is clearly an enforcement problem that may also carry over to PTA commitments. One reason for the enforcement problem in a WTO context may be that trade partner countries are not equipped to check the compliance of all other WTO members. Such a monitoring problem may be less severe in a PTA context. But another reason for an enforcement problem may be that trade commitments are made by trade negotiators who are divorced from what is really going on in their own countries. This problem may well carry over to PTAs, especially in countries where problems of coordination among different government ministries are endemic.

Roy et al. (2006) also attempt to assess whether PTA commitments lead to real liberalization. They do not make direct comparisons with regulatory practice, but look for instances where PTA commitments are phased in over time, using the phasing mechanism as an indication that real liberalization is taking place. They note that the group of countries making such phased commitments is fairly widespread, although it appears that financial services and telecommunications dominate. Most phase-out commitments have been contracted by countries as part of a PTA with the United States, although not exclusively.

Certainly, the PTA experience with partners other than the United States can be dramatically different. It is widely recognized that in the ASEAN countries, both WTO commitments and PTA commitments can lag behind actual practice by a considerable margin (see the discussion of the ASEAN Framework Agreement on Services by Stephenson and Nikomborirak 2002). And one of the recent PTAs to contain no services commitments whatsoever is that between ASEAN and China.

EVALUATING THE ECONOMIC SIGNIFICANCE REAL PTA LIBERALIZATION[2]

It is sometimes claimed that, because services trade barriers do not involve tariff revenue, preferential services trade liberalization cannot impose losses on PTA members through trade diversion. This claim is made explicitly by Roy et al. (2006), in their otherwise excellent paper, and is implied by the modelling treatment of services in papers such as Hertel (2000). The argument is fallacious, for the following reasons.

Some regulatory trade restrictions, particularly quantitative restrictions, create artificial scarcity. The prices of services are inflated, not because the real resource cost of producing them has gone up, but because incumbent firms are able to earn economic rents – akin to a tax, but with the revenue flowing to the incumbent rather than to government. Liberalization of these barriers would yield relatively small gains associated with better resource allocation, but also have redistributive effects associated with the elimination of rents to incumbents. Such rent-creating restrictions are tariff-like, with the redistribution of rent having effects similar to the redistribution of tariff revenue.

Alternatively, services trade restrictions could increase the real resource cost of doing business. An example would be a requirement for foreign service professionals to retrain in a new economy, rather than to pass an accreditation process. Liberalization would be equivalent to a productivity improvement (saving in real resources), and yield relatively large gains. This could increase returns for the incumbent service providers, as well as lowering costs for users elsewhere in the economy.

This distinction has two important implications. First, the gains from liberalizing cost-escalating barriers are likely to exceed the gains from liberalizing rent-creating barriers by a significant margin. Secondly, in the context of PTAs, the danger of net welfare losses from net trade diversion arises if the relevant barriers are rent-creating, since rent distribution can have the same effects as tariff redistribution (see also Pomfret 1997). So a key question for establishing the economic significance of any real services trade liberalization achieved in PTAs is whether it targets trade barriers that create rents or raise costs.

While many PTAs go further than the GATS, they have tended to be selective in two important ways:

- they have tended to be preferential, even in the provisions that go beyond goods trade; and
- they have tended to target only those provisions that explicitly discriminate against foreigners.

There are strong political economy explanations for both of these outcomes.

With some exceptions, recent PTAs have tended to do one of two things in the new age areas (including services) – either bind the status quo or make concessions on a preferential basis, even when logic suggests they could sensibly be made non-preferentially.[3] One very clear reason for this outcome is that countries with strong 'offensive' interests in the Doha Round are unlikely to give away negotiating coin by making defensive concessions on a non-preferential basis within a PTA, prior to a Doha Round settlement. In particular, Roy et al. (2006) note that the United States always lodges a broad exception for the market access obligation in its PTAs, with the purpose of ensuring that those PTAs do not go beyond its market access obligations under the GATS.

Partly because they have been preferential, recent PTAs have tended to target only those provisions that explicitly discriminate against foreigners. This is because, in many cases, the only provisions that can feasibly be liberalized on a preferential basis are those that discriminate against foreigners.[4] But even without this feasibility constraint, there are economic and political economy forces that tend to limit concessions within PTAs to those that explicitly discriminate against foreigners. The central one is the threat to sovereignty that is felt most strongly by countries when contemplating making reforms to non-discriminatory domestic regulatory regimes as part of a trade agreement. To many countries, both developed and developing, this may be viewed as too much of a threat to the 'right to regulate'.

Negotiating modalities have also contributed a focus on provisions that explicitly discriminate against foreigners, not just in PTAs but also in the WTO. The request-and-offer modality is currently being used in the Doha negotiations on services, and is the means by which many PTAs are negotiated. Under this modality, countries are asked to contemplate, not just reforms that are in their own best interests, but reforms that are in their trading partners' best interests. It will tend to be in a trading partner's best interests to target only those provisions that explicitly discriminate against foreigners – in this way, the foreign market share is maximized. Foreign producers would generally have little interest in unleashing competition from promising domestic new entrants. They would rather join a cartel on a far more selective basis! And in these circumstances, the liberalizing countries risk simply handing monopoly rents to foreigners. Indeed, this is the basis of the ASEAN desire to have safeguard provisions in the WTO services trade negotiations.

A further consideration is one of visibility. Regulatory regimes are always complex, and often not very transparent to insiders, let alone outsiders. The regulations that will tend to be visible to potential foreign entrants are those that discriminate against foreigners. A final point is the requirements for WTO consistency. As noted earlier, WTO disciplines only require PTAs to remove limitations on national treatment. They do not require them to address issues of market access or domestic regulation.

But this focus on measures that discriminate against foreigners means that PTAs are not concentrating on the trade barriers that matter most in an economic sense. As noted earlier, the barriers that are easiest to liberalize on a preferential basis are explicit quantitative restrictions. These create artificial scarcity, and hence generate rents. For example, one popular target for liberalization in PTAs has been barriers in banking and telecommunications. The limited empirical evidence suggests that in these sectors (where explicit barriers to entry are rife), barriers appear to create rents. In distribution services, where indirect trade restrictions also apply, barriers appear to increase costs. In air passenger transport and the professions, barriers appear to have both effects. In particular, discriminatory barriers in the professions appear to create rents, while the non-discriminatory restrictions (such as restrictions that require partnerships, and require both the investors and managers of professional firms to themselves be licensed professionals) increase costs.[5] And theoretical arguments suggest that barriers in maritime and electricity generation primarily affect costs.[6]

Dee (2007) shows that if an East Asian PTA managed to eliminate all discrimination against foreigners in these sectors where empirical evidence is available, the gains would be small compared to a moderately successful completion of the Doha Round. And they would be trivial compared to a comprehensive programme of unilateral regulatory reform, one that instead targeted non-discriminatory behind-the-border restrictions on competition. The reason is that there appears to be a reasonably strong correlation in practice between measures that discriminate against foreigners and measures that create rents.

What then is the source of the interest in PTAs? A major motivation by demandeur countries is to capture the first-mover advantage. Given the nature of services production, with its large sunk costs, first movers have a significant advantage. Mattoo and Fink (2002) compare the effects of 'sequential entry' to 'simultaneous entry'. A PTA negotiation might give a first-mover advantage to a supplier who is not competitive in world terms. The country giving the preference risks landing itself with a second-class supplier who is difficult to budge.

IMPLICATIONS FOR AN AUSTRALIA–CHINA FREE TRADE AGREEMENT

China comes to PTA negotiations in services from a slightly different perspective to many other countries. Its first waves of reforms in services focused on domestic regulation – converting sectors that were once monopolized by state-owned enterprises into sectors where some domestic competition could occur (Findlay and Pangestu 2004). It then went through the process of WTO accession, a process that saw it make significant commitments on all fronts, but with an important focus on removing discrimination against foreign suppliers (see also Mattoo 2004).

Despite the significant progress, Australian services providers have found that China still has significant barriers to trade. Australian officials have compiled a list of over 100 pages of services trade barriers that they would like to target in PTA negotiations, barriers that include derogations from national treatment, limitations on market access and restrictions imposed by China's domestic regulatory regimes. The exercise has contributed greatly to transparency in China, since coordination problems among Chinese government departments have been rife, and individual departments have been unaware of the restrictions and limitations imposed by others.

The question remains what real liberalization is likely to be achieved in practice. At the time of writing, it is unclear even whether services will be listed on a positive or a negative list basis. For its part, Australia will maintain its strategy of binding the status quo. China has so far been unwilling to include services provisions in its PTAs at all, or has been unwilling to go beyond its existing WTO accession commitments, arguing (with some cause) that these have already imposed a significant adjustment burden.

Australian officials will press China to go at least a little further. And they will press on all fronts – national treatment, market access and domestic regulation. What is significant is that they will do so on a preferential basis. They do not see themselves as negotiating on behalf of the rest of the world. Even when they make requests concerning domestic regulation, they will not be asking China to deregulate. Rather, they will ask for a waiver or an exemption of the current regulation for Australia.

Whether such preferential relaxation of domestic regulation affects rents or costs in China depends to a large extent on whether supply conditions from the Australian end are competitive (for example, Panagariya 2000 and Francois and Wooten 2001). If supply conditions are competitive, then the potential cost saving for Australian producers will attract new entry to bid the prices down to match the lower costs, for the benefit of Chinese users. If the supply conditions are not competitive, then selected Australian producers may be able to pocket the cost savings, generating greater rents in Australia for no benefit to Chinese users. Given the 'client focus' of Australian trade officials, which sees them happy to negotiate on behalf of individual services suppliers, rather than necessarily ensuring open entry for all Australian suppliers, it is not difficult to conceive of situations where the latter might occur.

Either way, Australia is clearly seeking a first-mover advantage for its services in China, or in some cases a second-mover advantage (behind Hong Kong and Macao). The gains to China are likely to be small, although so too are the adjustment costs. What is certain is that an Australia–China Free Trade Agreement will do nothing to further the cause of domestic regulatory reform in China. At worst, it may create a subset of Australian services suppliers earning rents in China, who then have an interest in opposing further regulatory reform.

TABLES

Table 6.1   Template for scoring cross-border trade in services

	Category	Score
Form of agreement		
Scope	Covers everything	1
	Excludes only air passenger transport or govt services	0.8
	Excludes air passenger transport and govt services (same as GATS)	0.75
	Excludes a little more than GATS (eg financial services)	0.5
	Excludes a lot more than GATS	0.25
	Endeavours with unspecified scope (cooperation or no detailed provisions)	0.2
	No services provisions	0
MFN	Negative list bindings	1
	Positive list bindings	0.75
	Best endeavours	0.25
	No commitment	0
MFN exemptions	None	1
	None for new bilateral agreements	0.5
	Some for new bilateral agreements	0.25
	For all existing and new bilateral agreements or no commitment on MFN	0
National treatment	Negative list bindings	1
	Negative list bindings – some sectors	0.75
	Positive list bindings	0.5
	Best endeavours	0.25
	No commitment	0
Market access (ie prohibition on QRs as in GATS)	Negative list bindings	1
	Negative list bindings – some sectors	0.75
	Positive list bindings	0.5
	Best endeavours	0.25
	No commitment	0

Local presence not required (right of non-estab.)	Has this provision	1
	Has this provision, but with some exemptions	0.5
	Doesn't have this provision	0
Domestic regulation	General provisions as in GATS plus necessity test (or equiv.)	1
	General provisions as in GATS (transparency, not a disguised restriction)	0.75
	Measures in a reasonable and impartial manner	0.4
	Provisions for specific sectors (eg professions)	0.25
	No provisions	0
Transparency (scores additive)	Prior comment	0.3
	Publish (as in GATS)	0.4
	National inquiry point (as in GATS)	0.3
Recognition	General provisions as in GATS (non-discrimination, based in international standards) plus provisions for all sectors	1
	General provisions as in GATS (non-discrimination, based in international standards) plus provisions for specific sectors	0.75
	General provisions as in GATS (non-discrimination, based in international standards)	0.5
	Provisions for specific sectors eg legal, engineering	0.25
	Encouragement	0.2
	No provisions	0
Monopolies and exclusive services providers	Stronger than general provisions in GATS	1
	General provisions as in GATS (not act inconsistently with commitments, not anti-competitive in other markets)	0.75
	General provisions as in GATS plus some exceptions	0.6
	Provisions for specific sectors eg telecommunications	0.5
	No provisions	0

Table 6.1   (continued)

	Category	Score
Business practices	Stronger than the GATS	1
	General provisions as in GATS (consult with a view to eliminating)	0.75
	Provisions for specific sectors	0.5
	No provisions	0
Transfers and payments	No restrictions except to safeguard balance of payments	1
	Restrictions in other prescribed circumstances	0.5
	No provisions	0
Denial of benefits (ie rules of origin)	Denial only to persons that do not conduct substantial (or any) business operations in other party	1
	Tougher treatment to specific sectors	0.75
	Tougher treatment to all sectors	0.5
	Total denial if owned by third party, or no provisions to prevent denial	0
Safeguards	General provisions	0
	Provisions for particular sectors	0.25
	Future negotiations	0.5
	No provisions or banned	1
Subsidies (may be in separate subsidies chapter but covers services)	Provisions limiting their use	1
	Consultation	0.5
	Future negotiations to limit their use	0.25
	No provisions	0
Govt procurement in services (could be in separate GP chapter)	Provisions on non-discriminatory access	1
	Provisions for access in some sectors	0.75
	Future negotiations	0.5
	No provisions	0
Ratchet mechanism	All subsequent unilateral liberalization to be bound	1
	Sectoral exceptions to ratchet mechanism	0.75
	No mechanism	0
Telecommunications (scores additive)	Interconnection (access to and use of PSTN and services by service suppliers of other party)	0.5
	Unbundling	0.1
	Particular services (eg leased circuits, resale, number portability)	0.1
	Competitive safeguards	0.1

	Universal service obligations	0.1
	Allocation of scarce resources (eg spectrum)	0.1
Financial services (scores additive)	Prudential carveout	0.4
	Provision for recognition of prudential measures	0.2
	NT for access to payments and clearing systems	0.1
	New financial services	0.1
	Privacy	0.1
	Data transfer	0.1
Content of agreement	For negative list agreements, look at non-conforming measures	
	For positive list agreements, look at specific, horizontal and MFN commitments.	
General reservations or exceptions – modes	No modes excluded by one or more parties	1
	One mode excluded by one or more parties (eg mode 4)	0.5
	Two or more modes excluded by one or more parties, or no provisions	0
General reservations or exceptions – measures	No measures (MFN, NT, MA) excluded by one or more parties	1
	One measure (eg MA) excluded by one or more parties	0.5
	More than one measure excluded by one or more party, or no provisions	0
Sectoral exclusions (out of 46 substantive sectors)	No sectors excluded by one or more parties	1
	1–10 sectors excluded by one or more parties (eg maritime, audiovisual)	0.8
(least generous treatment among members of FTA)	11–20 sectors excluded by one or more parties (eg maritime, audiovisual)	0.6
	21–30 sectors excluded by one or more parties	0.4
	31–40 sectors excluded by one or more parties	0.2
	More than 40 sectors excluded by one or more parties, or no provisions on services trade	0
Subnational exclusions	No measures at subnational (state or provincial) level excluded	1

Table 6.1   (continued)

	Category	Score
	Measures at local level excluded by one or more parties	0.7
	Measures at state level excluded by one or more parties	0.4
	Measures at all subnational levels excluded by one or more parties, or no provisions on services trade	0
Other general exclusions	No other general exclusions	1
	One other exclusion (eg for minorities, land purchases) by at least one party	0.5
	Two or more other exclusions (eg for minorities, land purchases) by at least one party	0

Table 6.2   Template for scoring investment

	Category	Score
Form of agreement		
Sectoral coverage	Beyond services (in separate chapter)	1
	Services only (mode 3 in services chapter)	0.5
	Based on bilateral treaties	0.4
	Endeavours without specified scope	0.25
	None	0
Scope of MFN, NT etc provisions (scores additive)	Establishment (ie greenfield)	0.3
	Acquisition (ie merger)	0.2
	Post-establishment operation	0.3
	Resale (ie free movement of capital)	0.2
MFN	Negative list bindings	1
	Positive list bindings	0.75
	Best endeavours	0.25
	No commitment	0
MFN exemptions	None	1
	None for new bilateral agreements	0.5
	Some for new bilateral agreements	0.25
	For all existing and new bilateral agreements, or no provisions to prevent exemptions	0

National treatment	Negative list bindings – all sectors	1
	Negative list bindings – some sectors	0.75
	Positive list bindings – all sectors	0.5
	Best endeavours	0.25
	No commitment	0
Nationality (residency) of management and board of directors (including exceptions)	Cannot restrict either	1
	Cannot restrict either, with sectoral exceptions	0.75
	Can partially restrict board of directors	0.5
	Can partially restrict management or both. Alternatively, sectoral promises to liberalize, but no general promise	0.25
	No provisions limiting restrictions	0
Performance requirements	No local content, trade or other specified requirements (eg on tech transfer, or where to sell)	1
	No local content or trade requirements ie as in TRIMS	0.75
	Provisions more limited than TRIMS	0.5
	No provisions	0
Transparency (in services or inv chap) (scores additive)	Prior comment	0.3
	Publish (as in GATS)	0.4
	National inquiry point (as in GATS)	0.3
Denial of benefits (ie rules of origin)	Denial only to persons that do not conduct substantial (or any) business operations in other party	1
	Tougher treatment to specific sectors	0.75
	Tougher treatment to all sectors	0.5
	Total denial if owned by third party, or no provisions	0
Expropriation etc (scores additive)	Minimum standard of treatment	0.2
	Treatment in case of strife	0.4
	Expropriation and compensation	0.4
Transfers and payments	No restrictions except to safeguard balance of payments	1
	Restrictions in other prescribed circumstances	0.5
	No provisions	0
Investor state dispute settlement	Yes	1
	No	0

Table 6.2   (*continued*)

	Category	Score
Safeguards	General provisions	0
	Provisions for particular sectors	0.25
	Future negotiations	0.5
	No provisions	1
Subsidies (may be in separate subsidies chapter but covers investment)	Provisions limiting their use	1
	Consultation	0.5
	Future negotiations	0.25
	No provisions	0
Government procurement (could be in separate GP chapter)	Provisions on non-discriminatory access	1
	Provisions for access in some sectors	0.75
	Future negotiations	0.5
	No provisions	0
Ratchet mechanism	All subsequent unilateral liberalization to be bound	1
	Sectoral exceptions to ratchet mechanism	0.75
	No mechanism	0
Content of agreement		
General reservations or exceptions	No measures (MFN, NT, MA) excluded by one or more parties	1
	One measure (eg MA) excluded by one or more parties	0.5
	More than one measure excluded by one or more party, or no provisions	0
Sectoral exclusions (out of 46 substantive sectors)	No sectors excluded by one or more parties	1
	1–10 sectors excluded by one or more parties (eg maritime, audiovisual)	0.8
	11–20 sectors excluded by one or more parties (eg maritime, audiovisual)	0.6
	21–30 sectors excluded by one or more parties	0.4
	31–40 sectors excluded by one or more parties	0.2
	More than 40 sectors excluded by one or more parties, or no provisions on investment	0
Subnational exclusions	No measures at subnational level excluded	1
	Measures at local level excluded by one or more parties	0.7

	Measures at state level excluded by one or more parties	0.4
	Measures at all subnational levels excluded by one or more parties, or no provisions on investment	0
Other general exclusions	No other general exclusions	1
	No other general exclusions, but some exclusions for some sectors	0.75
	One other exclusion (eg for minorities, land purchases) by at least one party	0.5
	Two other exclusions (eg for minorities, land purchases) by at least one party, or no provisions on investment	0

Table 6.3   Template for scoring movement of natural persons

	Category	Score
Form of agreement		
Sectoral coverage	Beyond services and investment (separate chapter)	1
	Services and investment (in both services and investment chapters)	0.75
	Services only (mode 4 in services)	0.5
	Endeavours	0.25
	None	0
Scope	Allows permanent immigration	1
	Includes access to labour market	0.75
	Temporary movement only	0.5
	No clear scope	0.25
	None	0
Immigration	Requires changes to immigration procedures (eg visa quotas or eligibility criteria)	1
	Subject to existing immigration laws and procedures, or no provisions	0
MFN for mode 4 delivery	Negative list bindings	1
	Positive list bindings	0.75
	Best endeavours	0.25
	No commitment	0
MFN exemptions	None	1

Table 6.3   (continued)

	Category	Score
	None for new bilateral agreements	0.5
	Some for new bilateral agreements	0.25
	For all existing and new bilateral agreements or no commitment on MFN	0
National treatment for mode 4 delivery	Negative list bindings	1
	Negative list bindings – some sectors	0.75
	Positive list bindings	0.5
	Best endeavours	0.25
	No commitment	0
Market access (ie prohibition on QRs as in GATS)	Negative list bindings	1
	Negative list bindings – some sectors	0.75
	Positive list bindings	0.5
	Best endeavours	0.25
	No commitment	0
Domestic regulation	General provisions as in GATS plus necessity test (or domestic regulation equivalent)	1
	General provisions as in GATS (transparency, not a disguised restriction)	0.75
	Measures in a reasonable and impartial manner	0.4
	Provisions for specific sectors eg professions	0.25
	No provisions	0
Transparency for mode 4 delivery (scores additive)	Prior comment	0.3
	Publish (as in GATS)	0.4
	National inquiry point (as in GATS)	0.3
Transparency for temp movt of people (scores additive)	Expedite procedures	0.3
	Publish	0.4
	Answer queries or comments	0.3
Recognition	General provisions as in GATS (non-discrimination, based in international standards) plus provisions for all sectors	1
	General provisions as in GATS (non-discrimination, based in international standards) plus provisions for specific sectors	0.75

	General provisions as in GATS (non-discrimination, based in international standards)	0.5
	Provisions for specific sectors (eg legal, engineering)	0.25
	Endeavours	0.2
	No provisions	0
Denial of benefits (ie rules of origin)	Denial only to persons that do not conduct substantial (or any) business operations in other party	1
	Tougher treatment to specific sectors	0.75
	Tougher treatment to all sectors	0.5
	Total denial if owned by third party or no provisions	0
Ratchet mechanism	All subsequent unilateral liberalization to be bound	1
	Sectoral exceptions to ratchet mechanism	0.75
	No mechanism	0

Content of agreement – service delivery

General reservations or exceptions	No measures (MFN, NT, MA) excluded by one or more parties	1
	One measure (eg MA) excluded by one or more parties	0.5
	More than one measure excluded by one or more party, or no provisions on movement of people	0
Sectoral exclusions (out of 46 substantive sectors)	No sectors excluded by one or more parties	1
	1–10 sectors excluded by one or more parties (eg maritime, audiovisual)	0.8
	11–20 sectors excluded by one or more parties (eg maritime, audiovisual)	0.6
	21–30 sectors excluded by one or more parties	0.4
	31–40 sectors excluded by one or more parties	0.2
	More than 40 sectors excluded by one or more parties, or no provisions on movement of people	0
Subnational exclusions	No measures at subnational level excluded	1
	Measures at local level excluded by one or more parties	0.7

Table 6.3   (continued)

	Category	Score
	Measures at state level excluded by one or more parties	0.4
	Measures at all subnational levels excluded by one or more parties, or no provisions on movement of people	0
Other general exclusions	No other general exclusions	1
	One other exclusion (eg for minorities, land purchases) by at least one party	0.5
	Two other exclusions (eg for minorities, land purchases) by at least one party, or no provisions on movement of people	0

Content of agreement – facilitation of mobility

Skill coverage (least generous treatment among members of FTA)	All groups (including unskilled)	1
	All business persons, traders and investors, intracorporate transferees, and professionals	0.5
	A subset of the above (eg specialists, managers and intracorporate transferees)	0.25
	No groups	0
Short-term entry (least generous treatment among members of FTA)	Over 90 days or no time limit mentioned	1
	Up to 90 days	0.75
	Up to 60 days	0.5
	Up to 30 days	0.25
	Unspecified	0.1
	No short term entry, or in the case of unbinding service provisions (eg endeavours)	0
Long-term entry (least generous treatment among members of FTA)	5 years or more or no time limit mentioned	1
	Up to 4 years	0.8
	Up to 3 years	0.6
	Up to 2 years	0.4
	Up to 1 year	0.2
	Unspecified	0.1
	No long-term entry, or in the case of unbinding service provisions (eg endeavours)	0

Quotas on numbers of entrants	No (or not mentioned)	1
	Yes, or in the case of unbinding service provisions (eg endeavours)	0
Local labour market testing or other criteria	All such tests prohibited or not required	1
	Some such tests prohibited or not required	0.5
	No prohibitions (or not mentioned or in the case of unbinding service provisions (eg endeavours))	0

Table 6.4   PTA agreements

Agreement	Date	Membership dynamics
EEC/EU	1958	Austria (joined 1995), Belgium-Luxembourg, Denmark (joined 1973), Finland (joined 1995), France, Germany, Greece (joined 1981), Hungary (joined 2004), Ireland (joined 1973), Italy, Netherlands, Poland (joined 2004), Portugal (joined 1986), Spain (joined 1986), Sweden (joined 1995), United Kingdom (joined 1973)
EFTA	1960	Austria (left 1995), Denmark (left 1972), Finland (joined 1961, left 1995), Iceland (joined 1970), Norway, Portugal (left 1985), Sweden (left 1985), Switzerland, United Kingdom (left 1972)
CACM	1961	Costa Rica (joined 1962), El Salvador, Honduras, Nigaragua
EC–Switzerland	1973	EU membership, Switzerland
EC–Iceland	1973	EU membership, Iceland
EC–Norway	1973	EU membership, Norway
Bangkok Agreement	1976	Bangladesh, China (joined 2001), India, Korea, Lao PDR, Sri Lanka
LAIA	1981	Argentina, Bolivia, Brazil, Chile, Colombia, Ecuador, Mexico, Paraguay, Peru, Uruguay, Venezuela
Sparteca	1981	Australia, Fiji, New Zealand, PNG, Solomon Is.
US–Israel	1985	Israel, United States
CER	1989	Australia, New Zealand
Mercosur	1991	Argentina, Brazil, Paraguay, Uruguay
EFTA–Turkey	1992	EFTA membership, Turkey
CARICOM–Venezuela	1992	Dominican Rep., Venezuela
Chile–Colombia	1993	Chile, Colombia

Table 6.4   (*continued*)

Agreement	Date	Membership dynamics
EFTA–Israel	1993	EFTA membership, Israel
CEFTA	1993	Hungary, Poland
EFTA–Romania	1993	EFTA membership, Romania
Chile–Bolivia[a]	1993	Bolivia, Chile
EEA	1994	EU membership, Iceland, Norway
NAFTA	1994	Canada (joined precursor in 1988), Mexico, United States (joined precursor in 1988)
COMESA	1994	Egypt (joined 1998), Madagascar, Mauritius,
EC–Romania	1995	EC membership, Romania
SAPTA	1995	Bangladesh, India, Nepal, Pakistan, Sri Lanka
Bolivia–Mexico	1995	Bolivia, Mexico
Costa Rica–Mexico	1995	Costa Rica, Mexico
Colombia–Mexico–Venezuela	1995	Colombia, Mexico, Venezuela
CARICOM–Colombia	1995	Colombia, Dominican Rep
ASEAN Framework Agt on Services	1995	Indonesia, Lao PDR (joined 1997), Malaysia, Philippines, Singapore, Thailand
EC–Turkey	1996	EU membership, Turkey
Chile–Mercosur[a]	1996	Mercosur membership, Chile
Canada–Israel	1997	Canada, Israel
Israel–Turkey	1997	Israel, Turkey
Canada–Chile	1997	Canada, Chile
Bolivia–Mercosur[a]	1997	Mercosur membership, Bolivia
Andean (decision 439)	1998	Bolivia, Colombia, Ecuador, Peru, Venezuela
ASEAN Framework Agt on Investment	1998	Indonesia, Lao PDR (joined 1997), Malaysia, Philippines, Singapore, Thailand
Mexico–Nicaragua	1998	Mexico, Nicaragua
Chile–Mexico	1999	Chile, Mexico
EC–South Africa	2000	EC membership, South Africa
EC–Israel	2000	EC membership, Israel
Mexico–Israel	2000	Mexico, Israel
New Zealand–Singapore	2001	New Zealand, Singapore
EC–Mexico	2001	EC membership, Mexico
EFTA–Mexico	2001	EFTA membership, Mexico
India–Sri Lanka	2001	India, Sri Lanka
US–Jordan	2001	United States, Jordan
Mexico–Northern Triangle	2001	El Salvador, Honduras, Mexico

EFTA–Jordan	2002	EFTA membership, Jordan
EC–Jordan	2002	EC membership, Jordan
Canada–Costa Rica	2002	Canada, Costa Rica
Japan–Singapore (services)	2002	Japan, Singapore
Central America– Republic of Chile[a]	2002	Chile, Costa Rica, El Salvador
Central America– Dominican Republic[a]	2002	Costa Rica, Dominican Republic (joined 2001), El Salvador (joined 2001), Honduras (joined 2001)
Panama–Central America[a]	2002	El Salvador, Panama
EFTA–Singapore	2003	EFTA membership, Singapore
EC–Chile	2003	EC membership, Chile
ASEAN–Chile	2003	ASEAN membership, China
Singapore–Australia	2003	Singapore, Australia
China–Hong Kong	2004	China, Hong Kong
US–Singapore	2004	United States, Singapore
US–Chile	2004	United States, Chile
EC–Egypt	2004	EC membership, Egypt
EFTA–Chile	2004	EFTA membership, Chile
Chile–Korea	2004	Chile, Korea
Mexico–Uruguay	2004	Mexico, Uruguay

Notes: [a]Not notified to WTO

Table 6.5   Comparing PTAs and the GATS – cross-border trade and general measures

	GATS	Averages across PTAs		
		All agree-ments	1994 and after	2000 and after
Form of agreement				
Scope	0.75	0.44	0.52	0.53
MFN	1	0.44	0.53	0.53
MFN exemptions	na	0.05	0.03	0.04
National treatment	0.5	0.45	0.56	0.56
Market access (ie prohibition on QRs as in GATS)	0.5	0.35	0.45	0.54
Local presence not required (right of non-establishment)	0	0.26	0.36	0.35
Domestic regulation	0.75	0.16	0.21	0.32

Table 6.5   (continued)

	GATS	Averages across PTAs		
		All agree-ments	1994 and after	2000 and after
Transparency	0.7	0.26	0.35	0.43
Recognition	0.5	0.28	0.38	0.38
Monopolies and exclusive services providers	0.75	0.22	0.27	0.29
Business practices	0.75	0.08	0.13	0.11
Transfers and payments	1	0.30	0.41	0.44
Denial of benefits (ie rules of origin)	1	0.47	0.61	0.71
Safeguards	0.5	0.88	0.83	0.85
Subsidies	0.25	0.05	0.05	0.07
Government procurement in services	0.5	0.20	0.27	0.36
Ratchet mechanism	0	0.27	0.33	0.29
Telecommunications	0.5	0.23	0.32	0.35
Financial services	0.6	0.15	0.23	0.25
Simple average of above	0.59	0.29	0.36	0.39
Content of agreement				
General reservations/exceptions – modes	na	0.49	0.60	0.63
General reservations/exceptions – measures	na	0.44	0.52	0.54
Sectoral exclusions	na	0.15	0.15	0.18
Subnational exclusions	na	0.46	0.55	0.60
Other general exclusions	na	0.48	0.59	0.59
Simple average of above		0.40	0.49	0.51

Source: Author's own calculations.

Table 6.6   Comparing PTAs and the GATS – investment

	GATS	Averages across PTAs		
		All agree-ments	1994 and after	2000 and after
Form of agreement				
Sectoral coverage	0.5	0.56	0.67	0.71
Scope of MFN, NT etc				
provisions	1	0.59	0.72	0.81
MFN	1	0.49	0.55	0.59
MFN exemptions	na	0.16	0.19	0.20
National treatment	0.5	0.55	0.65	0.70
Nationality (residency) of management and board of directors (including exceptions				
in Annexe)	0	0.11	0.14	0.10
Performance requirements	0.75	0.25	0.37	0.30
Transparency (in services or				
investment chapter)	0.7	0.33	0.45	0.54
Denial of benefits (ie rules of				
origin)	1	0.39	0.47	0.52
Expropriation etc	0	0.20	0.30	0.33
Transfers and payments	1	0.42	0.53	0.59
Investor state dispute				
settlement	0	0.24	0.35	0.34
Safeguards	0.5	0.94	0.93	0.91
Subsidies	0.25	0.05	0.04	0.05
Government procurement	0.5	0.20	0.27	0.28
Ratchet mechanism	0	0.27	0.36	0.34
Simple average of above	0.51	0.36	0.44	0.46
Content of agreement				
General reservations/				
exceptions	na	0.51	0.60	0.63
Sectoral exclusions	na	0.21	0.24	0.30
Subnational exclusions	na	0.54	0.65	0.77
Other general exclusions	na	0.42	0.49	0.52
Simple average of above		0.42	0.50	0.55

Source: Author's own calculations.

Table 6.7   Comparing PTAs and the GATS – movement of people

	GATS	Averages across PTAs		
		All agree-ments	1994 and after	2000 and after
Form of agreement				
Sectoral coverage	0.5	0.45	0.58	0.56
Scope	0.5	0.32	0.41	0.40
Immigration	0	0.02	0.00	0.00
MFN for mode 4 delivery	1	0.41	0.48	0.52
MFN exemptions	na	0.05	0.03	0.06
National treatment for mode 4 delivery	0.5	0.42	0.51	0.56
Market access (ie prohibition on QRs as in GATS)	0.5	0.38	0.47	0.54
Domestic regulation	0.75	0.16	0.21	0.32
Transparency of regulations governing service delivery via mode 4	0.7	0.30	0.41	0.48
Transparency of regulations governing temporary movement of persons	0	0.18	0.27	0.28
Recognition	0.5	0.27	0.36	0.35
Denial of benefits (ie rules of origin)	1	0.47	0.59	0.69
Ratchet mechanism	0	0.25	0.31	0.29
Simple average of above	0.50	0.28	0.36	0.39
Content of agreement – service delivery				
General reservations/exceptions	na	0.43	0.51	0.52
Sectoral exclusions	na	0.17	0.19	0.22
Subnational exclusions	na	0.49	0.60	0.65
Other general exclusions	na	0.51	0.63	0.67
Simple average of above scores		0.40	0.48	0.51
Content of agreement – facilitation of mobility				
Skill coverage	na	0.31	0.36	0.39
Short-term entry	na	0.50	0.63	0.69
Long-term entry	na	0.46	0.58	0.60
Quotas on numbers of entrants	na	0.55	0.68	0.74
Needs test	na	0.00	0.00	0.00
Local labour market testing or other criteria	na	0.08	0.11	0.07
Simple average of above		0.32	0.40	0.41

Source: Author's own calculations.

NOTES

1. The authors thank Ryo Ochiai for exceptional research assistance.
2. This section draws in part on Dee (2007).
3. For example, two of Australia's concessions in the AUSFTA were the lifting of Foreign Investment Review Board screening on inward foreign direct investment in non-sensitive sectors, and a commitment to provisions similar to those in the WTO Agreement on Government Procurement. Both measures were made preferentially, even though the arguments advanced by the Australian government would have applied *a fortiori* to non-preferential liberalization.
4. The converse does not hold. Because some provisions do discriminate against foreigners, it does not mean that they can be liberalized on a preferential basis. For example, when countries liberalize restrictions on foreign ownership, it may be very difficult to ensure that the new foreign owners are only from selected partner countries.
5. Gregan and Johnson (1999), Kalirajan et al. (2000), Kalirajan (2000), Nguyen-Hong (2000), OECD (2005), Copenhagen Economics (2005).
6. Steiner (2000); Clark et al. (2004).

REFERENCES

Barth, J., G. Caprio and R. Levine (2004), 'Bank regulation and supervision: what works best?', *Journal of Financial Intermediation*, **13**, 205–48.

Barth, J., J. Marchetti, D. Nolle and W. Sawangngoenyuang (2006), 'Foreign banking: do countries' WTO commitments match actual practices?', Economic Research and Statistics Division, World Trade Organization, staff working paper no. ERSD-2006-11, Geneva.

Clark, X., D. Dollar and A. Micco (2004), 'Port efficiency, maritime transport costs, and bilateral trade', *Journal of Development Economics*, **75**, 417–50.

Copenhagen Economics (2005), *Economic Assessment of the Barriers to the Internal Market for Services*, Copenhagen: Copenhagen Economics.

Dee, P. (2005), 'The Australia–US Free Trade Agreement: an assessment', Pacific Economic Papers no. 345, Crawford School of Economics and Government, Australian National University, Canberrra.

Dee, P. (2007), 'East Asian economic integration and its impact on future growth', *The World Economy*, **30**(3), 405–23.

Findlay, C. and M. Pangestu (2004), 'Services sector reform options: the experience of China', mimeo, University of Adelaide.

Francois, J. and I. Wooten (2001), 'Imperfect competition and trade liberalisation under the GATS', in R. Stern (ed.), *Services in the International Economy*, Ann Arbor: University of Michigan Press, pp. 141–56.

Gregan, T. and M. Johnson (1999), 'Impacts of competition enhancing air services agreements: a network modelling approach', Productivity Commission staff research paper, AusInfo, Canberra, July.

Hertel, T. (2000), 'Potential gains from reducing trade barriers in manufacturing, services and agriculture', *Federal Reserve Bank of St Louis Review*, July/August, 77–104.

Kalirajan, K. (2000), 'Restrictions on trade in distribution services', Productivity Commission staff research paper no. 1638, AusInfo, Canberra, August.

Kalirajan, K., G. McGuire, D. Nguyen-Hong and M. Schuele (2000), 'The price impact of restrictions on banking services', in C. Findlay and T. Warren (eds), *Impediments to Trade in Services: Measurement and Policy Implications*, London and New York: Routledge, pp. 215–30.

Mattoo, A. (2004), 'The services dimension of China's accession to the WTO', in D. Bhattasali, S. Li and W. Martin (eds), *China and the WTO: Accession, Policy Reform, and Poverty Reduction Strategies*, Washington, DC: World Bank, pp. 117–40.

Mattoo, A. and C. Fink (2002), 'Regional agreements and trade in services: policy issues', World Bank, Policy Research working paper no. 2852, Washington, DC, June.

Nguyen-Hong, D. (2000), 'Restrictions on trade in professional services', Productivity Commission staff research paper, AusInfo, Canberra, August.

OECD (2002a), 'The relationship between regional trade agreements and the multi-lateral trading system: services', TD/TC/WP(2002)27/FINAL, OECD, Paris.

OECD (2002b), 'The relationship between regional trade agreements and the multilateral trading system: investment', TD/TC/WP(2002)18/FINAL, OECD, Paris.

OECD (2002c), 'Labour mobility in regional trade agreements', TD/TC/WP(2002)16/FINAL, OECD, Paris.

OECD (2005), 'Modal estimates of services barriers', TD/TC/WP(2005)36, OECD, Paris.

Panagariya, A. (2000), 'Preferential trade liberalisation: the traditional theory and new developments', *Journal of Economic Literature*, **38**(2), 287–331.

Pomfret, R. (1997), *The Economics of Regional Trading Arrangements*, Oxford: Clarendon Press.

Roy, M., J. Marchetti and H. Lim (2006), 'Services liberalisation in the new generation of preferential trade agreements (PTAs): how much further than the GATS?', Economic Research and Statistics Division, World Trade Organization, staff working paper no. ERSD-2006-07, Geneva.

Steiner, F. (2000), 'Regulation, industry structure and performance in the electricity supply industry', OECD working paper no. 238, ECO/WKP(2000)11, Paris.

Stephenson, S. (2002), 'Regional versus multilateral liberalisation of services', *World Trade Review*, **1**(2), 187–209.

Stephenson, S. and D. Nikomborirak (2002), 'Regional liberalisation in services', in S. Stephenson, C. Findlay and S. Yi (eds), *Services Trade Liberalisation and Facilitation*, Canberra: Asia Pacific Press at Australian National University, pp. 89–124.

7. Resources sector and foreign investment

Yinhua Mai and Philip Adams

INTRODUCTION

The resource sector represents a natural complimentarity between Australia and China. Australia is a world leader in mining technology, and has rich energy and mining resources. China, on the other hand, has become a net importer of mining products due to its rapid industrialization in the past three decades. To secure the supply of energy and mining inputs to its manufacturing sector, China has invested heavily in resource assets around the world.

In this chapter, we discuss issues related to the resource sector under a bilateral free trade agreement (FTA) between Australia and China. In addition to border protection (tariff and non-tariff barriers) on bilateral merchandise trade of resource products, we also discuss the openness of the two countries' foreign investment regimes. The foreign investment issues discussed in this chapter are mainly those concerning foreign direct investment or portfolio investment with an interest in the management of the company. Bilateral investment issues are important to the resource sector for two reasons:

- most of Chinese investment in Australia is in the resource sector; and
- China's investment regime is important to the Australian providers of mining technology services as they establish their commercial presence in China.

In this chapter, we also discuss our quantitative estimates of the potential benefits of the trade and investment liberalization under the FTA, with special reference to the resource sector. However, as the resource products are mostly used as inputs into other industries, we consider the impacts of the FTA on the resource sector under a context of overall liberalization for all sectors instead of just for the resource sector.

The potential benefits of the FTA on the resource sector are estimated through simulations using the Monash multi-country (MMC) model – a

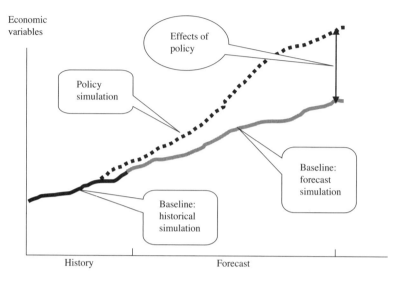

Figure 7.1   Estimating the effects of an Australia–China FTA

dynamic computable general equilibrium (CGE) model of the Australian, Chinese and rest-of-the-world (ROW) economies (for more details on the MMC model see Mai 2004).

To estimate the effects of the trade and investment liberalization under the Australia–China FTA, we first simulate a baseline scenario. This is a projection of how the Australian and the Chinese economies would evolve without the FTA. We then simulate the removal of border protection on merchandise trade that forms a policy scenario. The effects of the FTA are estimated as the deviations of economic indicators in the policy scenario away from the baseline projection (Figure 7.1).

The remainder of this chapter is organized as follows. In the next section we discuss issues related to border protection for the resource products. Bilateral investment issues are then discussed, followed by a review of the literature on quantitative estimates of the effects of investment liberalization. Next, we discuss the potential benefits of investment liberalization under the Australia–China FTA as estimated using the MMC model. Conclusions are in the final section.

FTA AND THE RESOURCE SECTOR

China's rapid economic growth since 1979 has placed significant pressure on its natural resources. China's self-sufficiency in oil ended in 1993 (Figure

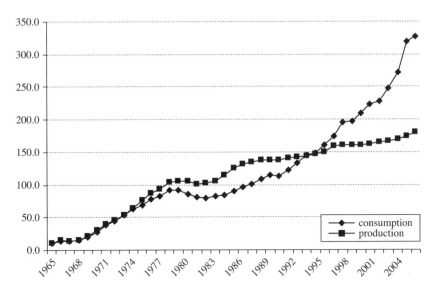

Figure 7.2   China: production and consumption of crude oil 1965–2005, million tonnes

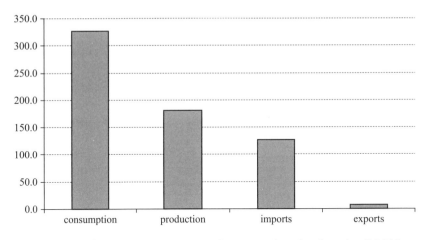

Figure 7.3   China: consumption, production and trade of crude oil 2005, million tonnes

7.2). Since then, imports have grown rapidly accounting for one-third of total oil consumption in 2005 (Figure 7.3). Similarly, rapid industrialization and urbanization in China has led to rapid growth in the imports of mining products. The total value of imports of mining and base metal

Table 7.1   China: imports from the world of resource products

HS88 code	Commodities	Value in 1992 (million USD)	Value in 2004 (million USD)	Average annual growth rates 1992– 2004 (%)	Shares 2004 (%)
270900	Petroleum oils, oils from bituminous minerals, crude	1724	33912	28.2	33.3
260111	Iron ore, concentrate, not iron pyrites, unagglomerated	705	10866	25.6	10.7
740400	Copper/copper alloy waste or scrap	242	2455	21.3	2.4
260300	Copper ores and concentrates	153	2228	25.0	2.2
281820	Aluminium oxide, except artificial corundum	145	2044	24.7	2.0
260112	Iron ore, concentrate, not iron pyrites, agglomerated	60	1824	33.0	1.8
760110	Aluminium unwrought, not alloyed	227	1069	13.8	1.0
750210	Nickel unwrought, not alloyed	38	895	30.2	0.9
260200	Manganese ores, concentrates, iron ores >20% Manganes	66	586	20.0	0.6
260700	Lead ores and concentrates	1	437	71.6	0.4
	Total	10357	101851	21.0	100.0

Source: United Nations, COMTRAD.

products[1] into China increased by over 20 per cent per annum from 1992 to 2004 (Table 7.1).

Australia, on the other hand, has been a major supplier of mining products to global markets. China's imports of mining and base metal products from Australia grew by about 20 per cent per year in value terms during 1992–2004. Overall, imports from Australia of these products accounted for over 7 per cent of imports into China. For certain items – such as iron ore (HS260111), aluminium oxide (HS281820), and lead ores (HS260700)

Table 7.2   China: imports from Australia of resource products

HS88 code	Commodities	Value in 1992 (million USD)	Value in 2004 (million USD)	Average annual growth rates 1992–2004 (%)	Shares of imports from Australia 2004 (%)
260111	Iron ore, concentrate, not iron pyrites, unagglomerated	402	3 281	19.1	30.2
281820	Aluminium oxide, except artificial corundum	140	1 103	18.7	54.0
270900	Petroleum oils, oils from bituminous minerals, crude	96	468	14.1	1.4
260200	Manganese ores, concentrates, iron ores >20% Manganese	10	226	30.1	38.7
760110	Aluminium unwrought, not alloyed	29	226	18.8	21.1
750210	Nickel unwrought, not alloyed	n.a.	194	n.a.	21.7
260300	Copper ores and concentrates	10	157	26.0	7.0
740400	Copper/copper alloy waste or scrap	4	132	35.0	5.4
260700	Lead ores and concentrates	n.a.	115	n.a.	26.3
260112	Iron ore, concentrate, not iron pyrites, agglomerated	22	68	9.7	3.7
	Total	855	7 529	19.9	7.4

Source: United Nations, COMTRAD.

– imports from Australia accounted for 26–54 per cent of China's total imports of these items (Table 7.2).

A projection using the MMC model shows that, from 2005 to 2015, the volume of Chinese imports of mining and base metal products from Australia is likely to continue to grow rapidly, at an average annual rate of around 8–10 per cent. This projection is based on an average annual GDP growth of 7 per cent for China, without the implementation of a bilateral FTA between Australia and China (Table 7.3).

Table 7.3   Baseline: the business-as-usual scenario (average annual growth rates, per cent)

	Australia		China	
	1997–2015	2005–2015	1997–2015	2005–2015
Macroeconomic indicators				
Real GDP	3.6	3.3	7.2	6.7
Real Consumption	3.6	3.4	6.0	5.8
Real Investment	3.8	2.9	7.5	6.6
Export volumes	3.5	3.9	10.1	9.2
Import volumes	4.2	3.7	9.0	8.2
Bilateral trade				
Australian imports from China	10.1	8.5	n.a.	n.a.
Chinese imports from				
Australia	n.a.	n.a.	9.2	8.8
of mining products	n.a.	n.a.	7.6	7.7
of non-ferrous metals	n.a.	n.a.	11.3	10.3
Output of aggregated sectors				
Agriculture	2.2	2.4	2.9	2.6
Mining	3.1	3.2	7.0	6.3
Manufacturing	2.2	2.1	8.0	7.4
Services	3.7	3.4	7.3	6.7

Source: Mai et al. 2005, Tables 2.1 to 2.3.

For mining and base metal products, Australian tariff equivalents on imports from China are below 5 per cent in 2005; Chinese tariff equivalents on imports from Australia ranged from 0 per cent for crude oil to 7 per cent for ferrous metals (Table 7.4). Table 7.4 shows that compared to other commodity groups, tariff equivalents on mining and base metal products are relatively low in China. However, the FTA affects bilateral trade in resource products not only through reducing or removing bilateral tariffs on these products, but also through reducing or removing bilateral tariffs on other products, especially those manufactured products that use mining products as intermediate inputs.

Our model simulation[2] shows that a complete removal of bilateral border protection presented in Table 7.4 has little impact on the output of the Chinese mining and base metal industries (see row 6 column 1 of Table 7.5) and on the Australian imports of these products from China (see row 1 column 4 of Table 7.5). This is mainly due to two factors. The first factor

Table 7.4   Levels of tariff-equivalent border protection on bilateral merchandise trade between Australia and China (ad valorem percentage rates estimated for 2005)

	Australia	China
Wheat	0.0	30.0
Cereal grains nec	0.0	3.0
Vegetables, fruit, nuts	0.7	5.9
Oil seeds	0.0	15.0
Plant-based fibres	0.0	3.0
Crops nec	0.0	3.1
Animal products nec	0.0	5.2
Wool, silk-worm cocoons	0.0	15.0
Forestry	0.4	2.2
Fishing	0.0	12.8
Coal	0.0	4.7
Crude oil	0.0	0.0
Gas	0.0	6.0
Minerals nec	0.0	3.0
Meat: cattle, sheep, goats, horses	0.6	12.0
Meat products nec	1.0	14.0
Vegetable oils and fats	0.6	13.0
Dairy products	12.0	9.9
Processed rice	1.7	10.6
Sugar	2.1	25.0
Food products nec	2.2	15.8
Beverages and tobacco products	3.4	26.0
Textiles (incl. lightly processed wool)	6.6	9.7
Wearing apparel	14.8	16.7
Leather products	7.4	9.0
Wood products	4.4	6.6
Paper products, publishing	1.8	4.9
Petroleum, coal products	0.0	6.3
Chemical, rubber, plastic prods	2.2	9.1
Mineral products nec	4.0	11.0
Ferrous metals	2.0	7.0
Non-ferrous metals	2.2	6.2
Metal products	3.8	11.0
Motor vehicles and parts	5.2	16.3
Transport equipment nec	0.3	7.5
Electronic equipment	0.3	7.0
Machinery and equipment nec	2.3	8.8
Miscellaneous manufactures	2.5	13.5

Source: Mai et al. 2005, Table 3.1.

The data in this table is based on data and information from the following sources: GTAP database, Australian Productivity Commission, Chinese Ministry of Finance, and the WTO.

Table 7.5 *Removing tariff equivalents on merchandise trade (full liberalization in 2006): effects on the resource sectors (deviations from baseline, 2015)*

	Output (%)	Output (US$ million)	Employment (%)	Imports from China (%)	Imports from China (US$ million)
Impact on Australia					
Mining	0.2	72	0.0	0.6	2
Minerals nec	0.7	86	0.5	1.7	1
Manufacturing	0.2	195	0.0	8.1	1977
Ferrous metals	0.0	1	−0.1	3.7	4
Non-ferrous metals	1.4	90	1.3	8.5	19
Impact on China					
Mining	0.0	0	−0.9	6.6	301
Minerals nec	−0.2	−47	−0.5	6.4	270
Manufacturing	0.1	1 150	0.0	20.3	2 282
Ferrous metals	0.1	40	0.0	10.5	41
Non-ferrous metals	−0.2	−41	−0.4	19.5	799

Source: Mai et al. 2005, Tables 4.3 and 4.4.

is that Australia imports little mining and base metal products from China. The second factor is that Australian tariff equivalents on mining and base metal imports from China are low (Table 7.4).

However, the removal of the border protection on merchandise trade leads to a large increase in the Chinese imports of mining and base metal products from Australia, resulting in an increase in the Australian output of these products, especially minerals not elsewhere classified (n.e.c.) (including iron ores) and non-ferrous metals (see rows 2 and 5 column 1 of Table 7.5). Table 7.5 shows that the removal of tariff equivalents is likely to increase Chinese imports of mining products from Australia by about 7 per cent (row 6 column 4 of Table 7.5) and non-ferrous metals by nearly 20 per cent in 2015 (row 10 column 4 of Table 7.5). Therefore, an FTA is likely to strengthen the role of Australia as a supplier of mining and base metal products to China.

BOX 7.1   KEY MODEL ASSUMPTIONS

Demands for inputs to be used in the production of commodities

In the MMC model, producers are assumed to choose the mix of inputs which minimizes the costs of production for their level of output. They are constrained in their choice of inputs by a three-level nested production technology. At the first level, intermediate-input bundles and primary-factor bundles are used in fixed proportions to output. These bundles are formed at the second level. Intermediate-input bundles are CES combinations of international imported goods and domestic goods. The primary-factor bundle is a CES combination of labour, capital and land. At the third level, the input of capital is formed as a CES combination of inputs of capital from domestic and foreign sources.

Household demand

In each region of the model, the household buys bundles of goods to maximize a Stone–Geary utility function subject to a household expenditure constraint. The bundles are CES combinations of imported and domestic goods. A Keynesian consumption function determines household expenditure as a function of GNP.

Inputs to investment

Capital creators for each country/region demonstrate optimizing behaviour in combining commodity inputs to form units of capital. Capital creators do not use primary factors. The use of primary factors in capital creation is recognized through inputs of construction (service).

International trade

The country/regions in MMC choose to supply to domestic versus foreign markets according to relative prices and therefore has an upward sloping export supply curve. The country/regions also choose to import from different foreign sources according to relative prices. Each of them therefore has a downward sloping import demand curve. The slopes of the export supply and import demand curves for each country/region depend on the structure of the economy concerned.

Capital market

In the MMC model, capital supply responds to rates of return. Capital ownership can cross country/regional borders so that each region's endowment of productive resources reflects relative rates of return. The accumulation of physical capital is through investment net of depreciation in each time period. In capital supply schedules, the expected rates of return are related to capital growth via reverse logistic functions (see Dixon and Rimmer 2002). There is a capital supply curve associated with each capital flow, that is, capital owned by country *s* in country *r*'s industry *j*, where *s* and *r* are the country/regions in MMC. In the current version of MMC, the expected rate of return is determined under static expectations. Under static expectations, investors only take account of current rentals and asset prices when forming current expectations about rates of return.

Labour market

In the model simulation, we assume that in the long run, national employment in each country is determined by demographic factors (for example, labour-force participation rates and population growth) that are unlikely to be affected by the implementation of an FTA. Thus we assume that the removal of protection on merchandise trade has no long-run effects on national employment in either Australia or China. The mechanism that keeps employment fixed in the long run is real-wage adjustment.

Trade-liberalization-induced productivity improvements

In the model simulation, we assume that producers react to increased import competition by cutting costs of production leading to an improvement in productivity. Table 7.6 presents the extent to which productivity improves when bilateral tariff-equivalent rates are cut. These improvements are endogenously calculated in the model (see Mai 2003 for further details). The calculation is based on empirical estimates (Chand, McCalman and Gretton 1998), taking into account bilateral trade flows between Australia and China, and China's characteristics as a developing country.

Source: Mai (2004).

Table 7.6 Removing tariff equivalents on merchandise trade (full liberalization in 2006): trade liberalization-induced endogenous productivity improvement (%)

	Australia	China
Agriculture	0.0	0.0
Wheat	0.0	0.0
Cereal grains nec	0.0	0.0
Oil seeds	0.0	0.0
Wool, silk-worm cocoons	0.0	0.0
Mining	0.0	0.4
Minerals nec	0.0	0.2
Manufacturing	0.1	0.1
Meat products nec	0.0	0.0
Dairy products	0.0	0.0
Sugar	0.1	0.3
Food products nec	0.0	0.1
Textiles (incl. lightly processed wool)	0.4	0.1
Wearing apparel	1.7	0.3
Chemical, rubber, plastic prods	0.1	0.0
Ferrous metals	0.0	0.0
Non-ferrous metals	0.0	0.1
Motor vehicles and parts	0.0	0.0
Machinery and equipment nec	0.0	0.0
Miscellaneous manufactures	0.2	0.1

Note: The numbers in this table show the percentage rates of change in output per unit of primary factor (labour, capital and land) input that arise from the removal of border protection shown in Table 7.4. For example, in our modelling we assume that due to the removal of tariffs and tariff equivalent protection on Chinese imports of wearing apparel into Australia, productivity (i.e. output per unit of primary factor input) in the Australian wearing apparel industry will improve by 1.7 per cent.

Source: Mai et al. 2005, Table 4.2.

RESOURCE AND INVESTMENT

The discussion in the previous section shows that removing bilateral border protection on merchandise trade between Australia and China reinforces Australia's role as a supplier of mining products to China – a trade pattern established in the past two decades. The influence of the FTA may also come from improved communication that deepens the economic cooperation between the two countries. One particular improvement in communication and cooperation may come from investment facilitation.

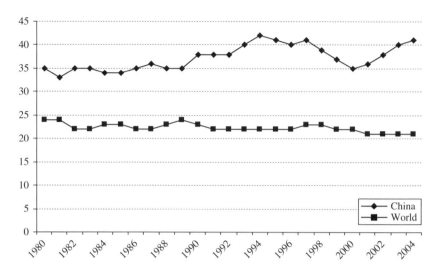

Source: World Bank, World Development Indicators.

Figure 7.4   *China's high gross domestic savings 1980–2004, as percentage of GDP*

The issue of investment facilitation is particularly relevant for the resource sector, since most Chinese investment in Australia is directed into resources.[3] The increasing demand for resource products following its rapid economic growth has become one of the most important factors shaping Chinese investment overseas. China is becoming an increasingly significant source country for foreign direct investment (FDI) because of its high rate of domestic saving (Figure 7.4) and large current account surplus (Figure 7.5).

Australia is a world leader in the development and provision of mining technology services including information technology, engineering and construction. Over 60 per cent of the world's mining operations now utilize software developed by Australian Companies (DFAT and MOFCOM 2005). China's foreign investment regime may have a significant influence on the provision of Australian mining technology services to China, as trade in services may involve establishing a commercial presence in destination countries.

Restrictions on investment flows can take various forms. These include restrictions on direct entry to an industry; restrictions on the operations and flexibility of foreign investors; discrimination between domestic and foreign businesses; and non-transparent regulations and standards that increase the costs of compliance.

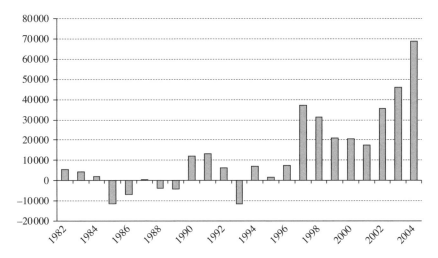

Source: World Bank, World Development Indicators.

Figure 7.5   China: current account surplus 1982–2004, million USD

According to the Foreign Acquisition and Takeovers Act 1975, foreign acquisitions and takeovers regulations and associated ministerial state-ments, certain types of investment proposals by foreign interests require prior notification and approval from the Australian government. The Foreign Investment Review Board screens the following types of proposals: foreign investment in existing businesses in excess of A$50 million; foreign invest-ment to establish new businesses in excess of A$10 million; direct investment by foreign governments or their agencies; foreign investment in the media sector, and foreign acquisitions of urban land. In particular, investment pro-posals made by companies with a greater than 15 per cent direct or indirect holding by a foreign government or agency are subject to screening. Most of the Chinese investment in the mineral and resource sector is likely to fall into this category and therefore be subject to the screening process.

Foreign investment in China is subject to notification and approval on a case-by-case basis. Foreign investment in excess of US$30 million is subject to approval of the Ministry of Commerce, while provincial and local gov-ernments can approve foreign investments of up to US$30 million that are on the list of the encouraged and permitted category. The Regulation on Guiding Foreign Investment and the Catalogue on Guiding Foreign Investment provide a list of encouraged, restricted and prohibited categ-ories of foreign investment; and foreign investment outside the three lists falls into a permitted category (DFAT and MOFCOM 2005).

Investment facilitation under a bilateral FTA can take various forms such as:

- enhancing the transparency of the investment rules and regulations;
- reducing or removing direct entry barriers to foreign firms;
- simplifying foreign investment screening procedures; and
- providing for better protection of bilateral investments.

In the next section, we review the recent literature that estimates quantitatively the effects of investment facilitation/liberalization.

THE CHALLENGE OF QUANTIFYING THE EFFECTS OF INVESTMENT FACILITATION/LIBERALIZATION

In the 1980s and the 1990s, multilateral and regional trade negotiations focused mainly on tariff and non-tariff barriers to merchandise trade – a topic that large-scale CGE models are well equipped to analyse quantitatively. Bilateral merchandise trade has been well represented in the database of various multicountry CGE models, such as the Global Trade Analysis Project (GTAP) model (see Hertel 1997 and Dimaranan and McDougall 2002). The response of economic agents to changes in relative prices – caused by a change in tariff or tariff equivalents of non-tariff barriers – is well represented in the equation system of CGE models.

However, the new wave of bilateral trade negotiations (examples being the Singapore–Japan FTA that took effect in 2002 and the Australia–China FTA that is currently under negotiation) gives emphasis on liberalization measures beyond border protection on merchandise trade. 'Non-price' measures such as investment facilitation and product standards have been brought under the spotlight. Furthermore, the General Agreement on Trade in Services (GATS) of the World Trade Organization (WTO) defined four modes of services trade: cross-border supply, consumption abroad, commercial presence and movement of natural persons. The third mode of services trade, commercial presence, refers to the services trade that occurs when an exporting country establishes service outlets in an importing country. This has brought the openness of member countries' foreign investment regimes onto the agenda of multilateral trade negotiations. Consequently, estimating quantitatively the effects of investment liberalization/facilitation has become a challenge to CGE analysis.

Recent empirical studies on the effects of investment liberalization started with attempts to quantify barriers to inward FDI flows. Hardin and Holmes (1997 and 2002) quantified restrictions to FDI using a weighted index approach. They calculated indices for FDI restrictions for 15 APEC countries. Using a similar approach, Golub (2003) estimated FDI restrictions for OECD countries. Under a similar method, a range of studies recently published by the Australian Productivity Commission estimated restrictions on services trade including commercial presence that involves establishing service outlets in importing countries (for examples, see Nguyen-Hong 2000 and Nguyen-Hong and Wells 2003).

The indexing approach summarizes information on the number and type of FDI restrictions imposed, by country and sector. A weight is assigned to each component of the index of FDI restrictions to reflect the relative importance of different barriers. For examples, the weight to the restriction 'no foreign equity permitted on all firms' is 1; and the weight to the restriction 'screening and approval: approval unless contrary to national interest' is 0.075. An overall index is calculated for each sector in each country. A score of zero indicates that there are no restrictions on FDI; while a score of one indicates that FDI is either completely banned or is highly restricted. The choice of the barriers to include in the index and the weights is to some extent arbitrary (Hardin and Holmes 1997). However, the index provides a reasonable comparison of restrictiveness to FDI between countries.

Itakura et al. (2003) incorporated efficiency gains associated with FDI into their simulation of the potential benefit of a Japan–ASEAN FTA using the GTAP model. Based on an econometric study on Taiwan (Chuang and Lin 1999), they associated a one percentage point increase in the foreign equity share with a 1.4 percentage point improvement in productivity.

Mai et al. (2003) conducted an historical simulation[4] for the Chinese economy for the period 1992–7, during which China experienced a surge of inward FDI into the light manufacturing industries[5] (Figure 7.6). The study estimated that, with the help of the FDI inflows, the liberalized light manufacturing industries experienced an annual productivity improvement of 3.6 percentage points faster than that of the 'pillar' manufacturing industries that were then not liberalized to FDI. CIE (2004) simulated the investment liberalization under the Australia–US FTA as a reduction in equity risk premium. In its estimation of the effects of an Australia–Japan FTA, CIE (2005) simulated the investment liberalization as an increase in FDI flows and associated productivity gains that are calculated in a similar way to Itakura et al. (2003).

In the above-mentioned empirical studies, the authors struggled with the lack of empirical estimation of productivity gains associated with FDI. However, there is a common consensus among these authors that an FTA is likely to lead to increased FDI flows and increased FDI flows lead to improved productivity.

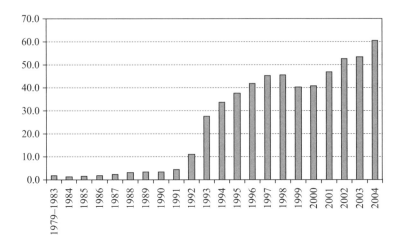

Source: China Statistical Yearbook, various issues, and Chinese Ministry of Commerce, accessed 18 May 2005, at www.mofcom.gov.cn/static.

Figure 7.6   China: total amount of FDI actually used, billion USD

A theoretical model developed by Helpman et al. (2004) provides background on how increased FDI flows may lead to improved productivity through spill-over effects. Their model of the organization of production incorporated firm-level heterogeneity in efficiency – a recent empirical finding by a number of studies (for example, Bernard and Jensen 1999 and Wagner 2002). Helpman et al. (2004) found that in equilibrium less efficient firms serve the local market, more efficient firms select exporting, while the most efficient firms engage in FDI.

There seems little doubt, based on our brief survey of the literature, that investment liberalization under an Australia–China FTA will have significant economic consequences for both economies. In the next section we present quantitative evidence based on projections from the MMC model showing the effects of liberalization on the overall size and structure of each economy. This modelling extends the indexing approach adopted by the Productivity Commission and others through the inclusion of general equilibrium effects which can be significant in areas of the economy quite distant from the resource sectors.

In our modelling we draw, in part, on empirical estimates by Mai et al. (2003) for productivity improvements associated with FDI inflows; and Productivity Commission estimates of relative restrictiveness to FDI in Australia and China (Hardin and Holmes 1997 and 2002; Nguyen-Hong 2000 and Nguyen-Hong and Wells 2003). These estimates provide a statistical foundation for inputs to our modelling which is an improvement on the quality of inputs used in other CGE-based studies (for example, CIE 2004).

ESTIMATING THE POTENTIAL BENEFITS OF THE INVESTMENT FACILITATION UNDER AN AUSTRALIA–CHINA FTA

To estimate the potential benefits of investment facilitation under an Australia–China FTA (Mai et al. 2005), we assume that the FTA would:

- enhance the understanding of Chinese investment rules and regulations by Australian investors and vice versa;
- lead to simplified foreign investment screening procedures; and
- provide for better protection of bilateral investments.

Such investment facilitation can be simulated as reductions in required rates of return on investment that encourage investment flows between Australia and China (see Figure 7.7). An inflow of foreign investment brings in more advanced technology and management and, therefore, improves productivity in the liberalizing countries.

In simulating the effects of investment liberalization, we assume that the liberalization is implemented fully by 2010, yielding:

- a reduction in the required rate of return on Australian investment in China of 0.5 percentage points (that is, a reduction from the current required rate of return of, say, 6 per cent to 5.5 per cent);
- a reduction in the required rate of return on Chinese investment in Australia of 0.4 percentage points (that is, a reduction from the current required rate of return of, say, 6 per cent to 5.6 per cent);
- a 0.12 per cent across-the-board improvement in primary factor productivity in China; and
- a 0.08 per cent across-the-board improvement in primary factor productivity in Australia.

In deriving the magnitude of the above changes we considered the following factors:

- empirical evidence derived from past investment liberalization in China (Mai et al. 2003);
- Australia's share in China's total trade and foreign investment;
- less scope for Australia to increase productivity because it is closer to the technology frontier than China;

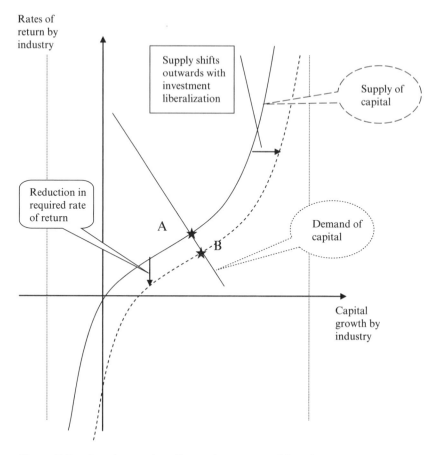

Figure 7.7   Simulating the effects of investment liberalization

- less scope for Australia to liberalize its investment regime because it has fewer barriers to foreign investment than China; and
- China's share in Australia's total trade and foreign investment.

It should be emphasized that the changes in required rates of return and productivity outlined above are, in our opinion, conservative. This is in keeping with the relatively high level of uncertainty associated with the estimates.

The long-run simulation results are presented in Tables 7.7 and 7.8. The numbers in Tables 7.7 and 7.8 show the deviation of economic variables from their baseline levels in 2015. For example, the first number in the Australia column in Table 7.7 shows that, in the long run, the level of real

Table 7.7   Australia–China FTA: effects of investment liberalization (deviations from baseline, 2015)

	Australia	China
Macroeconomic indicators		
Real GDP (%)	0.11	0.15
Real GDP (US$ million)	864	4616
Real GNP (%)	0.1	0.1
Real GNP (US$ million)	787	3737
Real Consumption (%)	0.1	0.1
Export volumes (%)	0.1	0.2
Import volumes (%)	0.1	0.1
Terms of Trade (%)	0.0	−0.1
Capital stock (%)	0.1	0.1
Real wage (%)	0.1	0.1
Volumes of investment flows		
Australian investment in China (%)	8.2	n.a.
Australian investment in China (US$ million)	235	n.a.
Chinese investment in Australia (%)	n.a.	7.1
Chinese investment in Australia (US$ million)	n.a.	197
Investment from the Rest of the World (%)	0.1	0.1
Investment from the Rest of the World (US$ million)	360	734
Volumes of trade flows		
Australian imports from China (%)	0.2	n.a.
Australian imports from China (US$ million)	58.0	n.a.
Chinese imports from Australia (%)	n.a.	0.2
Chinese imports from Australia (US$ million)	n.a.	38.6
Output of aggregated sectors		
Agriculture	0.1	0.1
Mining	0.1	0.2
Manufacturing	0.1	0.2
Services	0.1	0.1

Source: Mai et al. 2003, Table 5.1.

GDP for Australia is likely to be 0.1 percentage points higher than it would be without the bilateral investment liberalization.

The simulated reductions in required rates of return lead to increased bilateral investment flows (Table 7.7). Under the investment liberalization scenario, the volume of Australian investment in China increases to about 8 per cent (or about US$0.2 billion) above its baseline level by

Table 7.8   *Australia–China FTA: effects of removing border protection on*
              merchandise trade and investment liberalization (percentage
              deviations from baseline, 2015)

	Removing border protection on merchandise trade	Investment liberalization
Effects on China		
Real GDP	0.05	0.15
Real GNP	0.02	0.10
Effects on Australia		
Real GDP	0.12	0.11
Real GNP	0.22	0.10

Source: Mai et al. 2003, Tables 4.1 and 5.1.

2015. The volume of Chinese investment in Australia increases by about 7 per cent (or about US$0.2 billion). Increases in bilateral investment flows between Australia and China lead to productivity improvements in the two countries that, in turn, induce investment from the rest of the world. The induced investment flow from the ROW to Australia is estimated to be about US$0.4 billion; while the induced investment flow from the ROW to China is estimated to be about US$0.7 billion.

As a result of increased investment and hence increased capital and improved productivity, both Australia and China gain from bilateral investment liberalization in terms of real GDP (Table 7.7). Australia's real GDP in 2015 increases by slightly over 0.1 per cent (or about US$1 billion) relative to its baseline value, while China's real GDP increases by 0.15 per cent (or about US$5 billion).

For China, the effects on real GDP of investment liberalization are larger than those from the removal of border protection (Table 7.8). This is consistent with findings from studies on the effects of China's entry to the WTO – the impact of removing border protection on merchandise trade is found to be much smaller than the impact of investment liberalization (see, for examples, Fan and Zheng 2000; Ianchovichina and Martin 2001; Mai 2003; Ianchovichina and Walmsley 2003; Mai et al. 2003 and Walmsley, Hertel and Ianchovichina 2006). Mai et al. (2003) and Mai (2003) find that the GDP effect of investment liberalization due to China's entry to the WTO is five times larger than the GDP effect of removing protection on merchandise trade in line with WTO commitments.

Table 7.7 also shows that investment liberalization under a

Australia–China FTA will lead to increased bilateral trade in goods. The volume of Australian imports from China in 2015 increases by about 0.2 per cent (or about US$58 million) relative to its baseline level; while the volume of Chinese imports from Australia increases by about 0.2 per cent (or about US$39 million).

Increased investment and improved productivity increase the output of all industries, including the resource sectors (Table 7.7). Not all industries benefit significantly from the first-round impacts of the investment and productivity shocks. But all industries, especially consumption-oriented industries, benefit from the induced income effects arising from increased income and hence increased consumption expenditure. For most Australian industries output expansions are about 0.1 per cent of baseline levels. For Chinese industries, the range of output expansions is 0.1 to 0.2 per cent.

CONCLUDING COMMENTS

Although the bilateral border protection on the resource products is low, bilateral trade in the resource products can be significantly affected by the removal of border protection on merchandise trade for all products under an Australia–China FTA. In particular, Chinese imports of Australian resource products are likely to increase significantly as a result of the FTA, because the FTA leads to further expansion in a Chinese manufacturing sector that uses the Australian resource products as production inputs.

Bilateral investment flows facilitated through the FTA are also important for the resource sector. This is likely to be a more difficult area of negotiation than the border protection, as it touches upon the more sensitive topic of foreign ownership. The implementation of investment facilitation measures is also likely to be more difficult than the removal of tariffs on the resource products, because it involves institutional and legislative changes.

However, our estimation shows that, for Australia, a conservative estimation of the potential benefits of the investment liberalization delivers as large a gain as that of the removal of border protection on merchandise trade. For China, investment liberalization is likely to deliver a larger gain in terms of real GDP and GNP than the removal of border protection (Table 7.8). The key factor behind understanding this outcome is the productivity gains associated with the inflow of FDI.

Further understanding of the effects of investment liberalization would benefit from vigorous empirical studies of the magnitude of the productivity gains associated with the inflow of FDI. The productivity gains adopted in this study are rather conservative.

Theoretical models point to productivity gains from both removing border protection (Melitz 2003) and from inward FDI (Helpman et al. 2004). Due to the lack of empirical estimates of the magnitude of the productivity gains, CGE-model analyses tend to underestimate gains from trade liberalization.

NOTES

1. Mining and base metal products referred to in the text include coal, oil, gas, minerals n.e.c., ferrous metals and non-ferrous metals.
2. For a description of key modelling assumptions, see Box 7.1.
3. As at June 2003, Chinese resource and mining companies had invested US$328 million, agricultural enterprises US$13 million, and manufacturing enterprises US$60 million in Australia (DFAT and MOFCOM 2005).
4. For a systematic discussion of the methodology of a historical simulation, see Dixon and Rimmer (2002).
5. The surge of inward FDI occurred following Deng Xiaoping's southern tour, during which he encouraged the southern provinces to move ahead with their economic reform. As a result, Hong Kong and Taiwan clothing, footwear and electronic firms shifted their production rapidly to China's southern provinces marking the beginning of the surge of inward FDI.

REFERENCES

Bernard, A.B. and J.B. Jensen (1999), 'Exceptional exporter performance: cause, effect, or both?', *Journal of International Economics*, **47**, 1–25.

Chand, S., P. McCalman and P. Gretton (1998), 'Trade liberalization and manufacturing industry productivity growth', in 'Microeconomic reform and productivity growth', Productivity Commission and Australian National University, workshop proceedings, Canberra.

Chuang, Y.C. and C.M. Lin (1999), 'Foreign direct investment, R&D and spillover efficiency: evidence from Taiwan's manufacturing firms', *Journal of Development Studies*, **35** (April), 117–37.

CIE (Centre of International Economics) (2004), 'Economic analysis of AUSFTA: impact of the bilateral free trade agreement with the United States', report prepared for Department of Foreign Affairs and Trade, Canberra and Sydney: Centre of International Economics.

CIE (Centre of International Economics) (2005), 'Australia–Japan trade and investment liberalization: assessment of the economic impacts', report prepared for Department of Foreign Affairs and Trade, Canberra and Sydney: Centre of International Economics.

DFAT (Department of Foreign Affairs and Trade) and MOFCOM (Ministry of Commerce, China) (2005), 'Australia–China Free Trade Agreement' joint feasibility study, Canberra: Commonwealth of Australia.

Dimaranan, B.V. and R.A. McDougall (eds) (2002), *Global Trade, Assistance, and Production: the GTAP 5 Data Base*, West Lafayette, USA: Centre for Global Trade Analysis, Purdue University.

Dixon, P.B. and M.T. Rimmer (2002), *Dynamic General Equilibrium Modelling for Forecasting and Policy: a Practical Guide and Documentation of MONASH*, Amsterdam: North-Holland Publishing Company.

Fan, M. and Y. Zheng (2000), 'The impact of China's trade liberalization for WTO accession – a computable general equilibrium analysis', paper presented at the Third Annual Conference on Global Economic Analysis, Mount Eliza, Australia, June 2000.

Golub, S.S. (2003), 'Measures of restrictions on inward foreign direct investment for OECD countries', Paris: OECD Economics Department working paper no. 357.

Hardin, A. and L. Holmes (1997), 'Service trade and foreign direct investment', Australian Productivity Commission, available at www.pc.gov.au/ic/research/information/servtrad/index.html.

Hardin, A. and L. Holmes (2002), 'Measuring and modelling barriers to FDI', in B. Bora (ed.) *Foreign Direct Investment: Research Issues*, London: Routledge, pp. 252–72.

Helpman, E., M. Melitz and S. Yeaple (2004), 'Export versus FDI with heterogeneous firms', *American Economic Review*, **94**(1), 300–16.

Hertel, Thomas W. (ed.) (1997), *Global Trade Analysis: Modelling and Applications*, New York: Cambridge University Press.

Ianchovichina, E. and W. Martin (2001), 'Trade liberalization in China's accession to WTO', World Bank, policy research working paper no. 2623, Washington, DC, June.

Ianchovichina, E. and T. Walmsley (2003), 'Impact of China's WTO accession on East Asia', paper presented at the 6th Annual Conference on Global Economic Analysis, Scheveningen, The Hague, 12-14 June 2003.

Itakura, K., T. Hertel and J. Reimer (2003), 'The contribution of productivity linkages to the general equilibrium analysis of free trade agreements', Global Trade Analysis Project (GTAP) working paper no. 23, Center for Global Trade Analysis, Purdue University.

Mai, Y. (2003), 'China's entry to the WTO: the effects of reducing tariff and non-tariff barriers and endogenous productivity growth', in R. Smyth, O.K. Tam and C. Zhu (eds), *Institutional Challenges for the Global China*, conference proceedings, Melbourne, Australia, 13-14 November 2003.

Mai, Y. (2004), 'The Monash multi-country model', Centre of Policy Studies, Monash University, working paper no. G-150, Melbourne.

Mai, Y., P. Adams, M. Fan, R. Li and Z. Zheng (2005), 'Modelling the potential benefits of an Australia–China Free Trade Agreement', an independent report prepared for the Australia–China FTA Feasibility Study, Centre of Policy Studies, Melbourne.

Mai, Y., M. Horridge and F. Perkins (2003), 'Estimating the effects of China's accession to the World Trade Organisation', paper presented at the 6th Annual Conference on Global Economic Analysis, Scheveningen, The Hague, The Netherlands, 12-14 June 2003.

Melitz, M.J. (2003), 'The impact of trade on intra-industry reallocations and aggregate industry productivity', *Econometrica*, **71**(6), 1695–725.

Nguyen-Hong, D. (2000), 'Restrictions on trade in professional services', Productivity Commission staff research paper, AusInfo, Canberra, August.

Nguyen-Hong, D. and R. Wells (2003), 'Restrictions on trade in education services: some basic indexes', Productivity Commission staff working paper, AusInfo, Canberra, October.

Wagner, J. (2002), 'The causal effects of exports on firm size and labour productivity: first evidence from a matching approach', *Economics Letters*, **77**, 287–92.
Walmsley, T.L., T.W. Hertel and E. Ianchovichina (2006), 'Assessing the impact of China's WTO accession on investment', *Pacific Economic Review*, **11**(3), 315–39.

PART III

Key issues facing FTA negotiators

8. Intellectual property in a possible China–Australia free trade agreement

Kimberlee Weatherall

INTRODUCTION

Intellectual property (IP) laws – laws which grant and protect copyright, patent and trade mark, among other rights – are laws designed chiefly to promote creativity and innovation by providing creators and inventors with exclusive rights. A key feature of IP laws is that they are national in scope: patents or trade marks, for example, must be registered (and, if necessary, enforced) separately in each country where exclusivity is sought. IP law and the systems for registration and enforcement also vary from country to country. These facts create complications for IP-intensive and innovative industries, which have since the early 1980s pressed for the raising and harmonization of IP standards via trade negotiations. Today, countries negotiating bilateral trade agreements face several questions: should IP be included? If so, what, of the several kinds of IP provisions which could be included, will be useful? As this chapter shows, these issues are particularly complex and interesting in a negotiation between two countries such as Australia and China. From an Australian perspective, while IP-raising provisions may not be attainable, a more realistic, and still helpful alternative is to focus on creating obligations in dispute resolution and cooperation which are as specific as possible, and which seek to ensure that Australian IP owners are not disadvantaged by any future negotiations which China may have on IP matters with other, more powerful countries.

THE INCLUSION OF IP PROVISIONS IN BILATERAL FREE TRADE AGREEMENTS: MAPPING THE POSSIBILITIES

A question which commentators, particularly economists, often ask is why obligations in relation to IP law are included in FTAs at all. Their inclusion is counterintuitive, for two reasons. First, IP standards would seem to be a matter of domestic economic and innovation policy, not having direct implications for trade relationships – as compared, for example, to matters such as tariffs or import quotas. For a firm in country A deciding whether to export to country B, there will often be no direct, observable, increase in the price of its goods in country B attributable to IP policy in country B. In this respect IP policy is different from, for example, tariffs which add a fixed cost to imported goods, affecting their competitiveness. Nor does IP policy establish a set of regulatory barriers to imported goods, as might be the case, for example, with quarantine rules. Second, raising IP standards in some cases *increases* barriers to trade, by preventing goods legitimately sold in one country from being imported into another.[1] Commentators pointing to these facts have argued that IP standards should be left to domestic policy or to multilateral negotiations in dedicated forums, in particular, the World Intellectual Property Organization (WIPO).

In fact, however, there is a long history of IP standards being included in trade agreements: early examples date to the late 18th century (Ricketson 1987; Okediji 2003). And while the focus at an international level for much of the 20th century was on multilateral agreements, the 1980s saw an increase in lobbying efforts by transnational corporations to make IP a trade issue: both bilaterally and multilaterally. The trade–IP link was cemented with the negotiation of the North American Free Trade Agreement (NAFTA) in 1993, and the inclusion of the Agreement on Trade-Related Aspects of Intellectual Property Rights (TRIPS) as part of the World Trade Organization in 1994 (Drahos and Braithwaite 2002). TRIPS establishes a set of international minimum standards for IP rules that all WTO members must observe. TRIPS does not, however, prevent countries negotiating higher standards multilaterally or in bilateral agreements (TRIPS, Article 1.1). In recent years, both multilateral trade agreements, and multilateral IP treaties, have become much more difficult to negotiate: WIPO is caught up in a major debate over the effect of IP on development concerns (Mercurio 2007). It should be no surprise that we have seen a shift back towards bilateralism in IP, just as we have in international trade more generally (Okediji 2003; Mercurio 2007).

There are good reasons for including IP provisions in trade agreements. Academic economists have shown that IP standards can be a 'trade-related' issue. There is empirical evidence that differential IP standards have the potential to be trade-distorting, in the sense that they have an impact on firm decisions whether and where to export, as well as investment decisions (Maskus and Penubarti 1995; Maskus 2000; Mansfield 1994). This bare fact, however, tells us little about what kinds of IP matters are 'trade-related' or may be included in a trade agreement. IP is a complex area of law. It covers different kinds of rights (patent, trade mark, copyright, and more); and those rights may vary between countries in duration (how long the monopoly lasts), scope (what rights are given to owners), exceptions to rights (what acts can people do without permission of the owner), how rights are created (for example the registration system for patents and trade marks) and the methods of enforcement (civil and criminal; the level of penalties, whether administrative or court systems are used; whether infringing goods can be held by customs).

Untutored by experience, we might expect parties negotiating a free trade agreement to concentrate on amending those aspects of IP law which have the potential to interfere with the free movement of goods across borders. Harmonization of IP law in the European Union started from a recognition that IP rules could stand in the way of creating a common market for goods (Yusuf 1998). The first priority within the European Union was ensuring that goods, once produced legitimately (that is, with the authorization of any IP owners), could be sold anywhere in the European market (by allowing intra-European parallel importation[2]) and removing differences – such as variations in the duration of protection – that could stand in the way of cross-border trade. A second priority has been the creation and development of common systems for registration and enforcement of rights, via the Community Trade Mark and European Patent systems. European IP laws stand as an example of the kinds of IP developments we would expect to see if greater economic integration is sought by parties to a trade agreement. However, the European model of IP harmonization through reduction of barriers to trade seems to be the exception, not the rule. Arguably, this is because such an approach is only appropriate where countries already have broadly similar IP standards.[3]

Many IP chapters in trade agreements simply impose increases in IP standards and enforcement: requiring parties to grant longer terms of protection and more rights to IP owners, to limit exceptions, and to raise the penalties for infringement. Such expansions are justified on the basis that raising IP standards is needed to 'create a level playing field'. The argument goes something like this. Imagine two countries: country A has a strong innovation culture, and export strengths in advanced technologies; country B is less developed, and specializes in cheap manufactured goods and primary resources. Country A will likely have strong domestic IP laws, and local stakeholders who rely on legal protection for innovation. Country B, on the other hand, may have few local stakeholders arguing for IP law and hence weaker laws; indeed, country B may have local producers who survive through imitation, and who would be hurt by stronger IP rights or more enforcement. The difference in IP standards complicates trade between A and B. B's primary produce and manufactured goods can be sold into A's market; however, A's innovative firms may face competition from cheap local copies in B's market. A's firms may also hesitate to export technology to B for fear of copying. In short, without some IP protection in B, technologically advanced A is not on a level playing field, in the sense that it cannot make the most of its comparative advantage in research-intensive areas (Revesz 1999).

In practice, of course, IP chapters are not only about levelling the playing field. As Scotchmer (2001) has pointed out, profit from IP earned abroad 'is unambiguously a good thing: the more the better': any costs of such extensions are borne by foreign consumers; benefits flow back to local IP owners.[4] Trade negotiators for IP-rich countries with already strong IP law therefore have an incentive to negotiate increases in IP abroad, as long as changes to their own domestic law will not be required. As Scotchmer and others have further noted, this effect is exacerbated by the fact that in accordance with public choice theories of law reform, lobby groups for stronger IP rights are highly concentrated and hence tend to be effective in convincing trade negotiators and government officials to support stronger IP laws (Scotchmer 2001; Landes and Posner 2003).

This does not mean strong IP in trade agreements is a foregone conclusion. On the contrary, countries which are not significant exporters or owners of IP have corresponding incentives to resist IP chapters. Unlike provisions which raise tariffs, IP-raising provisions in trade agreements do not lead to gains for both parties; in this respect they differ from other measures normally included in FTAs, such as removal of tariffs, which at least in theory benefit consumers. Rather, IP chapters will tend to impose significant short-term costs on resource/primary producer countries, which must change their laws, shut down counterfeiting operations, devote more public resources to enforcement, and suffer increased prices for consumers and public institutions such as universities and schools to access new technologies or cultural items (for example, films or music). While it is sometimes argued that local innovation in B will be encouraged, any such benefits are long term, uncertain, unquantifiable, and may not be available at all to least-developed countries (Maskus 2000).[5]

A second complicating factor in any bilateral negotiation on IP is that a country which raises IP standards as a result of a bilateral trade agreement cannot confine the effect of the changes to nationals of the other party to the agreement. Under Article XXIV of the General Agreement on Tariffs and Trade 1994 (GATT 1994), agreements which create free trade areas are an exception to the most-favoured nation (MFN) principle enshrined in Article I of GATT. Thus tariff reductions or quota increases negotiated in a bilateral FTA apply only to goods originating in the partner country. However, this exception to MFN does not apply to changes which a party makes to its IP laws or enforcement provisions; on the contrary, MFN is enshrined *without* a free trade area exception in TRIPS Article 4. The result is that when countries A and B enter into a bilateral agreement that changes IP laws or enforcement systems, the same treatment must be given to the nationals of all WTO members. This has two effects: it increases the cost of raising IP standards and enforcement, and it removes the ability of a country in future multilateral or bilateral negotiations to trade off concessions in IP for better access to agricultural markets or other matters of importance.

Both the uneven distribution of benefits from raising IP standards and the need to 'multilateralize' any IP laws give countries which do not have a comparative advantage in IP-intensive industries reason to resist the inclusion of IP-raising in bilateral trade agreements. Such countries are generally better off negotiating on raising standards or enforcement levels in multilateral forums only, and only in return for concessions in other areas. To the extent that such countries *do* agree to bilateral IP provisions, it is likely to be as a cost, accepted in order to gain a concession in some other area of more immediate economic relevance to them: for example, access to agricultural or manufacturing markets. Evidence of this dynamic can be seen in trade agreements negotiated by the US, which increasingly include long, detailed IP provisions modelled on US laws (Mercurio 2007; Drahos 2001), or the EU's recently announced intention to make IP laws and enforcement a greater focus in its bilateral negotiations with countries outside the union (European Union 2006).

Thus far this chapter has discussed two approaches: an 'economic integration' approach following a European model, which removes barriers to cross-border movement of goods between countries already at a similar level of IP protection, and the 'IP-raising' approach following the US model, which seeks to create a level playing field, or perhaps ensure the maintenance of the US's comparative advantage. This discussion raises a real question: what, if any, IP provisions make sense in bilateral trade agreements which do not fit either of these situations?

One option, of course, is to leave out IP all together from a bilateral trade agreement. This would not be unusual at all: numerous examples of bilateral or regional trade agreements can be cited without any IP provisions: for example the bilateral FTA between China and Pakistan, or the India–Thailand FTA (2003). These may not be the kind of 'comprehensive' agreement that the Australian trade minister prefers, but they are a useful reminder that IP is not a necessary, or even usual inclusion in trade agreements (cf. Mauger and Stoianoff 2006). But further, if we take seriously the idea that bilateral trade negotiations are about removing barriers to trade and irritants or blockages in international trade relationships at least three further approaches are available relating specifically to IP:

1. A cooperation approach: drafting provisions to promote cooperation between patent offices and trade mark offices to ease difficulties faced by companies in one country in obtaining rights in the other party to the trade agreement (through, for example, staff exchanges or joint work efforts) and/or between enforcement and customs authorities (through, for example, provisions requiring cooperation between customs authorities in order to reduce cross-border trafficking in counterfeit goods).
2. A dispute-resolution approach: creating mechanisms for resolving specific IP-related disputes that are important to stakeholders within one or other of the parties to the agreement. Such an approach might, for example, require the establishment of administrative bodies, task-forces or officials tasked with assisting foreign IP owners to pursue enforcement.
3. A defensive approach: requiring parties to adhere to/implement multi-lateral IP treaties (such as TRIPS or other WIPO agreements). This approach can be characterized as 'defensive' in the sense that it does not seek to create any new rules or agencies, but does ensure that failure to meet basic international standards can be raised, and used as grounds for depriving a trading partner of other benefits granted under the bilateral trade agreement.

An important feature of all three of these approaches is that they have the potential to be significantly less costly than economic integration or IP-raising approaches, not least because, in so far as they relate to general matters of law enforcement or judicial assistance, they are arguably not subject to the requirement to apply benefits to all WTO members under the MFN principle.[6] All three approaches can also be drafted at any level on a spectrum from the general to the specific. For example, a 'cooperation' approach could be stated at a very high level of generality, where the parties undertake good faith efforts to cooperate on enforcement of IP rights (for one example, consider Chapter 11 of the India–Singapore Comprehensive Economic Cooperation Agreement 2005[7]). At the other end of the spectrum, an IP chapter could create a specific consultative mechanism, to meet on particular dates, and consisting of particular officials. Provisions at a higher level of generality may be easier to negotiate, but are likely to be less useful and much harder to enforce (Drahos and Braithwaite 2002, p. 139). In addition, different approaches can be combined in a single chapter. For example, Australia's 2004 trade agreement with Thailand combines a defensive provision (Article 1302), with obligations to cooperate on IP matters (Articles 1304, 1305).

A consideration of approaches to drafting IP chapters would not be complete unless it noted one final complicating factor which has a significant impact on the nature of IP provisions likely to be negotiated in any given bilateral agreement: that is, the 'horse-trading' aspect of comprehensive trade agreements. Any IP chapter will not be assessed in isolation for its benefits and costs, but rather as one aspect of an overall agreement where concessions will be made in one area to get agreement in another (I'll give you market access for pasteurized milk if you give up extension of patent terms).[8] In theory, a country which is considering how IP provisions will be negotiated ought to consider importance of IP issues as compared to other negotiating objectives, taking into account (a) the importance of IP-related issues in the partner country to affected industry sectors, and (b) the importance of the relevant industry sectors to the overall economy of the negotiating party. A full quantitative assessment even of the importance of the IP sectors of the economy is, however, rarely done in practice.[9]

THE IP INTERESTS OF AUSTRALIA AND CHINA

It has been argued that there are certain good reasons to include IP matters in trade agreements: but also that there are many different forms such agreements may take; what form is finally adopted depends on a series of factors, according to the IP issues being encountered in the relevant countries, the importance of those issues to industry, and the importance of IP-protected industries to the two countries involved. Thus far, discussion has been at a high level of generality. Two further important questions remain. First, does it make sense to include IP specifically in a trade agreement between Australia and China, and second, if so, what form should it take?

Considering the respective economies of Australia and China at a macro level, it might be expected that the two countries' interests would be relatively congruent. Neither Australia nor China is a world power in innovation. Both countries assert that development of a more innovative economy is a goal of public policy. Both countries might therefore be said to have similar aims, consistent with developing over time an IP regime which will support the development of an innovative economy. Comments by Australian negotiators to date have sought to emphasize this common ground. However, it is important not to underestimate the very real differences between the interests of the two countries.

Australian Interests

Australia, in part as a matter of deliberate policy, and in part as a result of its 2004 free trade agreement with the United States, has adopted very high standards of IP protection, extending well beyond the requirements of TRIPS in duration of both copyright and patent, the scope of rights granted, and the penalties for infringement. Australia for example has extensive digital copyright provisions, extended patent terms for pharmaceuticals to compensate for regulatory approval delays, and 'data exclusivity' laws which prevent government authorities from accepting applications to approve generic medicines based on clinical data used to approve the original drug for the period of exclusivity. As noted in the last section, these benefits apply to nationals of all WTO members, including China, even where China does not provide reciprocal protection to Australian innovators within its own borders. The combined effect is that Australia's self-interest in IP, considered in isolation, would be to see other countries adopt similar high standards to those which it is obliged to observe: such extensions would be 'pure benefit' to Australia, as discussed in the last section.[10]

On this reasoning, raising IP standards in China would be in Australia's interests regardless of any particular problems being experienced. However, the particular problems in China increase the importance of the issue to Australia. China is, notoriously, home to very significant IP infringements. While China has raised legal standards to accord with international minimums since acceding to the WTO, enforcement remains a significant problem. The Office of the US Trade Representative (USTR) cites industry estimates that levels of piracy in copyright businesses within China are between 85 and 93 per cent (USTR 2006). Moreover, China is the single largest source economy for counterfeit products in the world (OECD 2007); in 2005, 69 per cent of IPR infringing products seized at the US border originated in China (USTR 2006). General reports from private sector bodies indicate that counterfeiting may have increased, and that in general, enforcement efforts, particularly the administrative system, have been ineffective (American Chamber of Commerce 2006). Numerous submissions to the Australian government, made in the context of the Australia–China negotiations, have pointed out the impact of IP enforcement issues for Australian industries ranging from education providers to auto parts manufacturers and plant breeders. The major enforcement problems reported by the various government and private sector bodies reporting on the issue include:

- poor coordination of government ministries and agencies and bureaucratic delays;
- local protectionism and corruption which prevents enforcement of IP laws 'on the books' in the provinces of China;
- high thresholds which must be overcome before investigations or criminal prosecutions will occur;

- non-transparent processes;
- over-reliance on administrative enforcement, imposing fines which are too low to constitute an effective deterrent.

In addition, industry studies seem to place a high degree of importance on IP in the trade relationship with China. The Australian Industry Group (AIG) in 2006 reported that one in 16 manufacturing firms in Australia had a Chinese operation as at the first quarter of 2006, either as a foreign-owned company or a joint-venture partnership, and that the lack of IP protection was of the 'greatest concern' for Australian companies exporting to and investing in China, and for companies supplying the Australian and other markets (AIG 2006). The study was based on a survey of AIG members. Almost half of the firms (49 per cent) exporting to China identified shortcomings in IP as the number one issue of concern among non-tariff barriers to trade. On the other hand, such studies, based on self-reporting survey data, run at least some risk of overstating the issues. The same study found that 52 per cent of companies with business dealings with China stated that IP infringements did not prevent investment in China.

Despite these concerns, in the trade negotiation horse-trading, we would expect the Australian government to take into account the extent or size of Australia's interest in IP matters; it is still only as large as the increased profit Australian IP owners are likely to see from observance or better enforcement of IP rules in China. As Richardson has noted, overall, Australian imports of goods likely to have significant IP content dominate exports by a factor of 5 to 1; the cost to Australia of outgoing royalties and licence fees is three times the income received (Richardson 2004). While these figures are by no means conclusive of the value of IP to Australia – a full assessment would require an assessment of the role of IP in a whole range of industries – they provide some indication of the lower relative importance of these issues to the Australian economy overall. There is, of course, a further unquantifiable impact of poor IP enforcement in China, represented by the number of opportunities to do business in China *not* taken up by Australian industry for fear of IP infringement.

In summary, Australia certainly has some degree of interest in stronger IP enforcement and even higher IP standards in China. However to date, while there have been any number of assertions that IP is important in any bilateral dealings with China, there has been no attempt to quantify the significance of IP matters to Australia, relative to other matters which might be part of the horse-trading (but see Leahy et al. 2008).

Chinese Interests

China has indicated a clear preference for not negotiating IP chapters in bilateral trade agreements: none of its bilateral agreements to date have dealt with IP in any depth. Moreover, while it appears clear that the central Chinese government has adopted a policy in favour of more IP protection, there are many constituencies within China which oppose more enforcement. Chinese consumers, for example, have little interest in seeing more IP enforcement which will deprive them of the ability to buy copies of IP-protected material cheaply. Some Chinese businesses have little interest in laws which will prevent or restrict some of their activities – even though that activity is infringing. And some officials, particularly at a local or provincial level, may have little incentive to shut down counterfeiters who provide significant local employment and income (Mauger and Stoianoff 2006).

China faces a further issue in any negotiations with Australia: the impact on its dealings with other trading partners. Any raising of IP standards to which China agrees must be multilateralized. And while cooperation or dispute settlement provisions would not legally be required to be extended to other WTO members, they would nevertheless be seen as precedents. In future dealings with other countries such as the US or the European Union, provisions in an Australia–China FTA have the potential to be used as a starting point for negotiations. China therefore has a broader interest in keeping its IP commitments to a minimum. This is particularly true given the constant pressure to which China is subject from the US and Europe on enforcement matters; the US has consistently placed China on the 'Watch List' on IP matters (USTR 2006; Yu 2000 and 2006). The assorted threats and pressure emanating from the US in 2007 culminated in the US filing two WTO dispute settlement proceedings against China relating to IP matters (USTR 2007).

A third point must be noted in relation to Chinese interests in IP: and that is, the very rapid rate of change. According to commentators on the situation in China, it is inaccurate to characterize the country as a simple 'pirate nation'; rather, recent reports have noted the rise of local stakeholders concerned to explore and protect their IP rights (Yu 2006); even the USTR itself has noted that there is an increasing number of IP disputes being brought by Chinese plaintiffs in Chinese courts (USTR 2006). According to WIPO statistics, use of the patent system within China by Chinese inventors increased by 557 per cent between 1995 and 2004 (WIPO 2006); China was listed among the top ten countries for patent applications for the first time in 2005, recording an increase of 44 per cent compared with the previous year.[11] Any claims for more or better IP protection made by Australia need to take into account this changing reality, suggesting that there should be a focus on creating mechanisms to deal with future disputes or developments.

MODELS FOR AN AUSTRALIA–CHINA FTA IP CHAPTER

Bearing all this in mind, then, what kinds of IP provisions might we expect to see in an Australia–China FTA, and what kinds of provisions, in particular, might Australia reasonably aim for? One guide is to look at existing precedents. While China does not have IP chapters in its existing trade agreements, Australia does. Broadly speaking, they have so far come in two 'varieties':

1. The first variety is exemplified by Australia's agreements with Thailand and Singapore. These might loosely be termed 'defensive/cooperation' agreements: they are drafted at a very high level of generality, and simply require the parties to adhere to multilateral agreements, and to cooperate on enforcement, through exchange of information between relevant agencies, policy dialogue, and other initiatives.
2. The second variety is found in the Australia–US Free Trade Agreement: a comprehensive 'IP-raising' agreement on the way substantive IP law should look, plus detailed provisions on cooperation and provision for yearly meetings on the FTA as a whole.

Neither of these varieties provides a good model for a prospective Australia–China FTA. A very general 'cooperation/defensive' approach will not respond to the very real concerns that Australian stakeholders have expressed relating to the enforcement situation which currently pertains in China. On the other hand, a comprehensive agreement following the model of the Australia–US Free Trade Agreement is not attainable, since such an agreement would impose significant costs on China, and, in addition, would have to be applied multilaterally. The brutal fact is that Australia is not sufficiently important, nor are Australia's interests in IP sufficiently large or urgent that we are likely to see IP-raising standards, even though they would arguably be in Australia's interests. Nor, arguably, is the Australia–US model desirable given the impact of such an agreement in constricting local policy development. In any event, once again an IP-raising agreement would not truly respond to the main concerns of Australian stakeholders. Nor are Australia and China in a position where true economic integration provisions, European-style, would make sense.

An effective, useful IP chapter, therefore, from Australia's perspective, would adopt a combination of the defensive, cooperation, and dispute settlement approaches. In light of China's status as a current significant infringer, negotiators should aim for something far more specific than existing Thai or Singapore models, in order to create something enforceable. It would need to address any important, immediate concerns that have been identified by the industry. If, for example, trade mark applications are taking an inordinate time to be processed, then those delays could be specifically dealt with. This, on its own, however, is a rather 'static' approach. It deals with immediate issues, but free trade agreements are of their nature forward-looking documents. They need to make provision for future issues: a considerable challenge in the area of intellectual property where the market and the law change rapidly.

Thus as a second matter, an effective IP chapter would ideally contain a dynamic element: it must contain provisions that institute mechanisms for dealing with substantive and enforcement issues on an ongoing basis. A number of possible precedents may be found in the systems instituted between Europe and China, and between the US and China:

1. A *working group* in which Australian and Chinese officials, IP specialists and law enforcement authorities could consult on specific problems on an annual basis, modelled, perhaps, on the IPR Working Group of the Joint Commission on Commerce and Trade between the US and China.
2. Some form of *case referral* or specific *arbitration* system to deal with Australian IP disputes in China which does not rely solely on the existing, overworked and under-resourced enforcement systems.

The 'dynamic' aspects of the agreement would need, to be effective, to deal with both enforcement issues and problems, and possible future debate over substantive law. No doubt there are other even more interesting options available to create a 'dynamic' element to an IP chapter with China. It would appear, however, that only an agreement that contains such a dynamic element, that creates mechanisms for dealing with the new issues which are bound to arise as both Australian and Chinese interests in this field shift, will provide the kind of basis for ongoing cooperation that is required.

As a final matter, it should be recognized that an IP chapter in an Australia–China FTA would likely be one of the first negotiated by China, and seen as a precedent or starting point for future negotiations between China and other trading partners. It would therefore be in Australia's interests to include a most-favoured nation provision specifically addressing matters of dispute resolution and judicial assistance in relation to IP.

The purpose of such a provision would be to overcome any limitations in TRIPS Article 4, and to ensure that, if larger, more powerful negotiators such as the US or Europe do obtain 'special treatment' for their IP owners, Australian IP owners are given the same advantages.

The question that will remain is whether such a chapter can, in fact, be negotiated. Chinese preferences for no, or only very limited IP obligations, and the relatively low importance of Australian IP interests as compared with other industry sectors may see significant pressure towards a general, cooperation-type IP agreement. It is hard not to be pessimistic about the likely extent of Chinese concessions to Australian interests in this area.

NOTES

1. This can occur (a) where IP rights exist in the country of import which do not exist in the exporting country, and the IP owner prevents import, or (b) where an IP owner, holding rights in both countries, chooses to market its goods through exclusive distribution arrangements in each country, or to engage in price discrimination, charging different prices in the different countries.
2. 'Parallel importation', or grey market importation, refers to importation, without the permission of IP owners, of goods produced elsewhere with the authorization of any relevant IP owners. Parallel importation is an incursion into the IP owner's exclusivity, and limits their ability to engage in price discrimination, but does not prevent their being paid for the original production of the goods. International IP treaties give individual countries the right to choose whether to allow parallel importation or not. Australia allows some parallel importation (in particular, sound recordings and computer programs). The US does not allow parallel importation.
3. Removal of all IP-related barriers to movement of goods between countries of very different IP standards would pose a significant disadvantage to producers in a country with higher standards; the only reason a good might be 'legitimately' produced in a low-standard country is because IP rights are not recognized there; unfettered imports could undercut IP rights in the high-standard country entirely.
4. In framing domestic IP protection, a country must balance the gains to innovators against the costs to consumers who pay higher prices when intellectual property is protected. However, when IP protection is increased overseas, local inventors may obtain higher royalties, but the costs are all borne by foreign consumers. As long as the chapter does not involve increases in IP rights *domestically* for a country, IP chapters will appear to be costless to a negotiator (but see Burrell and Weatherall 2008 for a more detailed consideration of the costs of detailed IP chapters).
5. It is also argued that enforcing IP and shutting down counterfeit operations will tend to lead to increases in tax revenue: counterfeiters may not pay duties. However, given that the same countries often have more general issues with the effectiveness of their bureaucracies and tax collection agencies, it is not clear how significant the difference would be.
6. TRIPS, Article 4(a). In strict legal terms, there is room for argument whether the language of Article 4 of TRIPS, which requires that countries apply to all WTO members 'any advantage, favour, privilege or immunity granted by a Member to the nationals of any other country' would require 'multilateralizing' of IP-specific dispute bodies established in a bilateral trade negotiation. Nevertheless in practice countries are not applying such arrangements to all WTO members as a matter of course: for example, the US and China have established a series of committees to deal with IP disputes between nationals of their two countries and facilitate enforcement of US IP in China; these arrangements

have not been applied to other WTO members by China. The EU, too, has a number of arrangements in place which apply only to EU nationals. It should, however, be noted that a country which agrees to IP provisions in one FTA may find it more difficult, in future FTA negotiations, to resist inclusion of similar, or greater obligations.

7. This chapter consists of two articles: 11.1, which undertakes to 'develop and promote mutually beneficial cooperation between the Parties' in the area of IP, and 11.2, which states that such cooperation 'may' include the organization of symposia, seminars and training, or collaboration on projects to promote the effective use and application of IP rights.

8. IP is particularly vulnerable to this kind of barter because the costs of IP provisions are difficult to quantify, meaning that concessions in this area can be 'spun' as beneficial to both countries.

9. When Australia negotiated an FTA including an IP chapter with the US in 2004, much criticism was directed at the fact that there was no attempt to quantify the impact of that IP chapter (Dee 2004).

10. It is worth noting that this represents a change from the previous position as assessed by the Australian Productivity Commission (Revesz 1999). According to Revesz, Australia's interest in IP, at that time, was to see compliance with the international standards but not stronger standards. Now that Australia is committed to standards beyond the multilateral international framework, however, it has an interest in having other countries observe similarly high standards: extensions elsewhere are costless to Australia, but may bring some benefit; increases in IP protection elsewhere, beyond the international multilateral standards, represent 'pure benefit' for Australian IP owners (without any cost to Australian consumers).

11. China is also leading the developing world in trade mark applications from 2005, according to WIPO statistics. These figures may be found on the Chinese government's new intellectual property protection website, http://english.ipr.gov.cn/en/index.shtml.

REFERENCES

American Chamber of Commerce, People's Republic of China (AmCham China) (2006), White Paper 2006: American business in China, report, Beijing: American Chamber of Commerce, People's Republic of China.

Australian Industry Group (AIG) (2006), 'Australian manufacturing and China: deepening engagement', report, August, Australia: AIG.

Burrell, R. and K.G. Weatherall (2008), 'Exporting controversy? Reactions to the copyright provisions of the US–Australia Free Trade Agreement: lessons for US trade policy', *University of Illinois Journal of Law, Technology and Policy*, (2), 259–319

Dee, P. (2004), 'The Australia–US Free Trade Agreement – an assessment', report prepared for the Senate Select Committee on the Free Trade Agreement between Australia and the United States of America, June, Canberra, Australia.

Drahos, P. (2001), 'BITs and BIPs – bilateralism in intellectual property', *Journal of World Intellectual Property*, **4**(6), 791–808.

Drahos, Peter and John Braithwaite (2002), *Information Feudalism: Who Owns the Knowledge Economy?*, London: Earthscan Publications.

European Union (Directorate-General for Trade Policy) (2006), 'Global Europe: competing in the world', communication, 4 October, Brussels, Belgium.

Landes, William M. and Richard A. Posner (2003), *The Economic Structure of Intellectual Property Law*, Cambridge, MA: Belknap Press of Harvard University Press.

Leahy, A., D. MacLaren, D. Morgan, K. Weatherall, E. Webster and J. Yong (2008), 'In the shadow of the Australia–China FTA negotiations: what Australian business thinks about IP', *Economic Papers*, **27**(1), 1–18.

Mansfield, E. (1994), 'Intellectual property protection, foreign direct investment and technology transfer', International Finance Corporation discussion paper no. 19, World Bank, Washington, DC, USA, available from www.ifc.org.

Maskus, Keith E. (2000), *Intellectual Property Rights in the Global Economy*, Washington, DC: Institute for International Economics.

Maskus, K.E. and M. Penubarti (1995), 'How trade-related are intellectual property rights?', *Journal of International Economics*, **39**, 227–48.

Mauger, L. and N.P. Stoianoff (2006), 'Protecting Australia's trade mark interests through the Australia–China Free Trade Agreement', *LAWASIA Journal*, **2006**, 125–62.

Mercurio, B. (2007), 'TRIPS-plus provisions in FTAs: recent trends', in L. Bartels and F. Ortino (eds), *Regional Trade Agreements and the WTO Legal System*, Oxford: Oxford University Press, pp. 215–38.

Office of the United States Trade Representative (USTR) (2006), '2006 Special 301 Report', available from the USTR website, www.ustr.gov.

Office of the United States Trade Representative (USTR) (2007), 'United States files WTO cases against China over deficiencies in China's intellectual property rights laws and market access barriers to copyright-based industries', press release, 9 April 2007, available from USTR website, www.ustr.gov.

Okediji, R.L. (2003), 'Back to bilateralism? Pendulum swings in international intellectual property protection', *University of Ottawa Law & Technology Journal*, **1**, 125–47.

OECD (2007), *The Economic Impact of Counterfeiting and Piracy*, Paris: OECD.

Revesz, J. (1999), 'Trade related aspects of intellectual property rights', Australian Productivity Commission staff research paper, Canberra, May.

Richardson, D. (2004), 'Intellectual property rights and the Australia–US Free Trade Agreement', Parliamentary Library research paper no. 14 2003-2004, Canberra: Parliament of Australia, May.

Ricketson, S. (1987), *The Berne Convention for the Protection of Literary and Artistic Works, 1886–1986*, London: Centre for Commercial Law Studies, Queen Mary College.

Scotchmer, S. (2001), 'The political economy of intellectual property treaties', Center for Competition Policy, University of California at Berkeley working paper no. CPC01-24.

WIPO (2006), 'WIPO patent report: statistics on worldwide patent activity', available from the WIPO website, http://www.wipo.int/ipstats/en/statistics/patents/patent_report_2006.html.

Yu, P. (2000), 'From pirates to partners: protecting intellectual property in China in the twenty-first century', *American University Law Review*, **50**, 131–243.

Yu, P. (2006), 'From pirates to partners (Episode II): protecting intellectual property in post-WTO China', *American University Law Review*, **55**, 901–1000.

Yusuf, A.A. (1998), 'TRIPs: background, principles and general provisions', in C.M. Correa and A.A. Yusuf (eds), *Intellectual Property and International Trade: the TRIPS Agreement*, London: Kluwer Law International.

9. Rules of origin

Peter Lloyd and Donald MacLaren

INTRODUCTION

Rules of origin (ROOs) are a required feature of a China–Australia Free Trade Agreement (CAFTA), as they are for all free trade areas in which the member countries retain their own different systems of trade regulation. Yet, little attention has been paid in the past to rules of origin in Australia and, indeed, in most parts of the world. In a recent paper, Augier et al. (2005) state that 'Rules of origin are usually ignored for two reasons: they are dauntingly complex and at first sight appear mind-numbingly dull.' (p. 569) The technicality and complexity of the rules disguise their importance.

In fact, the tariff rate applied to any good entering a country is determined by:

- The tariff classification of the good,
- the rule of origin determining its origin,
- the tariff rate for the good from this origin,
- the value for duty of the good (unless duty is based on volume).

The first of these is settled by the harmonized system (HS) of tariff classification that is now used by all members of the World Trade Organization (WTO) giving a common classification down to the six-digit level. The value for duty system is used for all imports and is governed by Article VII of the General Agreement on Tariffs and Trade (GATT) 1994 and the Agreement on Customs Valuation concluded in the Uruguay Round.

Hence, the application of tariffs depends, practically speaking, on the tariff rates and the rules of origin. Since the tariff rates on goods entering from a preferential source under a free trade agreement (FTA) will be lower for many goods than those applying to goods entering from a non-preferential source, the determination of the origin of an import may substantially affect the tariff rate actually applied and the competitiveness of these imports. Similarly, the application of measures other than tariffs that restrict imports of goods depends on the rule of origin jointly with other rules that determine the conditions of entry for goods coming from a particular origin. This applies, for example, to quotas and tariff quotas.

Thus, in a free trade area, ROOs together with tariff rates and the conditions of entry for non-tariff measures jointly determine whether goods enter on preferential or non-preferential terms. Stringent ROOs take away some of the potential gains in an RTA resulting from the tariff preferences and improved market access that have been negotiated. ROOs are therefore a most important part of the total set of rules.

A corollary of this proposition is that ROOs matter only for goods which have a strictly positive most-favoured nation (MFN) tariff rate and goods where non-tariff measures restrict imports from MFN sources. If goods enter free of tariffs and other restrictions, the entry of goods from all sources is unaffected by ROOs. This has important consequences, as we see later.

Origin of goods is becoming increasingly difficult to determine in a globalized world as the processes of production are becoming more fragmented, particularly for manufactures and most particularly for product groups such as clothing, textiles and footwear (CTF) and telecommunications equipment. That is, the production processes that produce a traded good have been carried out in more than one country, upstream stages being carried out in one country and later downstream stages in one or more other countries. Typically, in making manufactured goods, countries now specialize not in the production of final goods but in the production of stages of goods, using materials or components or other intermediate inputs that have been produced at an earlier stage in another country. It is this fragmentation or dis-integration of production processes that makes the determination of origin difficult in many cases. (For general discussions of this phenomenon, see Feenstra 1998; Arndt and Kierzkowski 2001; and Cheng and Kierzkowski 2001). In some cases, the value added within the country from which a good is sourced may be small, certainly less than 50 per cent of the value at the point of exportation.

Australia fits this pattern. Australian exporters of manufacturers have always used many imported inputs. One feature of the Australian customs tariff has encouraged this, namely the system of by-law imports, or concessional imports as they are known today. This system allows imported intermediate inputs to enter free of duty or at a low concessional rate if the imported good does not compete with an Australian-produced substitute good. This has been a feature of the Australian tariff system since the first tariff was introduced in 1902. In the last two decades or so, Australian production of manufactures has become more limited both in terms of the range of goods produced and in terms of the stages carried out within the country for those goods it does produce. One part of this trend is the increasing use of 'offshore' production whereby an Australian manufacturer sets up an operation in another country as a foreign investor or joint venturer, or as a contractor. The semi-finished article or part is then shipped to Australia where it is finished off for sale in domestic or export markets. China is one of the countries where Australian 'offshore' production takes place.

Chinese production processes for manufactures tend to be more integrated than Australian processes and indeed than the processes of most countries in the global economy. This is because its manufacturing sector is large and diversified. Yet, there has been a similar increase there in the proportion of imported intermediate inputs as the Chinese economy has opened up.

The rules of origin in a CAFTA must deal with these realities of fragmented and offshore production.

THE BASIC PROBLEM

There is at present no set of rules or standard in the WTO which lays down preferential rules of origin. The original GATT 1947 and the GATT 1994 which was embedded in the rules of the WTO contain no rules of origin for free trade areas or customs unions. The Uruguay Round concluded an Agreement on Rules of Origin but this is confined to non-preferential rules. It contains a work programme for negotiations to harmonize non-preferential rules of origin. These negotiations have been going on in the WTO Committee on Rules of Origin for more than a decade but are a long way from complete (see Imagawa and Vermulst 2005).

Annex II of the Uruguay Round Agreement contains a common declaration on preferential rules but this is confined to a declaration of basic principles of transparency and administrative standards and procedures such as judicial review and non-retrospectivity, and it is non-binding. Thus members of the WTO are free to adopt what rules of origin they wish in negotiating free trade areas.

At present non-preferential ROOs are guided by the 1973 Kyoto Convention. This was made under the auspices of the Customs Cooperation Council, the predecessor of the World Customs Organisation, but it too is non-binding. The Kyoto Convention lays down several methods of assessing origin. Under the convention, the first question is whether the product is *wholly obtained or produced* in one country, or whether two or more countries have been involved in the manufacture of the product. If a product is wholly obtained or produced in one country, it clearly has the origin of that country. Origin has not proven controversial in this context.

If, however, more than one country is involved in the manufacture of the product, the product admitted into a country from an FTA partner country will incorporate some material originating in a non-partner country, or non-originating material as it is called. Here, the general concept is that the product will have the origin of the country where the *last substantial transformation* took place. Beyond this principle, the rules are very general.

There are three main methods that can be utilized to ascertain where the last substantial transformation took place:

- A percentage test,
- a change in tariff classification (CTC) test,
- a technical test.

The CTC test is sometimes known, inaccurately, as a change of tariff heading or CTH test. The third test is used for a few product groups only or as a supplement to either of the first two tests. The primary choice is, therefore, between a percentage test and a CTC test, or some combination of them. Within each of these tests there are many choices.

The percentage test comes in three forms:

- The import content method,
- domestic content (or regional value content) method,
- value of parts method.

The first two methods should, in principle, lead to the same result since the import content and the domestic content are complements, summing to 100 per cent of the value. One can, therefore, pose a test in terms of the maximum permissible import content or the minimum required domestic content. In practice, however, there are many differ-ences. In particular, the domestic content method requires an analysis of production costs. Production costs can be broken down into costs of manufacture and overhead costs, both manufacturing overheads and general overheads such as sales, outward freight and insurance. One must include profits in the domestic content for equivalence of the two methods. For the valuation of materials used in manufacture under the domestic content method, there is a question of at what stage materials and other expenditures should be valued, that is, in ascending order: ex works, free on board (fob), cost, insurance and freight (cif) or delivered (into factory).

Similarly, for the CTC test, there are many choices. These relate to the choice of aggregation in the classification of goods which is used to determine the change in classification and whether the test is used alone or supplemented by a percentage criterion or a technical test.

In fact, many different ROO systems are used in regional trade agreement (RTAs) around the world. WTO (2002) and Estevadeordal and Suominen (2003) provide excellent surveys of the overall picture. The WTO surveyed 93 RTAs that were in force in March 2001. Of the three tests, the CTC was the most common. Of the 93 RTAs, 89 used a CTC test, compared to 77 that employed a percentage test and 74 that employed a technical test. These three numbers add up to more than twice 93 because most RTAs use more than one test, and some employ all three for different product groups; for example, PANEURO and the North American Free Trade Agreement (NAFTA). Of those RTAs which use a percentage test, 70 use an import content method, 67 use a value of parts method and only nine (including Closer Economic Relations CER a free trade agreement between Australia and New Zealand) use a domestic content method.

In addition, all RTAs have general rules and most allow exceptions to some rules. Those using a percentage test may have general rules relating to, for example, tolerance or cumulation or outward processing or drawback. Those using a CTC may have *de minimis* or cumulation or absorption or drawback rules for example. Some of these make the rules less stringent (for example, tolerance or *de minimis*, outward processing and cumulation) and some make them more stringent (for example, disallowing customs drawback) than they would otherwise be.

The outcome is a great variety of rules with little uniformity among RTAs. Two ROO systems are widely used. One is the PANEURO system used by the countries of the EU, the European Free Trade Association (EFTA) states, the Central and East European states and the Mediterranean states with which the EU has separate agreements. This system applies only to trade between the areas as the EU itself is borderless. It is a completely harmonized system; all of the rules are identical across the areas. The other is the NAFTA system. The US has used NAFTA ROOs as a template and imposed NAFTA-style rules of origin in most RTAs which it has negotiated post-NAFTA. (There is, however, one notable exception; the US–Jordan Agreements use a percentage test. The US–Israel agreement also uses a percentage test but this was concluded before NAFTA). Canada and Mexico have done the same with their bilaterals (Estevadeordal and Suominen 2003, pp. 11–12). This has given a NAFTA family of ROO systems, with similar features though they are not harmonized.

The NAFTA and PANEURO families are based on CTC but use other tests for many product groups. The negotiations of a harmonized system of non-preferential ROOs are also based on CTC; the draft of the agreement allows a percentage or technical test as a 'supplementary criterion' only where the exclusive use of the HS nomenclature does not allow for the expression of substantial transformation (Imagawa and Vermulst 2005, p. 619). These features led Palmeter (1993, p. 329) to declare 'CTH appears to be the wave of the future'. Nevertheless, a number of well-known RTAs use some form of percentage test as the primary test; these include the European Free Trade Area, ASEAN Free Trade Area (AFTA), CER (currently) and the Andean Community. Moreover, the description of NAFTA as CTC-based is misleading. As noted above, ROOs do not matter when the applied MFN tariff rate is zero. When zero tariff rate items are removed from the list of products in the US tariff, around 70 per cent of tariff items are subject to a percentage rule (Productivity Commission 2004a, p. 33), and these include most of the heavily protected products in the CTF and automobile sectors. The PANEURO system determines the country in which the 'last working or processing' is carried out by product-specific rules which are a mixture of CTCs and percentage tests. In the event of insufficient work and processing in one country, origin is allocated according to the country with the highest percentage of value added. Thus, percentage tests are still a major part of ROO systems around the world.

In addition to choosing a test or tests, there is a second problem faced today by countries in negotiating rules of origin. Many countries now are members of more than one RTA. In the case of the EU and the US this does not pose a problem for ROOs as they are big enough in terms of markets to impose their primary EU and NAFTA rules respectively on other countries seeking to negotiate an RTA with them. Smaller countries, however, are not in this position. For example, Australia has currently a sole percentage test in the CER Agreement with New Zealand and in the Singapore–Australia Free Trade Agreement but when negotiating the Australia–US FTA it had to accept a variant of NAFTA ROOs.

AUSTRALIAN EXPERIENCE WITH ROO SYSTEMS

Australia has negotiated ROOs as a part of the negotiations of each of the FTAs of which it is a member; the CER agreement with New Zealand, the Singapore–Australia Free Trade Agreement (SAFTA), the Thailand–Australia Free Trade Agreement (TAFTA) and the Australia–United States Free Trade Agreement (AUSFTA). All have different ROOs. This section summarizes the main features only of each of these systems. For the full details of the method used, the agreements and any related documents and rulings must be consulted. The main sources are: for CER, the Joint

Australian/New Zealand Information Booklet; for SAFTA, the agreement itself; for TAFTA, Australian Customs Service, *Origin Manual*, volume 8D; for AUSFTA, Australian Customs Service, *Origin Manual*, volume 8C.

Table 9.1 sets out the main features of the ROOs in the four agreements. The features listed are the choice of primary test, the presence or otherwise of a supplementary test, and four other features which makes the rules less or more stringent. In all cases the tests outlined in the table relate to those products that are subject to a test because of the presence of non-originating materials. For example, in CER, there are three categories of goods:

1. Goods wholly the produce of the country (unmanufactured raw products),
2. goods wholly manufactured in the country,
3. goods partly manufactured in the country.

Goods in categories 1 and 2 enter without further conditions. Goods in category 3 are subject to the percentage test. That is, the features in Table 9.1 apply to category 3 goods only. Very similar categories apply in the other agreements.

For goods partly manufactured in one of the CER countries, the CER rules seem straightforward at first sight but they are not. CER uses a percentage test as the sole test.[1] These require:

- The 'last process of manufacture' be performed by a manufacturer in either Australia or new Zealand;
- not less than 50 per cent of the 'factory cost' (including materials, labour and overhead) associated with the process must be 'qualifying expenditures', that is, incurred in Australia or New Zealand.

Both parts are troublesome. The first requires a definition of manufacture and a determination of the last place of manufacture. This poses problems when the production system uses contracting out or commission work. The second requirement leaves out costs included in the country of manufacture but outside the factory. There are additional problems with materials supplied free of charge or at reduced cost and materials and containers of mixed origin. The Productivity Commission (2004a) reviewed this system in detail.

The ROOs in SAFTA are a variant of those in CER. The governments took the opportunity to refine the percentage test. SAFTA provides a definition of 'manufacture' whereas one is lacking in CER. It introduced the concept of the 'principal manufacturer' as '. . . the person in the territory

Table 9.1 *Main features of ROO systems*

Test	CER	SAFTA	TAFTA	AUSFTA
Primary test	Percentage test (Last process of manufacture + Domestic content method Factory cost basis 50 per cent for all goods)	Percentage test (Domestic content method Total cost of 'principal manufacturer' 50 per cent/30 per cent for goods specified in Annexe 2D)	CTC	CTC
Secondary test	No	No	Regional value content for goods specified in Annexe 4.1 (Build-down method) Or technical test in small number of lines	Regional value content for goods specified in Annexes 4-A and 5-A (Build-down method or build-up method) Or technical test in a small number of lines
General features				
Tolerance or *de minimis* rules	2 per cent tolerance in unforeseen circumstances	2 per cent tolerance in unforeseen circumstances	*De minimis* (up to 10 per cent) for all goods	*De minimis* (up to 10 per cent) for most goods
Cumulation	Bilateral + diagonal for materials originating in forum island countries	Bilateral	Bilateral	Bilateral
Outward processing	No	Yes (except for goods in Annexe 2C)	No	No
Customs drawback	Yes	Yes	No	

of a party who performs, or has performed on its behalf, the last process of manufacture of the goods'. This concept allows costs incurred by the principal manufacturer for work done outside the factory and on commission to be taken into consideration in assessing the percentage whereas they are not allowable under the CER definitions. This extends to materials processed outside the territories of the two parties to the agreement. These features allow outsourcing expenditures to be counted as domestic content. Outsourcing is a feature of many modern manufacturing operations; as a high-wage country, Singapore outsources parts of its manufacturing processes to plants in neighbouring Indonesia and Malaysia with much lower wage costs. All of the RTAs signed by Singapore contain outward processing provisions.

By contrast, TAFTA uses CTC as the primary method. All lines require a change of classification, except for a few in which a technical test is substituted. This CTC is, for some products, chapter-to-chapter (specified at the two-digit level), or parts thereof. For other products, heading-to-heading (specified at the four-digit level) or subheading-to-subheading (the six-digit level) or parts thereof are used or item-to-item. In less than 20 per cent of the total lines, there is a regional value content test, with the required minimum percentages being 40 or 45 or 55 per cent. In most cases, this is a supplementary test that makes the rule more difficult to satisfy. The most important area of application of a supplementary regional value content test is in the clothing, footwear and textiles and base metals product groups. In a few cases the regional value content test is an alternative to a CTC test. This makes the test less stringent. There is a *de minimis* rule that allows a specified maximum (10 per cent) percentage of non-originating materials to be used without losing origin. This also makes the test less stringent.

AUSFTA is the most recent of the RTAs that Australia has concluded. It is another agreement which is a NAFTA derivative. Most of the product-specific rules of origin require a CTC from the non-originating material to the traded good. This CTC is chapter-to-chapter or heading-to-heading or subheading-to-subheading or item-to-item. For a minority of goods, a specific rule of origin requires the good to meet an additional regional value content. Either the build-up or the build-down method may be used in most cases, but some are restricted to the build-down method. Where there is a choice of method, the percentage required for the build-up method is lower than that for the build-down method; for example, 35/45 per cent. The percentage for build-up and build-down varies across tariff lines. For a few goods, a regional value content test or a technical test is substituted for a CTC test. There are special rules for clothing and textile products (including a yarn forward rule), and for automotive products.

There is a *de minimis* rule that allows a specified maximum (10 per cent) percentage of non-originating materials to be used without losing origin, though this is not available for some products. Where applicable, this makes the test less stringent.

Thus Australia currently has four different ROO systems. Two use a percentage test as the primary test and the last two use a CTC test as the primary test. There are differences between the two systems that are based on a percentage test and between the two that are based on a CTC test. Comparing TAFTA and AUSFTA, the tests specified in many lines are the same, but some are different. All four agreements use some kind of percentage test as a primary or secondary test but the method of calculating the percentage, and the required percentage are different in all four cases. Across all four systems, there are differences in other general features. These differences among the four systems make it more difficult and costly for the customs officials to administer the systems and increase the costs of compliance for private traders.

Since the negotiation of SAFTA, the Australian government has been searching for an improved ROO system. In December 2004, the trade and economic ministers of the two CER countries announced a decision to replace the present percentage test by a CTC test. On 3 February 2006, the ministers announced that final agreement had been reached to adopt a CTC approach for the CER rules and the changes came into effect on 1 January 2007. Currently Australia is negotiating four trade agreements – bilateral agreements with the United Arab Emirates, Malaysia and China, and an agreement covering ASEAN and Australia and New Zealand. As a part of its consultation with the community, the Department of Foreign Affairs and Trade recently issued a Background Paper seeking views on the form of ROOs to be used in these agreements (DFAT 2006).

THE PROBLEM OF CHOICE OF ROOs

In this situation of non-uniform sets of rules, the obvious question is – which is the best set of rules? Unfortunately, it is generally agreed that no one system is best. For example, WTO (2002, para. 12) concludes 'In sum, there is no fully satisfactory methodology for origin determination, applicable to all products and serving all purposes.'[2]

Advantages and Disadvantages of a ROO System

Each test is commonly seen as having advantages and disadvantages (see, for example, LaNasa 1995; WTO 2002, para. 9–12; Lloyd 2003 and

Imagawa and Vermulst 2005). We list the advantages and disadvantages of the percentage and CTC tests.

When it is used as the primary test, the percentage test is not usually supplemented by another test. That is, it is the only test. Most ROO systems using the percentage test as the primary test use only one percentage rate. This has the advantage that the test is consistent across tariff items in that it sets out a single minimum percentage of domestic value added that applies uniformly to all imports. (This percentage varies among RTAs using a percentage test as the primary test from 30 to 70 per cent, the mode being 50 per cent; see Estevadeordal and Suominen 2003, Table 3). As a sole test with a sole percentage rate, it cannot be manipulated to give a higher hurdle for some products than for others. It is also the only one of the three main methods that easily allows cumulation across trading partners. This advantage is cited by Augier et al. (2005) as the reason for preferring this test.

Offsetting these advantages, a percentage test is more complex than the other two tests and, therefore, has higher compliance costs. It has greater uncertainty for traders, partly because of the complexity and partly because, for a given production process, the domestic content or the import content varies with the exchange rate applied to imported non-originating materials and parts. It provides a disincentive for greater efficiency in value adding in the domestic economy because greater efficiency lowers the domestic content and may, therefore, result in the loss of origin.

A CTC test has the advantages of being much simpler and easier to determine, provided there is no supplementary test. It tends, therefore, to have lower compliance costs and greater certainty for traders.

Offsetting these advantages, it has disadvantages. First,

> . . . the HS [Harmonized System of tariff classification] was not designed to serve the purpose of conferring origin; its basic aim is commodity classification and statistics. A simple change in tariff heading may therefore not be an adequate measure for fulfilment of the substantial transformation requirement: conversely, certain substantial transformations may not entail a change in tariff heading. (WTO 2002, para. 9).

As a result, the extent of transformation or value added will vary from tariff item to tariff item, even if the rules uniformly use the same digit levels to determine a change in tariff heading. In its review of the CER rules, the Productivity Commission (2004a, p. xxiii) found that, 'Unlike the CER ROO, the CTC method does not treat industries or products uniformly. This is because the extent of transformation involved in a change in tariff classification varies greatly between headings. As a result, it provides inconsistent origin determinations across industry sectors and can produce distortions in trade.' Second, it has the disadvantage, from an economic point of view, that it is easily manipulated to give more protection to local producers. By its nature, CTC is a product-specific rule. In an RTA that uses CTC as the primary test, every line requiring its own CTC specification or some alternative test. While a specified change of tariff classification by itself leaves no room for administrative discretion, the trade restrictiveness of the rule may be increased by using a lower level of digit to determine a CTC for a particular product and/or combining a CTC with a tight supplementary percentage or technical test. In this way it may protect either the domestic producer of a final product or producers of intermediate inputs used as originating inputs.

We can seek to quantify the effects of different ROO systems. For example, a number of studies overseas have been done of the compliance costs of ROOs. Compliance costs are important because they absorb real resources and because, as noted below, they restrict trade by reducing the incentive to apply for preferential access. These studies indicate that compliance costs range from 1.5 per cent to 6 per cent of the value of the products traded (see Productivity Commission 2004a, Chapter 6). The preference margin provides an upper bound estimate of the compliance cost as a percentage of the value of an import, as Goldfarb (2003, pp. 8–9) noted. For an import that is eligible for a preference, an importer always has the option of avoiding the compliance cost by paying the MFN rate.

The main focus has been on measuring the extent to which ROOs restrict the trade of the member countries. Unfortunately, it has not been possible to test directly the effects of ROOs on trade between the member countries at the digit level of the tariff classification or the calculations of the percentages at which the rules actually operate The ROO systems are too complex to do this.

A number of studies have adopted an index approach (see particularly, Estevadeordal and Suominen 2003 and Productivity Commission 2004a).[3] This consists of choosing the basic features of ROO systems, giving a qualitative assessment of each feature and then combining them in an index of the trade restrictiveness of different ROO systems. The most refined of these indices is that compiled by the Productivity Commission (2004a, Table A.2 and Figure 4.1). The Productivity Commission compiled the index score for 18 ROOS, including CER and SAFTA as well as NAFTA, PANEURO and other important systems.

The results show a considerable variation in the level of trade restrictiveness across RTAs. NAFTA has the highest index and SAFTA the lowest. Another feature is that the lowest seven scores are all achieved by systems which use a percentage test as the primary test; SAFTA, US–Jordan,

Singapore–NZ, AFTA and US–Israel, the Andean Community and CER in ascending order.

Another form of testing trade-restrictiveness is the study of preference utilization. As noted above, an importer will choose the MFN rate rather than the preferential rate if the compliance costs are greater than the preference margin. This indicates too that utilization rates should be calculated only for tariff items with non-zero tariff rates as the rules of origin are irrelevant to items with zero tariffs. For these items with non-zero tariff rates, non-utilization will be higher the lower the MFN rate and the preference margins are.

A number of studies have been done of utilization rates in different RTAs and also in non-reciprocal preference schemes; for example, Goldfarb (2003) and Anson et al. (2003) studied NAFTA; Augier et al. (2005) studied a range of Mediterranean countries and three Central and Eastern European countries which have agreements with the EU; Manchin (2005) studied the African, Caribbean and Pacific (ACP) countries' trade with the European Union (EU). Typically, these studies have found that preference utilization rates are generally low. For example, Goldfarb (2003, Table 1) finds that they are 55 per cent for Canadian exports to the US. As an extreme case, McKinsey (2003, p. 39), in a survey of intra-ASEAN imports in 2000, found that less than 5 per cent of intra-ASEAN trade entered under common effective preferential tariff rates. We need also to know if there is any correlation or statistical relationship between 'sector' utilization rates and the margin of preference for the sectors. (The margins equal the nominal MFN rates of protection if the preferential rates are zero.) In an impressive study, Manchin (2005) shows that, for trade between ACP countries and the EU, the utilization rate is positively and significantly related to the margin of preference, as predicted. Her study covered both tariff and preferential quota arrangements. We are currently trying to estimate the utilization rate for imports into Australia under the four agreements Australia has signed but this work is not completed.

Manchin also shows that there exists a minimum or 'threshold' value of tariff preference needed for traders to request preferences. This rate is 4 percentage points. If the preference margin is less than 4 percentage points, there is no incentive for traders to seek the preferential rate as the costs of obtaining the preferences are expected to be higher than the value of the preferences. This shows that compliance costs have an important trade-deterrent effect, as well as absorbing resources. For example, in the study of Mexican exports to the US, Anson et al. (2003) found that average preference margins available to Mexican exporters were 4 per cent while the compliance costs were 5 per cent: 'As a result compliance costs have largely eroded the preferential access afforded by the PTA.'

One may note that the decrease in average levels of tariffs in Australia and most countries around the world in the last decade as a result of the Uruguay Round and of unilateral changes in some countries has meant that compliance costs have risen relative to the margin of preference in RTAs generally. Consequently, ROOs are becoming more trade restrictive for this reason alone.

These empirical studies produce strong evidence of the trade-restriction effect of ROO systems and, as a consequence, of the importance of ROOs for determining the real improvements in market access coming from the formation of RTAs. To get a more precise appreciation of how we can devise better ROO systems, we need to consider principles of design of these systems. We should ask, what are the purposes or objectives of the ROO system? We should devise a ROO system for an RTA in order to advance these purpose(s) or objective(s). Unfortunately, this does not lead far. Rarely is a purpose declared; for example, none of the four ROO systems examined in Table 9.1 declare a purpose or objective.[4] However, accompanying documents make it clear that ROOs are intended to prevent trade deflection, that is, the deliberate routing of traded goods through a member country in order to qualify for a lower preferential tariff or better preferential access. Hence, they are an anti-circumvention device and nothing more.

Accepting ROOs as an anti-circumvention measure, we can take as our objective that a ROO system within an RTA should be operated so that, while preventing trade deflection, it should maximize the benefits to the member countries of the formation of the RTA. The economics literature on the benefits of a discriminatory regional liberalization of trade in goods is ambiguous in one respect. There is a category of trade within discriminatory trade agreements called 'trade diversion'. This is the diversion of imports into one member country that previously were sourced from a country outside the agreement to another member country within the agreement as a result of the preferences now given to this country. However, such diversion is not necessarily harmful to the country whose import trade is diverted because production and consumption effects may offset the higher cost of the imports. This ambiguity is an example of the economics of the 'second best'. A second best world is one in which some distortions remain after reform. The removal of one distortion does not necessarily improve welfare of the parties to the free trade area agreement because it creates new distortions.

There is a presumption that regional trade is beneficial to the member countries. (For a recent discussion of this theme, see Lloyd and MacLaren

2004). This does not deny that there may still be some products where trade is diverted *and* this diversion is harmful to the importing country. Trade diversion is, however, a smaller risk today as a result of the Australian government steadily lowering tariff rates in the last two decades. The average tariff rate on all imports in 2003–4 was 3.5 per cent and, of more relevance to ROO analysis, that on dutiable goods only (that is, excluding imports where there are no duties paid) was 9.5 per cent.[5] In the case of China, there is little risk of trade diversion as China is the least-cost supplier of a very wide range of goods. Moreover, in agreeing to a preference during the negotiations of an agreement, the member countries' governments have declared that they wish to promote trade in these items. Hence, one can interpret the objective of ROOs as one of maximizing trade between the members, subject to the prevention of trade deflection. The best ROO system is, therefore, that which is least trade restrictive, provided it prevents trade deflection.

Recently a literature has arisen which looks at ROOs as an instrument of protectionist policy rather than as a technical problem of determining origin. Pressure from protectionist groups has, in some RTAs, led to particularly trade-restrictive rules for some product groups (see Productivity Commission 2004a, Box 8.3 for examples). Estevadeordal and Suominen (2003) find that generally around the world the product-specific ROOs are most restrictive for agricultural goods and for the CTF group. As an example, the case of NAFTA rules is often cited. The more restrictive CTC and selective percentage tests in NAFTA apply to tariff items protected by higher MFN rates in the US (see Estevadeordal and Suominen 2003; and Productivity Commission 2004b, Chapter 4.1).[6] Very stringent supplementary percentage or technical tests are used for some products. Textiles and automobiles, among the most heavily protected of product groups, have especially highly trade-restrictive product-specific rules. These trade-restrictive rules maintain some of the protection for these groups. This is a form of hidden protection. This pattern is not surprising as the gains to domestic producers from this form of protection are the greater the greater the margin of protection.

ROOs may divert FDI flows as well as trade flows. FDI may be diverted to a country which is a member of an RTA in order to take advantage of preferential market access for exports from the FDI host and member country to another member; for example, foreign investors have chosen to relocate some of their international production to Mexico in order to gain preferential access to the lucrative US market. Jensen-Moran (1995) provides examples from the rules in force in the EU and NAFTA, mainly from high-tech industries. In the case of FDI, diversion is generally beneficial to the member countries as they gain additional FDI.

Looking at a ROO System as a Design Problem

To pursue this objective of maximizing the welfare gains from a free trade area agreement, we need to consider aspects of the design of a ROO system. How can we design a ROO system that has minimal trade-restriction effects and other desirable properties such as low compliance costs? Unfortunately, there is little literature to guide us here. The main concern should be with the trade restrictiveness of a potential ROO system. The trade-restriction effect is the most important effect of a ROO system. Substantial trade restriction denies the purpose of offering preferential access and the benefits of this access.

One design possibility is the establishment of common external tariffs. For example, there is a substantial movement in Canada in support of a common NAFTA external tariff and common measures for other trade barriers against third-party countries as a way of avoiding the costs of NAFTA ROOs (see Goldfarb 2003 and references therein). But this is a big step that the members of a free trade area have already chosen to avoid in negotiating a free trade area agreement rather than a customs union and they are, therefore, unlikely to revise this decision.

There are a number of features of the design of a ROO system which may mitigate the trade-restriction effects. Stephenson (1997) suggested that an RTA be required to opt for a single test only, except where necessary for technical reasons. This would rule out the use of supplementary tests in CTC-based systems that account for much of the trade restrictiveness of these systems.

Another design possibility is that of a waiver when the tariff rates on a tariff item are the same or close between the members of a free trade agreement. This is, in effect, a partial customs union type solution. A waiver has been proposed for NAFTA by Hufbauer and Vega-Canovas (2003) and independently for CER by the Productivity Commission (2004a, Chapter 8.5). Hufbauer and Vega-Canovas proposed a waiver when the difference was no greater than 1 per cent whereas the Productivity Commission proposed a maximum difference of 5 per cent. The proposal is made on the presumption that the costs of transhipment would make it most unlikely that goods would be deflected when the MFN tariff difference is small. This proposal can be applied to any ROO system: NAFTA is a system with CTC as the primary test and CER is a system with a percentage as the sole test. The difference tolerated should be somewhere between 0 and 5 per cent.

This proposal would, at a stroke, simplify any ROO system. The extent of the saving of compliance costs and the liberalization of trade will depend on the number of items with identical or near-identical positive tariff rates.

(There is no saving if the rate is zero). In the case of CER, the Productivity Commission (2004a, Chapter 6) estimated that 44 per cent of tariff items have a rate which is strictly positive in at least one country and the rates differ by 5 percentage points or less. This percentage is particularly high in the CER case because both countries have low tariffs and admit many goods free of duty.

Another design question relates to drawback of customs tariffs. In a free trade area goods exported from one member country to another will often contain non-originating materials and parts that have been imported from a third country and on which duty would ordinarily be payable. The question arises whether drawback of such duties should be allowed for trade within a free trade area. Some ROO systems allow drawback on intra-area trade and some do not (for example, PANEURO). Allowing drawback makes the ROO system less trade restricting. However, it is sometimes argued that drawback is not efficient in these circumstances because it gives a producer exporting to another member country and using drawback on inputs an advantage over two groups of producers of the same product: the competing producers in the same exporting country who sell on the home market rather than export the product, and the producers in the importing country who similarly sell on their home market, neither of whom can use drawback. This argument is true as far as it goes but it is incomplete. Disallowing drawback for intra-area trade would correct this anomaly but it would create new anomalies. For example, the exporter who exports to the member country would then be at a disadvantage vis-à-vis the exporter who exported to a third country where drawback is allowed. It is a strange outcome for a free trade area to treat exports within the area less advantageously than exports to destinations outside the area! (Some of these arguments are presented in Productivity Commission 2004a, pp. 95–8 and Driessen and Graafsma 1999).

The essence of the problem is that we are again in a second best world. Hence, one cannot state that in general the removal of drawback is necessarily better or worse for the countries. However, there is a presumption in favour of drawback. It moves prices in these economies into line with those faced by their competitors in the world as a whole. Area suppliers are, therefore, able to compete equally within the area and in third-country markets.

Another general feature is that dealing with cumulation. Cumulation adds areas where location qualifies for origin. 'Non-originating' now means not originating in the cumulation area. Cumulation is a feature of a ROO system which, in designated circumstances, allows exports to qualify as originating when they otherwise would not under the rules. It is, therefore, another feature which reduces the trade restrictiveness of an

RTA. We note that cumulation provisions can apply both to goods that are wholly produced in the free trade area and those that are partly manufactured in the area. They can apply both to ROO systems that use CTC as the primary test and those that use a percentage test as the primary test, though the modification of the test is more straightforward in the case of ROO systems that use a percentage test as the primary test (see WTO 2002, paras 14–16, 31–4 and Annex 1).

Bilateral cumulation treats inputs originating in an FTA partner country as domestic content for the exporting member country. This is not controversial. ROOs today routinely allow bilateral accumulation.

This raises the question as to how far cumulation provisions can be extended, that is, the definition of the cumulation area. *Diagonal cumulation* extends the area in which production may originate to a country or countries outside the RTA. Many countries now are members of more than one RTA. There is little debate in extending the area when the two (or more) countries that are members of one RTA both (or all) have free trade area agreements with a third country (or countries). In this case, the logic of free trade suggests that any product that is traded within the RTA and originates in the area which is the union of these sets of countries should be counted as originating in the exporting member country. The most important example by far of diagonal cumulation is the PANEURO agreement among the countries of the EU and other states with which the EU has separate agreements. (Some of the countries in the original 1997 agreement are now full members of EU-25). A similar case could arise in a free trade area with the People's Republic of China (PRC) as it might argue that the relevant territory for the purposes of defining origin is 'All China' (the PRC plus Hong Kong). The case for more extended cumulation is less clear cut when only one (or a subset) of the countries has a link to an outside country. *Full cumulation* occurs when a group of countries are all linked to each other by a network of agreements and the cumulation area is the whole area covered by the countries in two (or more) separate RTAs (a full cumulation system may differ from diagonal cumulation in other respects too). The problem of defining the extent of the cumulation area will become much more important and much more complex as the links between free trade areas are constantly expanding with the formation of new areas.

Beyond these general features, we have to look at the design of the primary test and other features of a particular ROO system. Consider first, an RTA which has a percentage test as the primary test. To start with, it should have a single percentage in order to avoid arbitrary differences in the percentage required across tariff items. Although economic theory does not indicate any percentage rate that results in a 'substantial' transformation, this rate should be less than 50 per cent and as low as possible. Then the most important feature is the choice of imported or domestic content. It is generally agreed that determination of origin is much simpler if an import content approach is used.

> In general, the import content seems preferable over the domestic content test because it is easier to apply and leaves the importing country administrators with less discretion. This is because it is simply based on the process paid by the producer, which can be easily checked through invoices, thereby obviating the need for complete cost of production calculations and allocations. (Imagawa and Vermulst 2005, p. 607)

Any ROO system with a percentage test will still, however, have an incentive at the margin, for some goods, to substitute domestic materials and parts for non-originating materials and parts. And it is not possible to eliminate the uncertainties associated with changes in exchange rates and foreign prices. These features are inherent in a ROO system based on a percentage test, though they may be mitigated by a lower percentage rate and a tolerance provision.

Consider now, an RTA which has a CTC test as the primary test. It should avoid a supplementary or replacement test, except where it is necessary to use one because of the nature of the transformation in the tariff item. Apart from this, it should avoid a selection of a low level of tariff classification change in order to protect domestic manufacturers. Unfortunately, it is not possible to insist on a single level, say the four-digit heading level, because the HS system was not devised for this purpose and the choice of any single level would leave anomalies.

Thus, product specificity and the danger of manipulation in a CTC-based system in order to restrict trade will remain. Any ROO system based on CTC will involve arbitrary choices and a variable transformation rule. It must also remain open to manipulation to restrict trade, especially when the MFN and, consequently the preferences margins, are high. These features are inherent in a system based on a CTC test.

CONCLUSION

ROO systems vary greatly among RTAs in their principal features. As a consequence, they vary greatly in their trade restrictiveness and in their effects on compliance costs, trade uncertainty and trade patterns.

The most important of these effects is trade restrictiveness. All ROO systems are trade restrictive to some extent. They have to be in order to prevent trade deflection. However, most ROO systems are much more trade restrictive then they need to be. Any ROO system with a single percentage test will have a uniform transformation rule. The lower the percentage rate the less trade restrictive the system and the lower the compliance costs. The system will still, however, have an incentive at the margin, for some goods, to substitute domestic materials and parts for non-originating materials and parts. And it is not possible to eliminate the uncertainties associated with changes in exchange rates and foreign prices. These features are inherent in a ROO system based on a percentage test. Product specificity and the danger of manipulation are inherent in a system based on a CTC test.

It is possible to design ROO systems with minimal trade restrictiveness. This holds both for those with a CTC as the primary test and those with a percentage test as the primary test. In this sense, the choice of CTC or a percentage test as the primary test is not the most crucial choice.

What is most crucial is that the details of the ROO system for an RTA be chosen in order to minimize trade restrictiveness and, as far as possible, other untoward effects on the costs of compliance, uncertainty and the pattern of trade. These details include the details of the primary test. They also include general features. The selection of features such as tolerance and *de minimis* provisions, cumulation and a waiver along the lines recommended by the Productivity Commission and Hufbauer and Vega-Canovas can greatly reduce trade restrictiveness and compliance costs.

NOTES

1. The architects of the agreement chose to follow the criteria that had been used in the previous New Zealand–Australia Free Trade Agreement. The two main features of these rules – the 'last process of manufacture' rule and the percentage of factory cost – can in turn be traced back to earlier preferential trade agreements with Great Britain and Canada (see Steele and Moulis, 1994).
2. Lloyd (1993) provides a solution. The basic problem arises because origin in these rules is treated as an all-or-nothing property, as if a good originates in one country, whereas the production is actually spread over two or more countries. His solution is a tariff that can be levied differentially on the value added by each country in the production chain, depending on whether it is in or out of the area qualifying for preferential treatment. In the context of free trade areas, this solution would require all member countries to adopt this form of tariff. See also Augier et al. (2005).
3. Another approach is to use a gravity model, for example, Estevadeordal and Suominen (2003) and Augier et al. (2005). However, this too must proceed at a level of aggregation well above that at which the actual rules apply. Tests based on gravity models can give only an indication of the trade-restriction effect.
4. For TAFTA, the Australian Customs *Service Manual* (current, Division 4) states 'ROO are necessary to provide objective criteria for determining whether or not imported goods are eligible for the preferential rates of duty available under TAFTA'. In almost the same language, the guide to determining the origin of goods for AUSFTA states 'We need rules to provide objective criteria for determining whether or not goods are eligible for the

benefit of preferential rates of duty that are provided under the Free Trade Agreement'. These statements describe what ROOs do, not what objective they serve.

5. From the Australian Bureau of Statistics time series of customs duty collected supplied to the authors. This average combines duties paid at both MFN and preferential rates.
6. According to Palmeter (1993, p. 329), 'no ascertainable rule or principle was employed in determining what level of change would be required for any particular product.'

REFERENCES

Anson, J., O. Cadot, J. de Melo, A. Estevadeordal, A. Suwa-Eisenmann and B. Tumurchudur (2003), 'Rules of origin in North–South preferential trading arrangements with an application to NAFTA', Centre for Economic Policy Research discussion paper no. 4166, London.

Arndt, S.W. and H. Kierzkowski (eds) (2001), *Fragmentation: New Production Patterns in the World Economy*, Oxford: Oxford University Press.

Augier, P., M. Gasiorek and C.L. Tong (2005), 'The impact of rules of origin on trade flows', *Economic Policy*, **20**(43), 567–624.

Australian Customs Service (current), *Manual – origin*, available at www.customs. gov.au.

Cheng, L.K. and H. Kierzkowski (eds) (2001), *Global Production and Trade in East Asia*, Oxford: Oxford University Press.

DFAT (Department of Foreign Affairs and Trade) (2006), Rules of origin and Australia's free trade agreement negotiations: a background paper on issues for consideration, DFAT, available at www.dfat.gov.au.

Driessen, B. and F. Graafsma (1999), 'The EC's wonderland: an overview of the Pan-European origin protocols', *Journal of World Trade*, **33**, 19–45.

Estevadeordal, A. and K. Suominen (2003), 'Rules of origin: a world map', Washington, DC: Inter-American Development Bank, (preliminary draft).

Feenstra, R.C. (1998), 'Integration of trade and disintegration of production in the global economy', *Journal of Economic Perspectives*, **12**, 31–50.

Goldfarb, D. (2003), 'The road to a Canada–U.S. customs union: step-by-step or in a single bound?', C. D. Howe Institute Border papers, commentary no. 184, Toronto, June.

Hufbauer, G. and G. Vega-Canovas (2003), 'Whither NAFTA: a common frontier?', in P. Andreas and T.J. Biersteker (eds), *The Rebordering of North America: Integration and Exclusion in a New Security Context*, New York: Routledge, pp. 128–52.

Imagawa, H. and E. Vermulst (2005), 'The agreement on rules of origin', in P.F.J. Macrory, A.E. Appleton and M.G. Plummer (eds), *The World Trade Organization: Legal, Economic and Political Analysis*, vol. I, pp. 601–78.

Jensen-Moran, J. (1995), 'Trade barriers as investment wars: the coming rules of origin debate', *Washington Quarterly*, **19**, 239–53.

LaNasa, J.A. (1995), 'An evaluation of the uses and importance of rules of origin, and the effectiveness of the Uruguay Round's agreement on rules of origin in harmonizing and regulating them', Jean Monnet Center, New York School of Law working paper 1/96.

Lloyd, P.J. (1993), 'A tariff substitute for rules of origin in free trade areas', *World Economy*, **16**, 699–712.

Lloyd, P.J. (2003), 'Rules of origin and fragmentation of trade', in L.K. Cheng and H. Kierzkowski (eds), *Global Production and Trade in East Asia*, Oxford: Oxford University Press, pp. 273–87.

Lloyd, P.J. and D. MacLaren (2004), 'Gains and losses from regional trade agreements: a survey', *Economic Record*, **80**, 445–67.

Manchin, M. (2005), 'Preference utilization and tariff reduction in European Union imports from African, Caribbean and Pacific countries', World Bank working paper series no. 3688, Washington, DC.

McKinsey and Company (2003), *ASEAN Competitiveness Study*, Jakarta: ASEAN Secretariat. (A summary of this report is provided by A. Schwarz and R. Villinger, 'Integrating Southeast Asian economies', *The McKinsey Quarterly*, **1**, 1–8).

Palmeter, D. (1993), 'Rules of origin in customs unions and free trade areas', in K. Anderson and R. Blackhurst (eds), *Regional Integration and the Global Trading System*, New York: Harvester Wheatsheaf, pp. 326–43.

Productivity Commission (2004a), 'Rules of origin under the Australia–New Zealand Closer Economic Relations Agreement', Productivity Commission research report, Melbourne.

Productivity Commission (2004b), 'Rules of origin under the Australia–New Zealand Closer Economic Relations Agreement: restrictiveness index for preferential rules of origin', supplement to Productivity Commission research report, Melbourne.

Steele, K. and D. Moulis (1994), 'Country of origin: the Australian experience', in E. Vermulst, P. Waer and J. Bourgeois (eds), *Rules of Origin in International Trade: a Comparative Study*, Ann Arbor: University of Michigan Press, pp. 195–256.

Stephenson, S. (1997), 'The economic impact of rules of origin in the Asia-Pacific Region', *Asia-Pacific Economic Review*, **3**, August, 14–27.

WTO (2002), 'Rules of origin regimes in regional trading agreements', Geneva: WTO Committee on Regional Trade Agreements WT/REG/W/45.

10. Settlement of disputes under free trade agreements

Jeff Waincymer

INTRODUCTION

This chapter examines the essential nature and role of dispute settlement (DS) obligations and processes within inter-governmental agreements. This is a subset of a broader question as to the role and utility of law in the international arena, an area often questioned due to the lack of any effective enforcement mechanisms akin to those within domestic political systems. The chapter does not address this issue.

Assuming instead that DS processes are considered to be a necessary element of an agreement, there are a number of other contentious sub-questions. What form should the processes take, diplomatic or adjudicatory and what persons should be utilized as neutral facilitators? Where formal adjudication is concerned, attention needs to be given to possible processes.

Negotiators also need to develop a clear understanding as to the central tasks of interpretation and fact finding lest they become unduly surprised at the outcomes in individual cases. This links in with an understanding of the legal uncertainties with the core concepts that are likely to be included in any free trade agreement (FTA), particularly non-discrimination and minimum standards protective devices. This chapter touches on the way these concepts have been interpreted through DS processes in other international fora with the dual view of providing insight into articulating such concepts within a proposed FTA and insight into the optimal DS processes that should be employed. The nature and role of any DS processes within the proposed FTA will be affected to a significant degree by the nature of the commitments that might ultimately be made. From a DS perspective, particular attention is given to special challenges in the fields of anti-dumping and intellectual property. This chapter will also consider the unique field of investor/state DS, which is incorporated into some FTAs. The most significant of these is the determination of whether to give private individuals and corporations direct rights to challenge foreign governmental behaviour.

Finally, the impact of various legal instruments upon one another must be examined. Significant problems can arise through the interaction of legal norms. This can flow from contract rights, national laws and international agreements to general principles of public international law dealing with host country obligations, whether emanating from treaty or custom. There may also be other recognized principles of law such as sovereign immunity, where limits are imposed on the ability of individuals to challenge governmental behaviour within domestic court structures. There is a need to consider how DS rights and obligations under a particular FTA relate to or are affected by rights and obligations under other FTAs or multilateral agreements, in particular the World Trade Organization (WTO) agreements. In order to devise an optimal model there is also a need for some comparative analysis of the different mechanisms.

NATURE OF INTERNATIONAL ECONOMIC LAW

Legal rules and institutions are part of the essential infrastructure required to enhance mutually beneficial trade and investment activities. These would be significantly reduced without the legal elements that we take for granted at the domestic level. Trade and investment build on principles of contract, property and corporate law among others, supported by a court system and some alternative dispute resolution mechanisms.

In domestic commerce, both the substantive and procedural building blocks are established as part of the normal fabric of society. While they may be tailored over time to meet the needs of international commerce, their operation is much broader. Furthermore, some of the DS processes are automatic. Domestic courts have automatic jurisdiction over disputes, except where parties have validly agreed to alternative DS procedures. In both cases there are strong enforcement mechanisms.

At the international level, these building blocks do not arise in this way as there is no comprehensive legal order. Traditionally, individual governments have sought to automatically apply their domestic regimes to international commerce. This is problematic as, under local systems and principles, there are likely to be conflicts between approaches. Each government may deny the territorial reach of the other and take a different view as to the way the issue should be resolved. Furthermore, gaps may appear if no domestic system accepts jurisdiction over a particular dispute. Finally, rules developed for domestic systems will not necessarily be desirable for international relations and transactions.

The last 50 years have seen a significant development in the number of international institutions and instruments in an attempt to provide the needed legal infrastructure.[1] These have looked to the development of desirable substantive norms, such as trade liberalization and investment protection, but need to be equally concerned with process norms, including dispute prevention and settlement.

THE NATURE AND ROLE OF DS UNDER FTAs, WTO AND INTERNATIONAL LAW

Legalist Versus Pragmatist Perspectives and Problems in Negotiating DS Norms

The gateway issue is what, if any, DS mechanisms should be added to an FTA. A discussion of DS and prevention raises conceptual questions about the nature of international treaties and the rights and obligations of parties to those treaties. At this level, one debate is often between those who advocate a legalist approach and those who prefer international organizations to behave in a more pragmatic manner.[2] Differing views have been taken by different countries about this issue. An analysis of present DS systems in other FTAs as well as the WTO indicates that the trend is towards an increasingly legalist perspective under a model that seeks to be part of and consistent with general principles of public international law. Consequently, it has been common to give greater attention to these issues when there are new inter-governmental initiatives in the fields of trade and investment.[3]

Nevertheless, in negotiation, it may be difficult to obtain true consensus on optimal DS models between states of different cultures, as there may be no natural points of compromise. As an example, China's traditional cultural attitudes are in favour of avoidance of conflict and the promotion of social harmony. In the past this has led to the promotion of dispute resolution by means other than third-party rights-based adjudication, particularly through the use of mediation (Zhiping 1989). Contrastingly, there is the Organisation of the Islamic Conference, that has proposed the creation of the International Islamic Court of Justice (IICJ), which while not yet established, would have a secular character and would consider a religious local code as the law to be applied for the resolution of international disputes (Lombardini 2001). It may be that those negotiating a cross-cultural FTA may have greater difficulty reaching consensus.[4]

The second concern is that negotiators are often non-lawyers and may have had little experience with DS. DS is often segmented out as a separate topic, handled by expert governmental lawyers on a discrete basis. Further, most negotiators are generally more concerned with compromises on substantive issues in the form of reciprocal concessions which are a natural part of trade and investment negotiations. Even if attainable, compromises on legal procedures cannot be presumed to have any efficiency value.

Thirdly, agreement difficulties may be increased if private groups lobbying governments are the primary parties in interest, and their various interests may not be compatible, although each may identify with and operate through the same government (Riesman and Weidman 1995). As a result of competing interests, 'designing a [dispute resolution mechanism (DRM)] for a binational or multinational trade agreement will have some clients with interests in an effective DRM and others with interests in a soft and relatively unenforceable agreement' (Riesman and Weidman 1995, p. 5).

Finally, those negotiating any agreement that is intended to be mutually beneficial often view the examination of the particular types of disputes that may arise to be unduly negative. Consequently, DS provisions tend to be general in nature, leaving much to be resolved on an ad hoc basis as disputes inevitably arise. While often this is unavoidable, the costs may be significant, particularly if this systemic problem is misunderstood and non-lawyers are unduly critical of the gap-filling that occurs in this way.

These problems may be overcome with greater integration of legal analysis into the negotiating process and greater understanding of the positive value of efficient DS norms. Examining prospective disputes should not be seen as negative and these concerns are a sign that the level of that interaction is significant. Intrinsic to success are the preparation of participants for mutually beneficial exchanges, which should involve sufficient preparation on DS, including details of the processes and preparing for emotional comfort with any ensuing disputes.

Attention must be given to the value of DS, optimal drafting of the norms and the procedures for formal and informal resolution of disputes. These are not mutually exclusive. When drafting, it is important to understand that substantive and procedural law are not separate social mechanisms. Those negotiating should consider how best to express the chosen policy norms so that they provide clarity and support consistent and reasonable interpretations and applications.

Analysis of Current Trends in FTA DS Models

Existing FTAs display a wide variety of approaches to these issues. DS models in FTAs range from completely informal arrangements to tightly structured frameworks. At the extreme of informality are the agreements that contain no DS mechanism whatsoever.[5] Although it is possible to sustain a productive trading relationship without any mechanism (see McCall Smith 2000), such an agreement must rely on diplomatic channels to resolve a dispute, or established international mechanisms such as the International Court of Justice. Since the agreement does not require a party to engage with a complaining party, there is no guarantee that a dispute would be resolved at all.

Most FTAs include at least basic DS options. Signatories may be required to engage in consultation with aggrieved parties when asked to do so. Despite it being simply compulsory diplomacy, FTAs generally emphasize amicable resolution through consultation as a primary and preferred settlement option (see, for example, SAFTA, Art. 2.1). Nonetheless, some FTAs provide for progression to conciliation and mediation, or 'good offices' if consultation is fruitless after a given period.[6] Conciliation may be facilitated by an organ of the agreement[7] or left to the parties to conduct. Other FTAs make conciliation available at any time and allow it to continue even during a later arbitration (for example the TAFTA, Art. 1803, and SAFTA, Art. 3.2).

DS remains a political and diplomatic process using these methods. If they do not yield a resolution, the agreement may provide for adjudicatory intervention by a third-party panel or tribunal. These may be organs of the agreement or independent arbitration tribunals. Such mechanisms fall closer to the centre of the spectrum of formality as diplomacy becomes less decisive in their outcome.

At the most formal end of the spectrum are FTAs that provide for final decision by standing adjudicatory bodies. These are more typical of regional FTAs such as the European Union (EU) or the Common Market for Eastern and Southern Africa. However, major regional agreements exist without any standing adjudicatory body, such as the North America Free Trade Agreement (NAFTA). The 2001 revision of the CARICOM Treaty[8] provides an illustration of a comprehensive approach to dispute resolution. It provides members with the usual array of options (consultation, conciliation and mediation, and arbitration) as well as a standing Caribbean Court of Justice.

Where a party fails to implement a decision of a panel that is binding, agreements vary on the action that other members may take. FTAs may stipulate that the retaliation must be 'equivalent'(for example TAFTA, Art. 1811, and SAFTA, Art. 20.11) to the disadvantage suffered by the complaining party, sometimes subjecting the assessment of what is 'equivalent' to panel review (for example, SAFTA, Art. 10.2). Others are broader, allowing the suspension of the party's trading privileges without any practical limit (US–Israel FTA, Art. 19.2). Generally a complaining party may obtain compensation for a failure to comply with a binding decision, but the compensation is frequently explicitly described as a temporary measure (for example, EU–China FTA, Art. 188.9). Some FTAs, however, contemplate compensation as a long-term solution, including guidelines for its collection and use (for example, US–Bahrain FTA, Art. 19.2; US–Morocco FTA, Art. 20.12).

Choices of forum clauses can differ between FTAs, sometimes allowing a choice between settlement under the FTA, or under another agreement to which both countries are party, or submission to the WTO. Importantly, the clauses generally state that although a complaining party may choose the forum, once chosen, the forum must be used to the exclusion of all others.[9]

FTAs almost exclusively call for closed hearings. However, hearings open to the public are typical of recent FTAs negotiated by the United States.[10] Additionally, some FTAs allow some access to proceedings by non-governmental organizations (NGOs) and persons (AUSFTA; US–Singapore FTA, Art. 20.4.2 (b); US–Jordan FTA, Art. 15.3 (b); CARICOM, Art. 222). It has been argued that public dispute settlement, and NGO participation, is the better approach if the public is to remain informed and democratic ideals perpetuated, although that remains a contentious issue (Mercurio and Laforgia 2005).

A survey of existing agreements and trends suggests that these issues may not be being given sufficient attention. While some countries are clearly promoting a consistent vision, others have such a broad variety that it is hard to conclude that they have a resolved and considered view as to which of these models to use as the basis for negotiations. The following section explores the broad stages that DS involves.

The Stages of DS

The first aspiration of any system is dispute prevention rather than settlement (Waincymer 2002, p. 64). This is best achieved through the realization of true consensus on the norms and their articulation with sufficient clarity. An important issue often overlooked by lawyers and non-lawyers is that formal adjudication is only one element of any legal system's DS mechanisms; it is simply the most visible and generally operates with winners and losers (Weiler 2001).

Therefore, where disputes inevitably arise, the preferable approach is to seek to resolve the dispute through consultation. This is the norm within the WTO and virtually all FTAs. Indeed most disputes are resolved amicably in this way. This can occur at the outset or at any stage of a formal process.[11] One important question is whether to include some express guidance on a possible mediation and conciliation process in the event that the dispute cannot be resolved bilaterally.[12] Thought could be given to whether a more elaborate model such as the UNCITRAL Conciliation rules could be a basis for an agreed format.[13] Thought could also be given to establishing a mediation panel of respected persons.

It is only if these stages are unsuccessful, that formal adjudication becomes important. Even then, it is desirable that such processes promote and allow for mutually agreeable settlements during formal processes. The desirability or otherwise of allowing an adjudicator to assist directly in achieving a settlement in an FTA would be an issue of consideration. As an example, Chinese arbitration strongly supports the role of mediator/ arbitrator, yet western traditions tend to raise concerns about the potential conflicts of interest, or claims of bias, where an adjudicator must make a formal ruling after receiving confidential information under an unsuccessful mediation process. It ought to be possible for negotiators to identify compromise procedures that minimize these concerns.

The final stage is enforcement. Where international law is concerned, the lack of natural enforcement mechanisms is obvious. Here there is a need to promote optimal surveillance and implementation norms within the constraints imposed by the international system. The balance of this section looks first at the issues within the adjudication stage and then looks at the implementation question.

Adjudicatory Bodies and Personnel

Many aspects of any DS model will significantly affect the implications of the initiative. One reason is that different models have different personnel, procedures and cultures depending on the norms and purposes of the organization involved. For example, in a normal WTO case, panellists are government officials, often non-lawyers who act voluntarily to settle the disputes between fellow WTO members (DSU, Art. 8). This provides significant scope for influence by legal secretariat officers. The same would not be the case with ad hoc arbitral tribunals under an FTA. There could also be a significant difference between ad hoc panels under international arbitral models on the one hand and a permanent panel on the other.

Procedure

A number of general principles of law relate to the procedural conduct of litigation rather than to substantive norms. Where the WTO is concerned, the bulk of these procedures are already incorporated expressly or implicitly into the DSU and other provisions. These include equality of parties before the arbitration tribunal, natural justice, equity, due process and abuse of rights, the requirement that no one must be a judge in their own case,[14] and the principle that a State is responsible for the acts of its agents. While FTAs rarely adopt such models, customary principles of international law that apply in any event would lead to similar outcomes on core issues.

A key question is whether an FTA should leave procedure to be determined on an ad hoc basis or should instead provide a model. The latter approach is more time consuming at the outset but can prevent wasteful and aggravating disputes at later stages. An FTA could refer to or modify the DSU or look to one of the arbitral models such as under the Permanent Court of Arbitration, UNCITRAL or International Centre for Settlement of Investment Disputes (ICSID).[15]

Standing

Generally, formal DS under public international law only allows for standing by governments.[16] Exceptions are commonly provided in the field of investor protection, which is discussed separately below. Nevertheless, where trade treaties are concerned, adjudicatory bodies such as the WTO and FTA panels are generally entitled to seek evidence from a broad range of persons and organizations.[17] Debate has arisen as to the extent to which they should do so and how they should deal with unsolicited submissions from private parties and NGOs. One approach is to treat them as *amicus curiae* briefs, that is, as submissions of friends of the court providing assistance to the adjudicator (Waincymer 2002, p. 328).

In *US – Shrimp* the Appellate Body decided to accept briefs from NGOs on the basis that it could accept information at any stage regardless of whether the information flowed from a request by it. The Appellate Body considered that it was authorized to accept the submissions but was not bound to do so.[18] This decision proved to be particularly contentious with a majority of developing country members. Some FTAs expressly allow for such submissions (see, for example, NAFTA, Chapter 11; AUSFTA, Chapter 21).

Appeals

To allow any form of appeal right in DS is significant and while it is not suggested as a model for an FTA, its mere existence within the WTO (DSU, Art. 17) signifies a shift in organizational legal culture (Weiler 2001) as traditional arbitral and international models provide for very limited rights of appeal.[19] While appeals are generally antithetical to the notion of arbitration, where the disputes deal with complex governmental regulatory powers, the lack of any kind of review or constraint mechanism is at least of significance. Either approach has benefits and costs. A one-stage process is faster and economical but might allow more erroneous results. Contrastingly, an appeal process raises integration issues.

Drafting, Adjudication and Interpretation

It is important for non-lawyers, particularly treaty negotiators, to understand the nature and challenges in legal adjudication. There is need for care in drafting norms and also caution against the expectation of high levels of precision as norms cannot always be drafted with such clarity that they will always ensure particular adjudicatory outcomes.

First, language is not mathematics. While the core substantive outcomes in an FTA negotiation are often able to be represented mathematically, non-tariff measures are invariably described using general language. Furthermore, there can be a range of ordinary meanings for many words and some may have technical or specialist meanings. Meaning can also be affected by context or by the purpose behind the words selected. Each negotiating party, in good faith, may attach different meanings to a particular agreed provision. A situation may arise which was simply not thought about when drafting the specifics of the agreement. There may have been contextual gaps and ambiguities in the drafting (Waincymer 2002, p. 387).

At times general language and concepts are used because that is the only proper way to articulate a norm. Examples might include most-favoured nation (MFN) treatment and other non-discrimination norms and investment protection requirements such as the proscription against expropriation without just compensation. At other times, general language hides a failure to agree on more concrete rights and obligations. In either circumstance, it is often left to adjudication to give greater clarity to the norms selected.[20] Such development of norms through clarification of general terminology will arise even in the absence of any doctrine of precedent as applies in common law legal systems.

When one looks at non-discrimination norms, it is also necessary to consider whether the norm will be applied formalistically or whether it will look to some economic standard. The WTO jurisprudence looks to measures which alter the conditions of competition.[21] This raises questions as to the ability of adjudicators, who are usually not economists, to make such judgements.

Drafting and adjudicatory problems are more difficult than ever because of the need to integrate trade and investment norms with other policy areas.[22] This has been central to the core constitutive documents of the EU and has also been a politically contentious aspect of NAFTA, given the high profile of some investor state disputes. The crucial point is that where trade and investment promoting agreements inevitably come into conflict with other regulatory norms, such as those within the fields of environment, health, labour relations, natural resource consumption, consumer protection and technology transfer, there will always be difficult drafting, interpretation and adjudicatory decisions to be made.

Seemingly innocuous differences to non-lawyers in drafting and interpretation can have fundamentally different effects on the ambit of the agreement. For example, if an FTA with differing DS provisions for trade and investment disputes has the investment protection provisions drawn broadly and, like NAFTA, indicates that it covers measures 'relating to' (NAFTA, Art. 1101: Scope and coverage) investment, many breaches of trade law obligations may be converted into investment claims and come within the ambit of the investment dispute processes.

Interpretation Methods in Public International Law

While there is no simple method that guarantees reliable outcomes, clear, consistent and predictable interpretative methods, are imperative. This is also a factor in all legal systems. FTAs, like the WTO Agreement, are international treaties subject to methods of interpretation under international law. Article 3.2 of the DSU refers to a requirement that panels utilize the customary rules of interpretation of public international law.[23] The Appellate Body has considered that this includes the principles contained in the Vienna Convention on the Law of International Treaties.[24] FTAs would also be interpreted utilizing these principles.

Article 31 of the Vienna Convention calls for a treaty to be interpreted 'in good faith in accordance with the ordinary meaning to be given to the terms of the treaty in their context and in the light of its object and purpose'. Subsequent agreements and practices can also be taken into account (Vienna Convention, Arts. 31.2 and 31.3). Article 32 allows for consideration of the background materials, (the *travaux préparatoire*), where ambiguity remains. When taken together, these provisions ensure that significant discretion is vested in adjudicators. This reduces the certainty and transparency of adjudicatory methodology (Waincymer 2002, pp. 387–8). This is not a criticism of such methods. It is another example of the inevitable tensions between flexibility and certainty and between intended and plain meaning in legal adjudication.

These legal techniques have to be considered within the political and cultural environment. For example, WTO Members are also very concerned that Panel decisions do not make new law, and as a result, the interpretative approach tends to be positivist and conservative in nature, relying on plain meaning, dictionary definitions and, ironically, decisions in earlier cases, as it looks much less activist to follow an earlier line of reasoning than adopt a new one. NAFTA arbitral panels have been different in approach, although not consistently so.

Hierarchy of Norms and the Role of Exceptions

One significant interpretative challenge is to consider whether there is a hierarchy of norms in the event that they conflict. The same question arises with application of express exceptions to the substantive obligations. Should they be interpreted narrowly, equally or as dominant? In the WTO context, the environmental and health exceptions in Article XX of GATT 1994 and in other instruments such as the Sanitary and Phytosanitary (SPS) Agreement, tend to be construed narrowly so as not to unduly interfere with the trade liberalizing norms. To assert that this is the tendency of WTO DS is itself a controversial proposition, yet any such biases, if evident, will have a significant impact upon state rights to regulate in the face of FTA obligations. If the negotiators are silent on this question, adjudicators will inevitably make determinations on this issue to resolve the conflict between otherwise binding norms. It is difficult to establish a mechanism for this purpose that does not at least appear to be biased towards either trade and investment or governmental social restrictions. Where that choice is made by adjudicators, it becomes particularly contentious, especially when the decisions are in the high-profile political fields of environment and health regulation.

Substance Versus Form Interpretation

Another contentious aspect of interpretation is the question of substance versus form. This relates to the analysis of evidence as well as interpretation of rules (Waincymer 2002, p. 389). The broader the coverage of the FTA, the more likely that domestic regulations will be considered as offending the spirit of the rules. For example, if an FTA covers investment, an import ban can be argued as constituting a de facto performance requirement if it can be said to commercially force corporations that have established investments to buy local substitutes, even though this was not expressly required. The argument is that it is in substance a purchasing requirement if not in form. NAFTA Article 1106 performance requirements have led to challenges that outright bans or the imposition of standards constitute illegal performance requirements. Arbitrators can always differ on these issues. The *Myers* NAFTA[25] tribunal split on whether there was a breach of

Article 1106, the majority held in the negative because the measure did not expressly require one of the prohibited elements. The dissenting arbitrator considered that this was the practical effect of the export ban.

There is no easy solution. An unduly formalistic approach encourages the search for loopholes. A search for the spirit of the law that conflicts with the plain meaning leads to criticisms that the Tribunal has imposed its own value judgements. Interpretative rules cannot readily constrain adjudicators from favouring one approach over another or varying their approach from case to case.

Adjudication Versus Interpretation Powers

It is clear that legal interpretation can commonly shape the law, yet it is desirable that the norms be predominantly shaped by negotiators rather than adjudicators.[26] Participating states can in theory amend an agreement to override the adjudicatory determination if adjudicators produce decisions that are not welcomed. Another approach is to provide a mechanism for authoritative interpretations. Comparative models may be found in the WTO and NAFTA; the latter also allows the Free Trade Commission to make binding determinations as to interpretation issues.

The Evidentiary Aspect of Adjudication

There are important policy and practical questions as to the method of finding and evaluating facts within public international DS.

Current disputes deal with complex evidentiary issues. Border barriers raise issues that include application of rules of origin, accounting calculations and questions such as 'likeness' in goods and circumstances. Customs and licensing procedures raise questions of procedural regularity, transparency and fair treatment. Standards and quarantine issues raise questions as to the evidentiary basis of governmental regulation. Intellectual property rights protection raises questions as to the adequacy of administrative and enforcement mechanisms. Investment-related issues include general concerns with the concept of expropriation and related questions as to 'conditions of competition'. Exempting provisions raise questions as to the 'reasonableness' or otherwise of health and environment safeguards. Residual protective mechanisms raise issues such as 'causation' analysis in anti-dumping and countervailing disputes.

In many disputes, the need for some sophisticated evidentiary analysis is ahead of the development of equally sophisticated and agreed evidentiary processes and methods. There are understandable reasons for this. Most refined legal systems give each party the right to present its case fully. The adjudicator may be given some independent fact-finding power. The task of any adjudicatory body is then to identify relevant evidence, evaluate it and weigh it against conflicting evidence. Yet there are many conceptual choices bound up in these general principles.

> Legal systems help resolve these questions with rules or principles as to burden and standard of proof and as to the admissibility and weight of evidence. Such rules provide a methodology for the adjudicator to try and determine the truth in the face of conflicting claims by the parties. Yet the processes by which truth is sought to be determined in a legal system are not absolutes. In setting the rules on evidence and burden of proof, legal systems choose between conflicting values. These include the pursuit of the correct outcome, the need to reduce time and costs, the need to compare probative and prejudicial aspects of potential evidence and even libertarian issues as to the obligation to provide information of use to an adversary. As a result, any system will display certain compromises and biases. (Waincymer 2002, p. 530)

As there is no absolute methodology of determining truth and no consensus as to the way these trade-offs should be determined, the policy choices have not been exercised in the same manner by different legal families. It would be particularly difficult to reach a consensus on the way evidentiary matters ought to be considered by an international adjudicatory body. Even the GATT/WTO system, with its long years of operation, like other international organizations, has not developed a substantial body of rules dealing with methods of proof, fact finding and admissibility and weight of evidence. Nor would we expect trade negotiators to devote significant time to debating these notions (Waincymer 2002, p. 530).

Once again, if consensus is not sought or reached on such rules and principles via direct negotiation, a definitive position will inevitably be reached simply because an adjudicator must resolve some of these questions when approaching the task of fact finding in actual disputes. The way adjudicators choose to exercise any such discretion can have an immense impact upon the outcome of particular disputes.[27]

SURVEILLANCE, REVIEW OF IMPLEMENTATION AND REMEDIES

Any legal system must pay particular attention to issues of remedies and implementation to prevent legal rights from being illusory. Implementation and compliance issues are even more important with international legal systems as they do not have direct enforcement mechanisms. WTO experience suggests that some improvements could be sought in this area.

Retrospective Remedies

The general principle in public international law is that a party in breach of international obligations must make full reparation in relation to any damage.[28] That can be modified by treaty and, as a result, is not the normal situation in the WTO. The GATT/WTO system is generally limited to orders for specific performance and termination of the unlawful measures. The question is not fully settled and, at the very least, is qualified in relation to prohibited subsidy disputes. An FTA needs to consider what approach to take to this policy issue. Again, such questions are rarely considered in negotiations. In the WTO context, Panels and the Appellate Body have had to deal with a fundamental policy issue without the clearest of guidance provided by the negotiators. The most contentious political aspect of this question to date relates to anti-dumping and countervailing duty decisions. Two GATT 1947 Panel reports had recommended that anti-dumping or countervailing duties be repaid if they were imposed in violation of GATT obligations.[29] This is not a clearly accepted view.

The situation is different where prohibited subsidies are concerned. Article 4.7 of the Subsidies and Countervailing Measures Agreement indicates that if a measure is found to be a prohibited subsidy, the Panel shall recommend that it be withdrawn without delay. In *Australia – Automotive Leather*,[30] the Panel resolved that 'withdrawal of a subsidy' contemplates repayment of the subsidy amount. The Appellate Body was not asked to rule on this issue. The parties had agreed in advance not to appeal the Panel's findings. While the Panel's view is arguable, it seems extremely unlikely that the negotiators during the Uruguay Round would have intended to have a niche area of retroactive remedies as part of a generally prospective system.

Compensation and Suspension of Concessions

A significant problem facing the WTO which should be uppermost in the minds of FTA negotiators is the lack of consensus as to the exact obligation on a losing party.[31]

One of the most contentious issues is whether a Member found to be in violation has a clear obligation to remove the offending measure or whether it has discretion to allow for retaliation instead. There are different views among Members flowing from a compromise set of words in the DSU. The system is better served by a proposition that there is no such discretion, otherwise advanced and large economies may ignore Panel recommendations. Retaliation is inefficient, harmful to small and developing economies and is philosophically suspect as it involves the aggrieved State choosing to harm its own importers and end users of the products targeted for retaliation.

APPLICATION OF COMMITMENTS IN FEDERAL SYSTEMS AND DS ISSUES

As modern international economic law regimes deal with a range of other regulatory obligations, particular difficulties are felt by federal legal systems. In many cases, federal systems leave some of these fields within the regulatory purview of sub-national governments. Yet the intergovernmental commitments are made at the national level. Because international trade agreements invariably affect the rights and obligations of national and sub-national governments where international trade and investment is concerned, they effectively perform a quasi-constitutional function, at least in a practical sense.

Additionally, national governments are at times made responsible for the behaviour of sub-national governments.[32] While the WTO Agreement is an intergovernmental agreement that cannot directly bind sub-national governments, signatories promise to take all appropriate action to ensure that sub-national governments will comply.[33] The same is commonly the case with FTAs. While the central government may feel concerned if it loses a case on the basis of the behaviour of a regional government, this may over time assist the central administration in having its policies fully implemented at the regional level.

WTO AND FTAs

Integration Issues

An important issue with any FTA is how it will interact with other international treaties. This primarily involves the WTO, but also a consideration of how different FTAs interact, even when they do not have common membership. This applies to both substantive and DS procedure overlap.

The first question is whether the FTA is compliant with WTO provisions, in particular, Article XXIV of GATT 1947. This goes to the legal validity of the FTA as a whole.[34] In practice, however, the WTO has not sought to systematically test the validity of FTAs even though it is contemplated in its norms.

The next question is whether any provisions are inconsistent with WTO norms and, if so, what is the hierarchy of norms, and which adjudicatory body can determine that. Negotiators should be mindful that if FTAs cover similar ground to the WTO, any slight differences in language provide inspiration for legal arguments that the norms have been intentionally changed. The third question is how DS systems of each are to be properly integrated.

This goes to processes and also to jurisprudence, as the differing adjudicatory bodies may say different things about the meaning of key obligations. The major question involves MFN obligations. MFN requires governmental measures and practices to not discriminate between different foreign countries and their nationals and investors. National treatment requires foreign investors and investments to be treated no less favourably than locals. These are norms of non-discrimination. If each FTA promises reciprocal MFN treatment, it is open for either party to examine treatment offered under other FTAs entered into by the other party, and argue for equal treatment where the other treaty is seen as providing greater benefits. MFN builds upon very broad notions of 'like goods' and 'like circumstances'. It must inevitably consider cases where formally identical treatment is still argued to be discriminatory because of an adverse impact upon conditions of competition. Due to this, it can at least be predicted that the vast increase in use of FTAs will make such MFN claims of some significance in the foreseeable future.

Choice of Forum

It is possible for disputes to be brought concurrently before FTAs, the WTO and domestic courts unless there are express prohibitions. WTO Members have direct rights under its DSU that could not be pre-empted by any side agreement, at least where third-party Members of the WTO are concerned. If there was an agreement between two members of an FTA not to pursue a dispute at the WTO, that could be seen as an acceptable agreed settlement of a particular dispute. That could also be treated as an agreement to use DSU arbitration provisions as an alternative to the Panel process.

One important element found within FTAs involving the US is the use of choice-of-forum provisions (see, for example, NAFTA, Art. 2005(1) or AUSFTA, Art. 21.4). The party bringing the complaint is allowed to choose the forum if more than one breach is alleged to arise under more than one agreement. In the absence of such a clause, they may well have been entitled to choose in any event, as the two treaties independently set up those rights unless one is expressed to be subordinate. Expressing the choice also removes the uncertainty in that regard. Without such a provision, the defendant might argue that the treaty language requires resort to the other forum, either through its own words or through the provisions of the Vienna Convention[35] which has provisions for reconciling conflicts between treaties. Such a choice could be seen as a prior exercise of the right under the DSU to choose arbitration rather than a Panel procedure.

The converse view is that this kind of clause may unduly undermine the centrality of WTO DS and minimize the ability of weaker States to benefit from third-party involvement or Dispute Settlement Body (DSB) control in WTO cases. Providing for a choice of forum clause in an FTA favours the complaining country over the defendant.

Whatever the view on the policy merits, uncertainty as to forum is itself an undesirable feature, so some express rule should be considered. The contrary approach is to state expressly that WTO DS prevails.[36]

Exhaustion of Local Remedies

In some circumstances, treaties require exhaustion of local remedies before an international dispute can be pursued.[37] Common areas for such provisions include anti-dumping and countervailing disputes.[38] There do not appear to be strong arguments in favour of such provisions at a general level and it would depend on the parties, the nature of the domestic avenues, the likely number of disputes and the attitudes to DS at the inter-governmental level.

Even where no obligation to exhaust local remedies exists, this can affect other claims. For example, the NAFTA tribunal in *Loewen*[39] considered that there is no violation of the obligation to provide 'fair and equitable treatment' in terms of a claim of denial of natural justice where local remedies had not been fully pursued.

Jurisdiction of Adjudicators

Whichever forum is chosen, one issue that has arisen in the WTO is whether adjudicators of a WTO dispute are either allowed or required to consider other treaties besides WTO provisions. The argument against is that they only have jurisdiction under the WTO for the purposes of WTO DS. They have no general jurisdiction under international law, unlike the International Court of Justice. The contrary argument is that no branch of international law should operate in a vacuum. If there truly are a range of treaties applicable between the parties or which are relevant to their individual actions, an adjudicator must consider these.[40] At times it is not a question of jurisdiction but merely a question of evidence.

WTO adjudicators have proceeded cautiously towards a broader consideration of treaties although the possibility of dual fora taking different approaches is hard to fully remove, yet if this was considered important enough, it could be dealt with in the drafting.

Jurisprudence and Acquis

Related to this is the degree of influence of interpretative decisions of one forum on adjudicators in another. In a technical sense, no one is bound by such decisions but the possibility of influence and inconsistency are unavoidable (Waincymer 2002, p. 510). A difficulty would arise if the loser in an FTA dispute argued that the result was inconsistent with WTO or other obligations and should not be complied with. Again, methods should be imposed to ensure that whichever forum is chosen, problems are minimized.

SPECIFIC DISPUTES

While this chapter does not intend to focus on substantive issues, it is important to illustrate some of the concerns raised above through select examples from substantive areas. An analysis of jurisprudence in a range of fora shows the inevitable uncertainty when seeking to interpret and apply broad substantive concepts.

MFN and National Treatment

MFN and national treatment are relative standards expressed broadly. They require a range of interpretative and evidentiary questions to be considered. As non-discrimination is a relative concept, there is a need to consider who to compare to whom and what differences constitute proscribed behaviour. WTO jurisprudence has shown that there is a difficulty with the notion of 'like products' when considering whether there has been unreasonable discrimination in relation to trade in goods. The notion of 'like circumstances' between domestic and foreign service providers and investments is even more problematic. A particularly important issue is whether equal treatment is to be judged substantively or formally. SAFTA services provisions enshrine a WTO principle that discrimination can arise through measures applying to all parties, where they alter the conditions of competition in favour of locals. Such an approach makes the norm more far reaching and the disputes more uncertain and complex but more economically defensible.

Anti-dumping, Countervailing and Safeguards Disputes and Administrative Review Generally

Where DS mechanisms deal with anti-dumping and countervailing issues, they become elements of an administrative review system. Because WTO Agreements include numerous transparency and notification obligations, it is also possible that the matter in dispute is the extent to which a Member has notified certain developments as required. It is important to consider questions of the appropriate standards of review and the evidentiary basis upon which complaints should legitimately be brought.

Negotiators should consider special rules for such disputes, either as alternatives to domestic or intergovernmental disputes or as additional mechanisms. For example, Chapter 19 of NAFTA provides for national review panels as an alternative to challenges in domestic courts. There is also an appeal mechanism to an extraordinary challenge committee on certain specified and limited legal grounds. The Chapter 19 process has dominated the field and few parties resort to domestic courts.

The WTO provisions specify clear obligations on Members and their bureaucracies in terms of evidence gathering, evidence submission, ambit of relevant factors for consideration and levels of proof before some domestic trade restricting decision can be taken. WTO jurisprudence provides a further guide, indicating that when a Panel reviews factual determinations by domestic bureaucrats:

> an objective assessment would entail an examination of whether (i) the [national authority] had examined all the relevant facts before it (including facts which might detract from an affirmative determination . . .), (ii) whether adequate explanation had been provided of how the facts as a whole supported the determination made, and, consequently, (iii) whether the determination made was consistent with the international obligations of the [Member concerned].[41]

Intellectual Property

There can be significant debates about the optimal extent of intellectual property protection, the range of property that ought to be covered, philosophical issues as to technology transfer in favour of developing countries and even the justification for including such domestic standards in international treaties. These issues are connected with some challenging DS issues such as uniformity of interpretation, the ways in which intellectual property rights are employed in civil law as well as common law countries, the sophistication of the administrative structure and the enforcement mechanisms available in the event of breach of intellectual property rights.

Investment Protection and Investor State Disputes

If some form of investment protection is agreed, the issue to consider is how to draft these provisions, what DS processes should be employed and what the outcomes are likely to be. Since the OECD failed to promote successfully the adoption of a Multilateral Agreement on Investment, protective devices have been experimented with in bilateral investment treaties (BITs) and within broad FTAs.

From the adjudicatory perspective, it is important to understand that BITs and comprehensive FTAs generally give rights to foreign citizens over and above those normally provided to citizens of the host country. While this may look to be unequal treatment, it may be a sensible response to dealing with the differences between local and foreign investors. Local investors theoretically have an ability to challenge their governments politically when they disagree with measures taken, while foreign investors require greater levels of protection.

It is important to understand the way customary international law applies to issues of investor protection.[42] This is so as to determine whether the obligations provided for under FTAs are broader than is currently the case under customary international law. The classical approach of international law to investment and commercial issues looks for a compromise between two potentially conflicting principles: territorial sovereignty, which allows a state to exercise full and exclusive jurisdiction over its territory, and the principle of nationality, which confirms a state's right to protect the interests of its nationals abroad. Customary international law does not provide for many of the protections within investment treaties such as MFN, national treatment, repatriation rights or limitations on performance requirements.

An exception to the general rule of standing in FTAs has at times been made with investment protection norms (such as NAFTA, Art. 11, Part B). Given that a treaty-based DS system is an alternative to domestic litigation, its importance depends on how adequate the domestic processes are seen to be.

There are some general arguments in favour of providing for investor/state DS. First, real or imagined bias of host country judges would be a disincentive to wealth-enhancing investment or would add to its cost. The second benefit is to remove the need to have the host government agree to take an action under international law. Lastly, providing for equivalent protection to that provided in other international treaties puts prospective investments on the same footing. Generally, it is preferable that those contemplating investment make decisions based on commercial criteria and not on differences in legal infrastructure.[43]

On the other hand, the potential for private parties to seek very broad notions of rights and obligations, such as expropriation by indirect means, is concerning. Technically, this argument is not against investor/state DS mechanisms per se, but rather an argument for more carefully prescribed substantive norms, although the practical reality is that private corporations and their lawyers might push the limits of interpretation in ways which would not have been contemplated by the states themselves.

There is also the related question of whether a large number of costly and unmeritorious challenges are likely to be brought. While the likelihood of success is important, even unsuccessful claims can be politically damaging and costly. Uncertainty can easily deter governments from undertaking desired policy measures for fear of legal claims by foreign investors. Lastly, private party rights lead to retrospective damages for the offending behaviour in nearly all cases whereas inter-state actions tend merely to call for changes to the offending measure.

At times the real issue with a foreign investor will be a contract dispute rather than a challenge to some governmental regulatory behaviour. This will commonly be the case where the process of gaining a permit to invest has involved complex negotiations and documentary representations and agreements and where the final investment is via a contract with a governmental agency. Experience with ICSID and BIT dispute resolution has shown there to be complex issues in determining jurisdiction and applicable law.[44]

A key issue is the ambit of the expropriation provisions. Virtually all BITs ensure that expropriation must be for a public purpose, be non-discriminatory, follow principles of due process and be accompanied by appropriate compensation. The expropriation norm is problematic as a broad concept is asked to cover a range of reasonably distinct government measures. This range is from complete takings of property, removal of fundamental licences, discriminatory regulations that favour locals over foreign investors, lack of adequate protections for such things as intellectual property rights and outwardly non-discriminatory measures that nevertheless have a more serious impact on foreign investors. Each of these regulations can be further divided into those that seek consciously to affect foreign investors and alternatively, those that do so without the government having that intent.[45] An indirect expropriation norm will vary significantly depending on whether it is based on an intent test or an economic effect test. The jurisprudence has displayed inconsistent approaches to this question.

If there is to be such a norm in an FTA, consideration must be given to how it might be drafted and adjudicated upon so as to make appropriate distinctions between compensatable expropriations and fully acceptable regulatory behaviour. Relevant issues in distinguishing between expropriation and acceptable regulatory behaviour would include considerations of due process, discrimination, intent, good faith and reasonableness, both in terms of the regulatory aim and the proportionality of the interference with commercial interests.

CONCLUSIONS

DS is an inevitable aspect of complex interactions between economies. Adjudication, where required, has inevitable challenges that must be understood. A consensus-based international rule-making system with divergent interests and which builds on reciprocal commitments is never likely to present an adjudicator with optimal drafting of norms. Such a system must present well-reasoned and respectable conclusions even where there are competing tenable positions that can be reached about the proper interpretation of the rules or the application of them to contentious factual situations.

International negotiators cannot be expected to establish a comprehensive and elaborate procedural model along the lines of those found in the most advanced domestic systems. Yet in the absence of any such model, adjudicators must deal with exactly the same contentious questions without sufficient guidance from negotiators. In doing so, adjudicators will tend to follow broad principles of fairness and efficiency, particularly through concepts such as reasonableness and due process.

Participants should accept that the increasing role of law and legalist perspectives are appropriate if the system is to operate to promote compliance in the face of protectionist pressures. It is to be hoped that a proper understanding of the difficulties of such a legalist model should assist in keeping legitimate and ongoing evaluation and criticism within appropriate and reasonable bounds.

NOTES

1. Such as the United Nations (UN) and the International Court of Justice, the Permanent Court of Arbitration, the International Monetary Fund (IMF) and World Bank, the WTO, World Intellectual Property Organization (WIPO), United Nations Commission on International Trade Law (UNCITRAL), International Institute for the Unification of International Law (UNIDROIT), the Hague Conference and the unsuccessful Organization for Economic Cooperation and Development (OECD) initiative, in relation to a multilateral agreement on investment and the burgeoning web of regional trade and investment agreements.
2. 'It is very clear that the law and legal norms play the most important part of the institutions which are essential to make markets work' and that the 'rule-oriented' approach can lead to 'greater certainty and predictability which is essential in international affairs'. Jackson 2000, pp. 7–8, citing J. Jackson (1998), 'Global economics and international economic law', *Journal of International Economic Law*, **1**, 1–23.
3. The GATT/WTO experiences provide a rich body of data for this debate upon which to build their cases and provide a useful frame of reference for negotiators of an FTA.
4. It is suggested that the NAFTA undertook a more minimalist approach where as MERCOSUR and the EU, by contrast, adopted a more interventionist approach, and that this may reflect the prevalence of common law in the USA and Canada, while

MERCOSUR and the EU have a prevalence of civil law traditions in their member states. See Duina 2006, p. 63.
5. ANZCERTA is one example.
6. The US–Jordan FTA is one exception, proceeding directly to adjudication by a joint committee.
7. Such as the Conciliation Panel in the US–Israel FTA, or the Association Committee in the EU–Chile FTA.
8. Revised Treaty of Chaguaramas Establishing the Caribbean Community Including the CARICOM. Single Market and Economy (CARICOM) (entered into force 5 July 2001).
9. Art 17.2(b) of the US–Jordan FTA is unusual in that allows for different claims under the same dispute to be heard in different fora.
10. See the FTAs to which the United States became a party after October 2000.
11. At most, there is a need in the WTO to notify settlements in order to allow other members to consider whether their rights have been nullified or impaired, see the Understanding on Rules and Procedures Governing the Settlement of Disputes (DSU), Annex 2 of the WTO Agreement, Art. 3(5).
12. NAFTA provides model clauses for private mediation and arbitration for use in international contracts.
13. Adopted by UNCITRAL on 23 July 1980. The rules cover all aspects of the conciliation process, providing a model conciliation clause, defining when conciliation is deemed to have commenced and terminated and addressing procedural aspects relating to the appointment and role of conciliators and the general conduct of proceedings.
14. *Mosul Boundary Case*, at p. 32.
15. Refer to the Permanent Court of Arbitration, Model Arbitration Clause for use in connection with the permanent court of arbitration optional rules for arbitrating disputes between two states, the 1985 UNCITRAL Model Law on International Commercial Arbitration and the ICSID model clauses.
16. Individuals as a general rule lack standing to assert violations of international treaties in the absence of a protest by the state of nationality; see Shaw 1997, p. 183, citing *US v. Noriega*, 746 F. Supp. 1506, 1533 (1990); 99 ILR, p. 349 and *infra*, Chapter 14.
17. DSU Art 13(1). Each panel shall have the right to seek information and technical advice from any individual or body which it deems appropriate.
18. Appellate Body Report, *United States – Import Prohibition of Certain Shrimp and Shrimp Products* WT/DS58/AB/R, paras 79–91.
19. The WTO was the first international organization to develop a binding and comprehensive appeal process within its DS provision (Waincymer 2002, p. 693).
20. A related problem is that there is a significant challenge if treaty signatories try and use the DS system to articulate commitments that were not negotiated clearly in the FTA itself.
21. A similar principle has been included in the SAFTA services chapter, Art. 4.3.
22. 'More issues are now regarded as trade related in the narrow sense that the norms governing those issues affect trade' (Leebron 2002, p. 5).
23. There are two elements in identifying customary law for interpretation. First is the material fact of the common behaviour. The second is the subjective belief that the behaviour amounts to law (Waincymer 2002, p. 382).
24. Vienna Convention on the Law of International Treaties, done at Vienna, 23 May 1969, 1155 UNTS 331, 8 ILM 679. The Vienna Convention entered into force on 27 January 1980. See Appellate Body Report *United-States – Standards for Reformulate and Conventional Gasoline* (*US – Gasoline*) WT/DS2/AB/R.
25. *S.D. Myers, Inc. v. Government of Canada*, UNCITRAL [NAFTA].
26. In the international sphere, sovereign nation states are less inclined to allow judges in some international forum to behave this way because they do not concede such powers to those persons (see Waincymer 2002, p. 390).
27. 'Early cases that dealt with such questions of degree were not particularly well handled.

See, for example, GATT Panel Report, *European Communities – Refunds on Exports of Sugar* (*EC – Sugar*) and the analysis of the applicant's claim that the subsidy had led to more than an equitable share of world trade; BISD 27S/69 at 96; BISD 26S/290 at 319 (see Waincymer 2002, p. 530 and fn. 3).

28. See, for example, *Chorzow Factory Case*, p. 4.

29. See GATT Panel Report, *New Zealand – Imports of Electrical Transformers from Finland* L/5814, GATT Panel Report, *United States – Measures Affecting Imports of Softwood Lumber from Canada* SCM/162. Other cases that dealt with inconsistent taxes or duties, for example under Articles II or III have not made such recommendations.

30. *Australia – Subsidies Provided to Procedures and Exporters of Automotive Leather* WT/DS126/R.

31. For example, Art. 21.11 of the AUSFTA addresses compensation.

32. The DSU does not expressly provide for responsibility over sub-national behaviour. That responsibility is determined by particular substantive provisions.

33. For example see Article XXIV: 12 GATT 1994.

34. This chapter will not cover the details of WTO compliance, but indicates that to be consistent with Article XXIV of GATT 1994 regulations dealing with trade in goods must be sufficiently comprehensive for the FTA to be acceptable.

35. That would also be a key method in resolving disputes as to conflicting substantive provisions.

36. This is the EU preferred provision in its recent FTAs, still allowing the parties to select DSU arbitration in any event.

37. There is no such rule to this effect in any WTO provisions (see Waincymer 2002, p. 203).

38. The NAFTA has provision for investor/state DS claims to be brought without first exhausting local remedies. For evaluation of this debate see Dodge 2005.

39. *The Loewen Group Inc. v United States*.

40. The wider view is presented in Palmeter, Mavroidis and Schoenbaum 1998. Contrary views are suggested in Trachtman 1999.

41. Panel Report, *United States – Restrictions on Imports of Cotton and Man-Made Fibre Underwear* (*US – Underwear*), WT/DS24/R para 7.13.

42. Under Article 38(1)(b) of the ICJ Statute, customary international law can in part be described as 'a general and consistent practice of states that they follow from a sense of legal obligation . . .'.

43. For an analysis of the benefits and disadvantages of private rights in investor/state dispute settlement between developed countries see Dodge 2005.

44. ICSID cases are inconsistent in the way they see the relationship between BIT claims and contract claims. One approach is to see them as wholly distinct. The other is to interpret BITs broadly to cover all claims. The latter approach may look for justification from general principles of treaty interpretation (or may be criticized from that perspective), or from notions of implied consent, in particular presumptions that parties at the outset would not have wanted expensive and potentially conflicting bifurcated DS processes. At times umbrella clauses are utilized in BITs. These expressly state that states are required to comply with contract obligations. The intent is thus to incorporate those obligations as treaty obligations giving rise to treaty DS processes.

45. In the US–Singapore FTA and the US–Chile Free Trade Agreement, both of which were concluded after NAFTA, there has been some modification to the wording used in the appropriation article. The aim was to limit the ability of the article to support actions which interfere with normal governmental regulatory activities.

REFERENCES

Books and Journal Articles

Dodge, W.S. (2005), 'Investor–state dispute settlement between developed countries: reflections on the Australia–United States Free Trade Agreement', Vanderbilt *Journal of Translational Law*, **39**(1), 1–37.

Duina, F. (2006), *The Social Construction of Free Trade, the European Union, NAFTA, and MERCOSUR*, Princeton: Princeton University Press.

Jackson, J. (2000), *The Jurisprudence of GATT and the WTO: Insights on Treaty Law and Economic Relations*, Cambridge: Cambridge University Press.

Leebron, D. (2002), 'Linkages symposium: the boundaries of the WTO', *American Journal of International Law*, **96**(1), 5–6.

Lombardini, M. (2001), 'The International Islamic Court of Justice: towards an international Islamic legal system?', *Leiden Journal of International Law*, **14**, 665.

McCall Smith, J. (2000), 'The politics of dispute settlement design: explaining legalism in regional trade pacts', *International Organization*, **54**(1), 137–69.

Mercurio, B. and R. Laforgia (2005), 'Expanding democracy: why Australia should negotiate for open and transparent dispute settlement in its free trade agreements', *Melbourne Journal of International Law*, **6**, 487–514.

Palmeter, D. and P. Mavroidis (1998), 'The WTO legal system: sources of law', *American Journal of International Law*, **92**(3), 398–413.

Riesman, M. and M. Weidman (1995), 'Contextual imperative of dispute resolution mechanisms', *Journal of World Trade*, **29**(3), 5–6.

Schoenbaum, T.J. (1998), 'WTO dispute settlement: praise and suggestions for reform', *International and Comparative Law Quarterly*, **47**, 647–53.

Shaw, M. (1997), *International Law*, 4th edn, Cambridge: Cambridge University Press.

Trachtman, J.P. (1999), 'The domain of WTO dispute resolution', *Harvard International Law Journal*, **40**, 333.

Waincymer, J. (2002), *WTO Litigation Procedural Aspects of Formal Dispute Settlement*, London: Cameron May Ltd.

Weiler, J.H.H. (2001), 'The rule of lawyers and the ethos of diplomats reflections on the internet on the internal and external legitimacy of WTO dispute settlement', *Journal of World Trade*, **35**(2), 191–207.

Zhiping, L. (1989), 'Explicating "law": a comparative perspective of Chinese and Western legal culture', *Journal of Chinese Law*, **3**, 55–91.

Cases

Permanent Court of International Justice
Chorzow Factory Case (*Germany v Poland*), PCIJ, Series A, No 17 (1928).
Mosul Boundary Case, PCIJ, Series B, No 12 (1925).

WTO
Australia – Subsidies Provided to Procedures and Exporters of Automotive Leather (*Australia – Leather*) WT/DS126/R.

United States – Standards for Reformulate and Conventional Gasoline (*US – Gasoline*) WT/DS2/AB/R.
United States – Import Prohibition of Certain Shrimp and Shrimp Products (*US – Shrimp*) WT/DS58/AB/R.
United States – Restrictions on Imports of Cotton and Man-Made Fibre Underwear (*US – Underwear*) WT/DS24/R.

GATT
European Communities – Refunds on Exports of Sugar (*EC – Sugar*) L/4833.
European Communities – Refunds on Exports of Sugar – Complaint by Brazil (*EC – Sugar(Brazil)*) L/5011.
New Zealand – Imports of Electrical Transformers from Finland (*NZ – Transformers*) L/5814.
Thailand – Restrictions on Importation of and Internal Taxes on Cigarettes (*Thailand – Cigarettes*) DS10/R.
United States – Measures Affecting Imports of Softwood Lumber from Canada (*US – Softwood Lumber*) SCM/162.

NAFTA
S.D. Myers, Inc. v. Government of Canada (UNCITRAL) 21 October 2002.
Pope & Talbot, Inc. v. Government of Canada (UNCITRAL) 31 May 2002.
The Loewen Group Inc. v United States, No. ARB(AF)/98/3.

Treaties

Agreement between the Government of the United States of America and the Government of the Kingdom of Bahrain on the Establishment of a Free Trade Area (US–Bahrain FTA) (entered into force 1 August 2006).
Agreement between the United States of America and the Hashemite Kingdom of Jordan on the Establishment of a Free Trade Area (US–Jordan FTA) (entered into force 17 December 2001).
Agreement on South Asian Free Trade Area (SAFTA) (entered into force 1 January 2006).
Agreement on the Establishment of a Free Trade Area between the Government of Israel and the Government of the United States of America (US–Israel FTA) (entered into force 19 August 1985).
Australia New Zealand Closer Economic Relations Trade Agreement (CER) (entered into force 1 January 1983).
Australia–United States Free Trade Agreement (AUSFTA) (entered into force 1 January 2005).
The Common Market for Eastern and Southern Africa Treaty (COMESA) (entered into force 8 December 1994).
Chile–United States Free Trade Agreement (Chile–US FTA) (entered into force 1 January 2004).
Convention establishing the European Free Trade Association (EFTA) (entered into force 4 January 1960).
EU–Chile Association Agreement (EU–Chile FTA) (entered into force 1 February 2003).

Revised Treaty of Chaguaramas Establishing the Caribbean Community Including the CARICOM Single Market and Economy (CARICOM) (entered into force 5 July 2001).

Singapore–Australia Free Trade Agreement (Singapore–Australia FTA) (entered into force 26 July 2003).

Thailand–Australia Free Trade Agreement (TAFTA) (entered into force 1 January 2005).

North American Free Trade Agreement (NAFTA) (entered into force 1 January 1994).

United States–Morocco Free Trade Agreement (US–Morocco FTA) (entered into force 1 January 2006).

United States–Singapore Free Trade Agreement (US–Singapore FTA) (entered into force 1 January 2004).

11. Safeguards, anti-dumping actions and countervailing duties

Martin Richardson

INTRODUCTION

In the interests of 'fair trade', the General Agreement on Tariffs and Trade/ World Trade Organization (GATT/WTO) multilateral trade agreement contains a number of provisions that swim directly against its general current and allow countries to protect their import interests.[1] These provisions fall under the general heading of Administered Protection, meaning that a member country simply has to put in place the relevant administrative structure to operate in accordance with WTO guidelines, and the imposition of protective duties or quantitative restrictions then becomes an administrative matter. This is in contrast to the more usual tariff protection that generally requires legislative intervention each time and requires a country to consider its international obligations in each case. Consequently, administered protection provides a much easier and less costly route to protection for a firm and these measures have very much become the 'new new protectionism'.[2] Furthermore, once enabling legislation is in place, the imposition of trade restrictions via administered protection is essentially a unilateral decision with (at least for anti-dumping and countervailing duties) no obligations for compensation. This sits very uneasily in the WTO/GATT multilateral framework of reciprocity.

The WTO/GATT provisions regarding so-called safeguards (SG), anti-dumping (AD) and countervailing duties (CVD), find no justification on purely economic grounds. The one rationale provided for AD – the prevention of predatory behaviour – in fact is not articulated in the GATT provisions at all, nor is it any longer contained in the enabling legislation of any countries of which I am aware. (It was a feature of the original US AD provisions, interestingly, but the inability of complainant firms to use the legislation led to its removal after a few years, at which point the legislation became much more popular.) AD has now become simply a means of protection from efficient rivals or of preventing domestic consumers from taking advantage of the largesse of foreign firms or governments. This is shown clearly in the numbers of AD complaints brought worldwide and also in the nature and practice of AD actions. The role of CVD is even less economically motivated, if possible: as Dixit has noted, the appropriate response to a foreign subsidy is usually a thank-you note, not a retaliatory measure.

It is clear, however, that the real purpose of both of these measures in the multilateral system is the same as that which is explicitly recognised in the case of actual Article XIX SG measures (which are temporary GATT-legal import restrictions) and that is to make reform tolerable to policy makers: they are sops to domestic interests that enable countries to implement welfare-improving agreements that might otherwise be rejected by sectoral interests.[3] In acknowledging this, the question then arises as to how they should be handled in a bilateral deal. Countries making such deals still have similar political pressures to those faced in the multilateral case (although, typically, these will be more focused) but one might assume that the very fact that two countries are sitting at a bilateral negotiating table means that there is some recognition of a mutual coincidence of interests and that might mitigate the needs for safeguards against the unpredictable actions of the other.

In this chapter I want to argue that free trade areas should seize the opportunity to remove these remedies (and I use the term reluctantly) entirely from their bilateral trade relationship. While I use the proposed Australia–China Free Trade Agreement (FTA) as a vehicle for these arguments, they apply to preferential trading areas generally. Indeed, given the impasse in multilateral negotiations, it may be that bilateral deals are the only medium through which administered protection can be addressed. A number of commentators have noted, on the occasion of the recent centenary of anti-dumping (2004), that AD, in particular, seems to have become an almost intransigent problem at the multilateral level (see, for example, Barfield 2005; Deardorff and Stern 2005; Prusa 2005 and Staiger 2005) and the nature of many proposed solutions is such that they may be more implementable at the bilateral level.

In the rest of the chapter I first consider the background to the Australia–China economic relationship in terms of these safeguard measures and then suggest some possible approaches to the negotiation of FTA terms concerning these measures.

THE PROBLEM WITH 'SAFEGUARDS'

It is clear that AD law has nothing to do with preventing predation, either *de jure* (as noted, countries' enabling legislation for AD never mentions the intent of the dumper) or *de facto* (the US steel industry, for example, can launch AD complaints against over 30 foreign rivals simultaneously: odd monopolists, these!). A compelling piece of evidence on this comes from Australia and New Zealand's experience in the Closer Economic Relations (CER) FTA: in a fit of enlightenment these countries abolished trans-Tasman AD from mid-1990, noting that predatory behaviour could continue to be dealt with by the relevant country's competition policies. Since that epiphany not a single case of trans-Tasman predation has successfully been prosecuted, to the best of my knowledge.

So proponents of administered protection generally justify it in terms of fairness: creating a 'level playing field'. But as *The Economist* once tartly observed, continuing the sporting metaphor, the only acceptable evidence of a level playing field seems to be that equal numbers of goals are scored at each end; sectoral trade imbalances, rather than confirming the value of trade, are instead evidence of its unfairness. The interests of consumers are totally ignored in this and it is interesting that they are almost totally ignored in the negotiations of FTAs as well, so that increased import volumes are always perceived as a cost, not a benefit, of an FTA, and differences in productivity are problems rather than the very basis for mutually beneficial trade. But, whatever the original intention of provisions such as AD,[4] it is simply not clear that they achieve anything like fairness: 'the antidumping law, as it currently stands, has nothing to do with maintaining a "level playing field." Instead, antidumping's primary function is to provide an elaborate excuse for old-fashioned protectionism' (Lindsey and Ikenson 2002, p. 1).

This is apparent both from the explosion of AD initiations and findings worldwide[5] – suggesting that trade has become unfair very suddenly – and from the practices surrounding implementation of AD codes. The litany of outrageous practices produced by various countries' AD authorities is long and well known (see Bovard 1991 for an extensive account of US practices) but again one piece of evidence on this is very suggestive. When the US and Canada first signed the Canada–United States Free Trade Agreement (CUSFTA) in 1988 they introduced a disputes settlements procedure under which an ad hoc binational panel could be convened on a case-by-case basis that could review decisions of a country's relevant administrative bodies, but only on the basis of the relevant country's own domestic administrative law. Such a panel had no power to revoke duties but could simply return decisions that it felt were incorrectly made – by the country's own standards, note – to be re-examined by the relevant administrative authorities. Nevertheless, of 14 cases brought by Canadian firms against US determinations before 1995, a reduction of duties followed in nine cases.[6] So, despite the deck being so heavily stacked against foreign respondents in administered protection anyway, domestic agencies still frequently abuse the law in reaching their decisions.

AUSTRALIA AND CHINA

Australia is currently 'celebrating' 100 years of anti-dumping, having introduced its first AD legislation in 1906 (the third country in the world to do so, after Canada and New Zealand). After a century of practice, it is clear that Australian industries have really got the hang of using AD – according to one study (Messerlin 2004) Australia is by far the biggest user of AD amongst developed countries (as measured by AD measures in force per value of imports, 1995–2001). On the other hand, China, by the same author's calculations, is the world's biggest target for AD actions (as measured by AD measures in force by value of exports, 1995–2001). Interestingly, however, China is largely a victim of AD levied by other developing countries and only 7 per cent of Australia's AD measures over the period 1995–2001 were imposed on China (which is substantially lower than the corresponding figure for the US – for whom about 15 per cent of AD measures were against China – and the EU (over 21 per cent)).

As a main target for AD actions, China would seem to have a very clear interest in reducing the operation of AD laws globally (and, indeed, its trade negotiators have stated just this) but there is a tension here with the global trend in AD use by developing countries, a trend from which China is not exempt. Figure 11.1 shows the number of AD measures initiated by China from 1997 to 2005 and the notable features are, first, the increase over time and, second, the big spurt in initiations since China's WTO accession in late 2001. Since that accession, China's AD activity has been quite sector specific and relatively concentrated against a few countries, as Figure 11.2 illustrates.

So, in the abstract, it seems that both China and Australia might have a fair bit to 'lose' if AD were to be sacrificed: historically Australia has been a very heavy user of AD provisions and, while China has been a common victim of such provisions, it is increasingly becoming a user itself. But in terms of AD actions between Australia and China, it is notable that China does not appear to have ever brought an AD case, while the WTO reports that Australia initiated 21 AD investigations of Chinese products from 1995 to 2005 inclusive.[7] Bown's dataset and ACS reports indicate some of the Chinese products investigated by Australia, as shown in Table 11.1.

Ignoring terminated and withdrawn cases and those in which no dumping (or injury) was found, we have only 16 cases in Table 11.1 of affirmative AD findings by Australian authorities against China from 1989

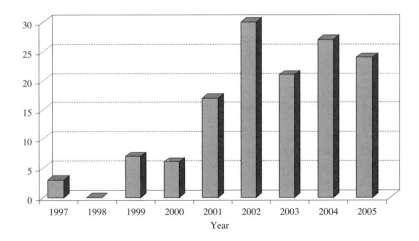

Source: Constructed from AD-CHN-v2.0.xls: AD dataset compiled by Chad Bown, accessed 7 June 2006, at people.brandeis.edu/~cbown/global_ad/.

Figure 11.1 AD initiations by China

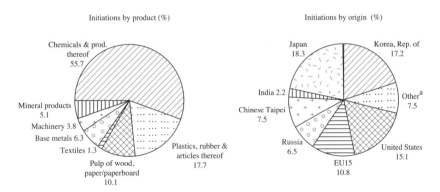

Source: WTO Trade Policy Review: China (WT/TPR/S/161 28 February 2006) p. 85.

Note: Including Iran, Kazakhstan, Malaysia, Mexico, Singapore, Thailand and the Ukraine with one case each.

Figure 11.2 China's anti-dumping cases, 2002–4

to 2004. Again, it does not seem that Australia would sacrifice much by forgoing AD actions against China.

This argument misses two potentially important points, however. First, AD is renowned for its harassment value[8] and it is not clear that it is

Table 11.1   Australian AD initiations against China, 1989–2006

Product under investigation	Date (d/m/y)	Dumping?	Injury?
Woven polyolefin bags	03/04/1989	N	N
Silicon	10/07/1989	N	N
Canned pears	27/02/1991	A	A
Canned peaches	27/02/1991	N	N
Dibutyl phthalate	08/05/1991	A	A
Certain glass fibre products	09/07/1991	A	A
Canned whole tomatoes	27/08/1991	A	A
Raw and blanched peanut kernels	25/09/1991	N	N
Clear float glass	31/01/1992	A	A
Polyvinyl chloride	05/02/1992	A	A
Certain cast iron manhole covers grates and frames	15/05/1992	N	N
Disposable plastic cutlery	29/09/1992	A	A
Further processed glass products	18/12/1992	N	N
Fibreglass insect screening	29/03/1993	N	N
Fibreglass gun rovings	11/10/1993	A	A
Disposable plastic cutlery	03/06/1994	A	A
Steel and steel/concrete access floor panels	16/12/1994	A	A
Glyphosate acid	27/03/1996	A	A
Laminated glass	09/08/1996	N	N
Certain toughened glass rectangular panels	22/11/1996	A	A
Gun rovings	13/02/1997	W	W
Certain picture frames	07/07/1997	W	W
Cotton blankets	04/02/1998	T	T
Ordinary portland cement	09/12/1999	MI	MI
Certain steel shelving kits	15/09/2000	A	A
Certain disc brake rotors	20/09/2000	T	T
Glyphosate	12/06/2001	MI	MI
Carpet Gripper	23/07/2001	N	N
Sodium Metabisulfite	12/09/2001	A	A
Steel Ladders	26/10/2001	MI	MI
Dichlorophenoxy-Acetic Acid	02/04/2002	A	A
Uncoated White Cut Ream Copy Paper	11/08/2003	T	T
Certain Hot Rolled Plate Steel	20/08/2003	A	A
Certain Silicon	19/05/2004	N	N
*Preserved mushrooms	2005	-	-
*Sodium Hydrogen Carbonate	2005	-	-

*Certain laminated Safety Glass	2006	-	-
*Pineapple fruit	2006	-	-

† A(ffirmative), N(egative), W(ithdrawn), T(erminated), MI(ssing data).
Source: Constructed from AD-AUS-v1.0.xls: AD dataset compiled by Chad Bown, http://people.brandeis.edu/~cbown/global_ad/ accessed 07/06/06. Asterisked items compiled from ACS Initiation Reports, http://www.customs.gov.au accessed 06/06/06.

appropriate to ignore withdrawn and terminated AD cases – these may well serve the purpose of their initiators nevertheless. The second point is that the mere existence of the AD architecture may intimidate foreign firms and deter them from pursuing dumping behaviour. If so, abolishing the AD system would trigger a lot more dumping behaviour. Now, one might respond that this is simply a further benefit of any such abolition but it is not clear that sectoral interests would share that optimistic perspective!

Notwithstanding these arguments however, recent experience does not suggest that AD has been of critical importance in Sino-Australian trade relations and it does seem that AD could successfully be put aside in an FTA with little real cost to either partner. The situation regarding CVDs and SGs is even clearer, in that there has apparently been no use of them at all between China and Australia.[9] One might retort that the lack of action on CVDs is a consequence of the lack of transparency in the operation of subsidies. Indeed, this is an explicit complaint of the US about Chinese commercial practices, with a recent Office of the US Trade Representative (USTR) review suggesting that China has failed, 'to fully implement its WTO subsidy obligations, particularly with respect to (i) prohibited subsidies and (ii) providing notification of its subsidies to the WTO' (USTR 2006, p. 15). To the extent that Chinese legal processes are opaque,[10] however, surely this militates even more strongly for sidestepping them entirely by removing these remedies from a bilateral deal: attempting to deal with them introduces a costly layer of procedure with no obvious payoff.

A MODEST PROPOSAL[11]

First, I would take issue with the common rationale for administered protection as a political sop to sectors that would otherwise oppose a deal that is in a country's overall interests. Even to the extent that this argument has some validity, vested in the realpolitik of trade negotiations in practice rather than in the textbook, one might still object that this is a very blunt instrument to deal with the problem. If we wish to 'buy off' specific sectors, simple targeting principles tell us that the most efficient instrument to do so will be one that addresses those specific sectors only. But the architecture of AD and CVDs presents a protectionist mechanism that is available to all industries and sectors and, as such, is not targeted at all. Now, one might retort that it will only be used by the 'squeaky wheel' sectors so, *de facto*, it delivers protection to sectors most likely to be harmed by trade liberalization, but that simply underlines the fact that a far better approach to buying off sensitive sectors is to do so explicitly; this also has the advantage of making the costs of such special treatment more transparent and therefore more subject to political contest.

I have already suggested that neither China nor Australia has a lot to lose by completely proscribing administered protection in the FTA negotiations, on the basis of historical usage of these tools. One concern that has been raised with respect to China's trade policy execution (post-WTO accession as well as prior to 2001), particularly by the US, is that procedures are frequently not transparent and appear to be biased in favour of domestic complainants. For example, the aforementioned USTR Top-to-Bottom Review of US–China trade relations also notes concerns with China's administration of its AD laws, which it suggests is not consistent with its WTO obligations. Of course, China is certainly not alone in this (and in Australia, for instance, there is no specific legislation covering the use of Article XIX Safeguard measures), but the key point here is that abolition of bilateral Australia–China AD, SG and CVD provisions completely sidesteps this issue and avoids all the administrative costs of attempting to grapple with it.

Nevertheless, certain industries are likely to object to the removal of their protection from more efficient foreign producers. Messerlin (2004) notes that, globally, there are a few 'antidumping-intensive sectors', notably metals, chemicals, machinery and electrical equipment, textiles and clothing and plastics, which jointly account for 75 per cent of AD measures while constituting less than 50 per cent of world trade (Messerlin 2004, p. 111). He suggests that the prevalence of AD actions in sub-sectors characterized by fairly standardized products but frequently oligopolistic structures hints at the use of AD actions by large firms as a means of segmenting international markets. To the extent there is some truth in this globally, it seems to be reflected in the context of Sino-Australian trade. Reference back to Table 11.1 confirms this: while there are a number of complaints from producers of processed foodstuffs, these have generally been unsuccessful[12] and the main successes have come in chemicals, plastics, glass and steel. This presents an alternative perspective on AD actions and an alternative interpretation of their welfare consequences; if their purpose is to facilitate the segmentation of markets internationally, then global welfare will typically be enhanced by their removal. Messerlin (2004, p. 111) writes,

> In sum, the observed sectoral pattern of antidumping reflects the increasing 'privatization' of trade policy by firms that have enough initial oligopolistic power to use the 'procollusion' bias ... embedded in antidumping regulations – a key lesson that should be kept in mind when implementing these regulations, in China as elsewhere.

Another issue that is pertinent to the Australia–China case lies in the details in China's WTO accession agreement. There are two significant features of special terms negotiated for that accession. First, if countries treat China as a non-market economy (NME) then they are entitled (for 15 years) to use proxies (usually prices in third countries) for Chinese home prices or costs in AD cases. As Messerlin (2004, p. 123) notes, this makes the existence of dumping easier to prove. Second, Section 16 of China's Accession Protocol (which applies for 12 years) contains a number of provisions that make the imposition of Article XIX Safeguards on China a lot easier than against other WTO members. For example, the emergency nature of Article XIX remedies is weakened, with no requirement that they be imposed only in 'unforeseen circumstances', there is no MFN requirement and the evidence on links between import surges and domestic injury (which need only be 'material' rather than 'serious') is weakened (Messerlin 2004, p. 127). Furthermore, there is an entirely novel 'trade deflection' clause that gives third-party WTO members the right to enforce their own Article XIX Safeguard measures on China if they fear that another member's measures will deflect Chinese exports to their own market – to do this requires no investigation or prior notification to be provided! (Messerlin 2004, p. 127).

Now, these terms cannot be a bargaining chip for Australia, given that recognizing China as a market economy was a pre-condition to negotiating an FTA and such recognition involves a permanent waiver of Sections 15 and 16 of China's Accession Protocol, the relevant sections that contain these terms. But it should be recognized that other countries that do not grant market economy status to China do have the option of invoking these terms and the longevity of these clauses – 15 and 12 years, respectively, for Sections 15 and 16 – means that they could be a significant factor in world trade for some time.[13] To the extent that there is anything to the trade deflection concerns behind Section 16.8 of the Accession Protocol, of course, this means that countries in FTAs with China will be even more subject to such deflection of trade. Now, to stiffen Article XIX-type Safeguards within the FTA in reaction to this prospect would be a retrograde and very mercantilist prospect; nevertheless, it does suggest that further study of the likelihood of such deflected trade flows would be sensible.

And what of any precedent for treating safeguards in this fashion in a bilateral deal – that is, removing them from the set of trade remedies available in an intra-FTA dispute? As noted above, Australia and New Zealand were sufficiently farsighted to remove trans-Tasman AD entirely within the CER FTA,[14] but that was a decision taken between two countries with harmonized legal practices and competition policies.[15] One might object that the systems of China and Australia are sufficiently different that such a far-reaching reform is infeasible. But, again, historical usage of AD in this relationship is sufficiently low that it would not appear to be much of a sacrifice to lose AD anyway, even if no alternative anti-predation remedies were made available. What is more, as the problem of predatory behaviour can be handled by courts internally within the country of destination of a product – that is, Australia can prosecute foreign firms acting anti-competitively within Australia under Section 46 of the Trade Practices Act[16] – the only real concern that might arise in negotiations in an FTA is that one's partner will use such domestic remedies inappropriately. To the extent that there is a lack of transparency in a partner's judicial processes, this is a real concern. Nevertheless, Australian judicial experience demonstrates that predatory behaviour is very unlikely domestically and it is clearly even less likely in a world market where it would require a global monopoly to be effective.

As far as Article XIX Safeguards are concerned, there is also already strong precedent in other FTAs that Australia has signed for them to be excluded on a bilateral basis, as in the CER and SAFTA, the Australia–Singapore FTA. This is a little ironic in the sense that if one had to allow one administered protection mechanism for countries to persuade them to sign trade deals, Article XIX Safeguards are more attractive than the alternatives such as AD. This is so for a number of reasons but particularly because no ad hoc attempts need to be made to measure price differences internationally and ascribe domestic injury to them. Nevertheless, it is this relatively less harmful instrument that has most easily been negotiated away! This example, incidentally, illustrates that precedent may be of limited use in guiding the negotiation of an FTA as each FTA is very much *sui generis*: Australia does not have SGs in its deals with Singapore or New Zealand, for example, but does have them in deals with the US and Thailand.

TWO EVEN MORE MODEST PROPOSALS[17]

If the complete abolition of administered protection in the FTA is considered too extreme a step, two alternative intermediate reforms are still attractive. First, one might couple the abolition of Article XIX Safeguards with the retention of AD and CVD measures, but augmented by a

CUSFTA-style arbitration procedure. To preserve notions of economic sovereignty, such a body would, as in the CUSFTA, be empowered to review administrative decisions only on the basis of the relevant country's own administrative law and procedures. This would have the added attraction of requiring both parties to be explicit about the nature of those procedures – as noted above, the opacity of Chinese procedures and questions of their GATT consistency have been an issue internationally and this would be resolved under this proposal, at least in the context of Australia–China economic relations.

Furthermore, if sector-specific options are essential to enable the negotiation of a comprehensive FTA, then it would behove negotiators to consider sector-specific safeguards (carefully modelled on the principles of Article XIX to ensure their temporary nature); these at least have the benefit of being targeted, in light of the earlier discussion.

An alternative – but quite different – halfway reform would be to recognize that Article XIX Safeguards are more consistent with the principles of the WTO/GATT system and to retain these while either abolishing AD and CVD measures entirely or reforming them in such a way that they effectively become SG actions.[18]

SOME FURTHER ISSUES

I finish with a brief mention of two related issues. The first concerns third parties; in particular, are there concerns that arise in writing an FTA from the fact that the partner countries may each have – now or in the future – separate deals with other countries? The concern here is one of 'bilateral opportunism': country A might offer some 'concession' to country C that induces an FTA but then, in subsequent negotiations with country B, undermines the value of the concession offered to C by offering a similar (or more extensive) concession to B.[19] Now, in itself this is not a problem – A is liberalizing its trade at each step – but the concern arises from the chilling effect that fears of such opportunism might have on C's interest in signing a deal in the first place.

From the Australian perspective, the dominant role of resources in the export mix to China suggests that this 'concession diversion' (Ethier 2004) should not be a particularly serious concern. More generally, however, while such opportunism has been interpreted (in the context of multilateral negotiations) as undermining incentives to cut tariffs in the first place, another possible interpretation is that it actually militates in favour of more extreme liberalisation than might otherwise be considered: the deeper the initial 'concession', the lower the incentive A has to offer further deals to C. Accordingly, an FTA that incorporates the removal of administered protection remedies, by constituting an 'extreme' liberalization, might mitigate the problems associated with bilateral opportunism.

The second issue I wish to mention is the interrelationship between international investment flows and trade policy measures, such as the safeguards instruments discussed here. There is some international evidence that AD actions have triggered AD-jumping international investment (see Belderbos et al. 2004 and Blonigen 2002). That is, to avoid the imposition of AD duties incurred when exporting to a foreign market, exporters have simply relocated to that market and produced internally. Again, the pattern of Australian exports to China suggests that this is unlikely from Australian firms and the relative insignificance of the Australian market to China suggests it is unlikely to occur in the other direction. Nevertheless, any such investment flows are clearly inefficient and again are best avoided by simply removing the barrier which they seek to overcome.[20]

CONCLUSION

To sum up, the arguments in favour of abolishing AD, CVD and SG actions in the Australia–China bilateral relationship are:

- The 'principled' argument based on underlying economic welfare that these administered protection devices are standard, welfare-reducing protection; consequently they do nothing for 'fairness' in that they invite procedural abuse.
- The 'practical' argument that, to the extent that their current use indicates their value, they are little used in the bilateral trading relationship so their loss is unlikely to be significant.
- That abolition sidesteps the direct costs of administration of these schemes as well as the mistrust that these procedures can introduce into a relationship (indeed, it has been argued that the central reason for Canada to sign up to the CUSFTA originally was nothing to do with the gains from trade; rather it was the insurance against future fickle US trade policy that the disputes settlement mechanism of the CUSFTA provided).
- That if the rationale for these schemes is political, they are nevertheless very blunt instruments, and explicit recognition of 'sensitive' sectors is a more efficient means of achieving the same political goal.
- That abolition removes the use of AD, in particular, as a 'facilitating device' to segment international markets.

I have also noted that there are examples of tightening administered protection clauses in FTAs – certainly on the Australian side, at least – and that objections to these arguments should carry little weight, except that more study is needed on the prospective consequences of other WTO members invoking the 'trade deflection' terms of Section 16.8 of China's WTO Accession Protocol. Finally, if the full revocation of these instruments is simply unfeasible, I have suggested that partial reforms might also be attractive.

NOTES

1. Many observers have noted the oddly mercantilist thrust and language of the GATT and there is a further oddity in the notion of 'fair trade', which, in GATT-speak, takes precisely the opposite meaning to that in everyday language. When most people speak of getting a fair trade they mean getting more in return for they are giving up: their export. But when GATT lawyers talk of fair trade they typically mean getting *less* for exports: fair trade here always means paying more for imports.
2. The old 'new protectionism' was the wave of non-tariff barriers such as voluntary export restrictions (VERs) that spread in the 1970s and 1980s.
3. Given this commonality of motivation, I shall refer in this chapter to 'safeguards' as a general catch-all phrase to refer to all three administered protection measures generally and use 'Article XIX Safeguards' or SG in reference to actual GATT Article XIX actions.
4. The suggestion has been made that Article VI of the original GATT, permitting AD, was inserted simply as recognition of the reality that a number of signatory countries already had domestic AD laws and were not willing to give them up.
5. Irwin (2005) suggests that US historical use of AD has had other periods – the late 1930s and late 1950s – of high use as well.
6. Trebilcock and Howse (1999, p. 85). It should be noted, however, that a partial explanation of this is that US administrative law procedures are much less deferential to agency decisions than are Canadian procedures, so this system was always going to favour Canadian complainants. In recognition of this and in response to US complaints, the system was somewhat diluted in the formation of NAFTA in 1992.
7. WTO, 'Anti-dumping measures: reporting member vs exporting country', MS Excel sheet www.wto.org/english/tratop_e/adp_e/adp_stattab8_e.xls, accessed 7 June 2006, at www.wto.org/english/tratop_e/adp_e/adp_e.htm.
8. See Prusa (1992).
9. This is not the global experience. Canada, for instance, initiated only one Article XIX Safeguards action in the first ten years of the WTO but the relevant Canadian tribunal made two recommendations in 2005 while considering three further complaints, with, 'Chinese imports . . . the primary target' Purchase (2005, p. 3). Nevertheless, Article XIX Safeguard actions are generally pretty rare in the WTO. Perhaps because they must be temporary and must be gradually reduced, they are blanket and non-discriminatory measures and, most significantly, they require that compensation be paid – typically in the form of other 'concessions' – to the countries affected by them.
10. See also Killion (2004).
11. For preventing trade negotiators in Australia and China from being a burden to their citizens or country, and for making them beneficial to the public.
12. At least in the sense of leading to AD duties; as noted earlier, however, the harassment value of AD complaints may mean they are successful from a complainant's perspective, even when terminated.

13. Another criticism made of these sorts of arrangement is that, if extensively used, they will reinforce the reliance of non-competitive industries in the rest of the world on administered protection as a means of avoiding competition with Chinese firms (Groombridge 2001, p. 4). Evidence from WTO figures on Article XIX initiations over the last decade, however, does not support the contention that these actions will increase dramatically, Canadian experience notwithstanding (see fn. 9 herein).

14. Interestingly, the Australia–China FTA Joint Feasibility Study (DFAT 2005) notes the possibility of so-called third-party AD (TPAD) in Australia and New Zealand: that Australian firms, for example, can complain of dumping by third parties in New Zealand that damages the Australian interest. This bizarre route for protection (requiring, as it does, that a country prosecute cheap imports even if it has no domestic production presence of its own) has been accessed a number of times by Australian firms but never with any success. The reason, presumably, is that GATT conditions require approval of any TPAD actions by the Council on Trade in Goods and this is a WTO body that operates by consensus; accordingly, if the respondent is a WTO member it can quash any approval of such an action at the CTG. See Richardson (2006) for a more complete discussion.

15. Vautier and Lloyd (1997) provide a comprehensive discussion of these issues in the context of the CER FTA.

16. Of course, there are always issues concerning the ability of domestic laws to discipline foreign companies – in particular, concerning the extent to which a country's competition authorities can penalise foreign entities in terms of reaching their assets etc. As the CER experience has shown, this can be solved through harmonization of competition policy, but this is an unrealistic goal in the context of an Australia–China FTA.

17. Others have proposed reforms of AD law that might be implemented at the multilateral level but, for the reasons given earlier, these might be more successful at a regional or bilateral level. For instance, Barfield (2005) argues that countries should move from AD to SG actions but, in the meantime, that the evidentiary proof required of complainants should be tightened and a 'national interest' override should be allowed on all AD cases (as is, in fact, the case in New Zealand).

18. A further alternative might be to bring AD and CVD measures into line with Article XIX Safeguards by imposing explicit (and restrictive) time limits on their application while also requiring compensation to the trading partner (see Staiger 2005). Effectively, however, this would transform such actions into Article XIX Safeguard actions (except that the proximate cause of actions would be different).

19. See Bagwell and Staiger (2004). Lest it be thought that this is purely a theorist's concern, the following passage is to be found in the background paper – 'Resources and investment', prepared by DFAT for the Australia–China FTA Conference in Shenzhen, 27-8 June 2006: 'One of the benefits for China in an FTA with Australia is the *possibility of capturing the preferences we have given to other FTA partners*' (p. 4, emphasis in original).

20. See Ranjan (2006) for a recent analysis of FDI incentives in a model of FTAs and multinationals.

REFERENCES

Australian Customs Service (2006), ACS initiation reports, accessed 6 June 2006, at www.customs.gov.au.

Australian Department of Foreign Affairs and Trade (DFAT) (2005), 'Australia–China FTA Joint Feasibility Study', Canberra: AGPS, accessed 6 June 2006, at www.dfat.gov.au/geo/china/fta/feasibility_full.pdf.

Bagwell, K. and R. Staiger (2004), 'Multilateral trade negotiations, bilateral opportunism and the rules of WTO/GATT', *Journal of International Economics*, **63**(1), 1–29.

Barfield, C. (2005), 'Anti-dumping reform: time to go back to basics', *The World Economy*, **28**(5), 719–37.

Belderbos, R., H. Vandenbussche and R. Veugelers (2004), 'Antidumping duties, undertakings, and foreign direct investment in the EU', *European Economic Review*, **48**(2), 429–53.

Blonigen, B. (2002), 'Tariff-jumping antidumping duties', *Journal of International Economics*, **57**(1), 31–49.

Bovard, J. (1991), *The Fair Trade Fraud*, New York: St Martin's Press.

Bown, C. (2006), 'Global antidumping database version 2.0', mimeo, Brandeis University.

Deardorff, A. and R. Stern (2005), 'A centennial of anti-dumping legislation and implementation: introduction and overview', *The World Economy*, **28**(5), 633–40.

Ethier, W. (2004), 'Political externalities, non-discrimination and a multilateral world', *Review of International Economics*, **12**(3), 303–20.

Groombridge, M. (2001), 'Economic relations after China's accession to the WTO: an American perspective on shared goals and challenges confronting the US and the EU', mimeo, Washington, DC: Cato Institute, accessed 8 June 2006, at www.cap.lmu.de/transatlantic/download/groombridge.pdf.

Irwin, D. (2005), 'The rise of US anti-dumping activity in historical perspective', *The World Economy*, **28**(5), 651–68.

Killion, M.U. (2004), 'Quest for legal safeguards for foreign exporters under China's anti-dumping regime', *North Carolina Journal of International Law and Commercial Regulation*, **29**, 417–56.

Lindsey, B. and D. Ikenson (2002), 'Antidumping 101: the devilish details of "unfair trade" laws', Cato Trade Policy Analysis no. 20, Washington, DC: Center for Trade Policy Studies, Cato Institute.

Messerlin, P. (2004), 'China in the World Trade Organization: antidumping and safeguards', *The World Bank Economic Review*, **18**(1), 105–30.

Office of the United States Trade Representative (USTR) (2006), 'U.S.-China trade relations: entering a new phase of greater accountability and enforcement. Top-to-Bottom Review', Washington, DC: USTR, accessed 6 July 2006, at www.ustr.gov/assets/ Document_Library/Reports_Publications/2006/asset_upload_file921_8938.pdf.

Prusa, T. (1992), 'Why are so many anti-dumping petitions withdrawn?', *Journal of International Economics*, **33**(1), 1–20.

Prusa, T. (2005), 'Anti-dumping: a growing problem in international trade', *The World Economy*, **28**(5), 683–700.

Purchase, K. (2005), '2005 – the year of the safeguard?', *Blake's Bulletin on International Trade – China Focus*, December, accessed 8 June 2006, at www.blakes.com / english / publications / InternationalTrade / Dec2005 / International Trade_ChinaFocus.pdf.

Ranjan, P. (2006), 'Preferential trade areas, multinational enterprises, and welfare', *Canadian Journal of Economics*, **39**(2), 493–515.

Richardson, M. (2006), 'Third-party anti-dumping: a tentative rationale', *European Journal of Political Economy*, **22**(3), 759–70.

Staiger, R. (2005), 'Some remarks on reforming WTO AD/CVD rules', *The World Economy*, **28**(5), 739–43.

Trebilcock, M. and R. Howse (1999), *The Regulation of International Trade*, 2nd edn, London: Routledge.

Vautier, K. and P. Lloyd (1997), *International Trade and Competition Policy: CER, APEC and the WTO*, Wellington, New Zealand: Institute of Policy Studies.

World Trade Organization (WTO) (2006), WTO statistics on antidumping, accessed 7 June 2006, at www.wto.org/english/tratop_e/ adp_e/adp_e.htm.

World Trade Organization (WTO) (2006), 'WTO trade policy review', report by the Secretariat, People's Republic of China, WT/TPR/S/161, 28 February 2006, accessed 9 June 2006, at www.wto.org/english/ tratop_e/tpr_e/tp262_e.htm.

12. Ensuring compliance between a bilateral PTA and the WTO

Andrew D. Mitchell and Nicolas J.S. Lockhart

INTRODUCTION

The global trading system is now comprised of an interlocking, ever-growing, network of bilateral, regional and multilateral trade agreements. It would be easy to assume that any form and combination of trade agreement is necessarily beneficial for trade. After all, such agreements pursue the common goal of trade promotion through liberalization. More trade agreements of whatever type might, therefore, translate into more trade liberalization. The short-coming of this assumption is, however, that multilateral and other agreements pursue this goal in different and often conflicting ways. A core objective of the multilateral trading system is 'the elimination of discriminatory treatment in international trade relations'.[1] In pursuit of this objective, World Trade Organization (WTO) Members must accord equal treatment to the goods and services of all other WTO Members (through 'most-favoured-nation' or MFN treatment).[2] In contrast, preferential trade agreements (PTAs), such as free trade agreements (FTAs) and customs unions, pursue trade liberalization through precisely this type of discrimination. The parties to a PTA liberalize trade solely among themselves, creating a network of special preferences within the PTA that are not available to other WTO Members. PTAs, therefore, entrench the very discrimination that WTO rules seek to eliminate. This key difference in approach makes the relationship between multilateralism and regionalism both complicated and controversial. In this book, other contributions examine whether in economic terms maintaining an ever-growing network of PTAs alongside multilateral rules produces an overall increase or decrease in economic welfare. In legal terms, the coexistence of the WTO and PTAs among WTO Members creates a complex system of competing international rights and obligations.

As PTAs involve discrimination contrary to the general MFN obligation, they would normally give rise to inconsistencies with WTO rules. However, the WTO agreements contain a series of exceptions for PTAs that allow limited derogation from WTO rules for PTAs meeting certain conditions. Only PTAs falling within one of these exceptions are valid under WTO law. In other words, a WTO Member must ensure that any PTA to which it is a party complies with the conditions of the relevant WTO exception. Otherwise, the Member risks acting inconsistently with its WTO obligations. The PTA exceptions are contained in: Article XXIV of the General Agreement on Tariffs and Trade (GATT) 1994; paragraph 2(c) of the Enabling Clause;[3] and Article V of the General Agreement on Trade in Services (GATS). The first two exceptions apply to PTA provisions relating to goods, while the third applies to PTA provisions relating to services. A PTA covering both goods and services would generally need to comply with the relevant exceptions for both goods and services. This chapter focuses on the goods exception contained in GATT Article XXIV in particular the exception for FTAs because the Australia–China FTA is not a customs union.

Few provisions of the WTO Agreements have inspired as much controversy and disagreement as the PTA exceptions. The WTO Members themselves are divided on almost every issue of significance in these exceptions, with the result that the process for WTO review of PTAs has broken down. Although 175 PTAs have been notified to the WTO since it was established in 1995,[4] none has completed the GATT or GATS examination process to determine its WTO consistency. Ironically, this systemic failure comes at a time when the WTO exceptions for PTAs should have taken on increasing importance because of the unprecedented proliferation of PTAs among WTO Members.[5] In addition, although the Appellate Body has issued its first decision on the Enabling Clause,[6] the Appellate Body has provided very little substantive guidance on Article XXIV of GATT 1994 or Article V of GATS. Therefore, it is worth examining these exceptions to identify the main areas of controversy and uncertainty, because they are relevant to an Australia–China FTA and other FTAs being negotiated, and because they are subject to negotiation in the current Doha Round and may arise in future disputes.

This chapter focuses on the substantive aspects of the exception for FTAs in relation to goods under Article XXIV, examining in detail the conditions with which FTAs must comply in order to fall within the exception. These conditions relate to the elimination of restrictions on trade between the parties to the FTA, and to the nature and level of restrictions that the parties to the FTA impose on trade with WTO Members that are not party to the FTA. The chapter goes on to discuss the activities of the Committee on Regional Trade Agreements as well as the lack of enforcement of the rules before WTO Tribunals. This puts into context the likelihood of any legal challenge to an Australia–China FTA.

ELIMINATING RESTRICTIONS ON TRADE WITHIN THE FTA: ARTICLE XXIV:8(B)

Introduction

Article XXIV:8(b) of GATT 1994 defines a 'free-trade area'. To benefit from the exception in Article XXIV:5(b), a PTA must meet this definition. An FTA is defined by the elimination of internal trade restrictions as follows: 'duties and other restrictive regulations of commerce (except, where necessary, those permitted under Articles XI, XII, XIII, XIV, XV and XX) are eliminated on substantially all the trade between the constituent territories in products originating in such territories.'

Thus the definition of FTAs: (a) requires the elimination of restrictions on 'substantially all the trade' between the FTA parties 'in products originating' within the FTA; (b) defines the restrictions that must be eliminated as duties and 'other restrictive regulations of commerce' (ORRCs); and (c) expressly allows the maintenance of certain restrictions, 'where necessary', namely 'those permitted under Articles XI, XII, XIII, XIV, XV and XX' of GATT 1994.

Measuring 'Substantially all the Trade'

1 Members' views

The meaning of 'substantially all the trade' in Article XXIV:8 has given rise to much discussion over the years. To date, WTO Members have been unable to agree on the proportion of trade that amounts to 'substantially' all trade,[7] or how 'all the trade' within an FTA is to be measured.[8] However, two overlapping approaches have gained currency. First, a qualitative approach, which would require the elimination of restrictions with respect to every major sector of the economies of the FTA parties. Second, a quantitative approach, which relies on a statistical threshold, for example requiring the elimination of restrictions with respect to a predefined percentage of trade.

The qualitative approach is designed to prevent FTA parties from maintaining restrictions to protect important sectors from competition within the FTA. The rationale would seem to be that an exception to WTO rules should only be granted when the parties to a regional agreement have shown commitment to closer economic integration. If the parties exclude major economic sectors from liberalization, that commitment is deemed lacking. If this approach were adopted, it would be likely to operate in conjunction with a quantitative criterion, and rules would be required to determine what constitutes a major economic sector.

Under the quantitative approach, one suggestion is that internal restrictions should be eliminated on 95 per cent of all Harmonized Commodity Description and Coding System (HS) tariff lines at the six-digit level. Tariff lines can be used as a criterion to ensure that liberalization covers all possible or potential trade between the FTA parties, because all goods fall within a tariff line. However, using tariff lines may give a misleading impression of the extent to which trade has been liberalized, for instance where actual trade flows between the FTA parties are concentrated in a few tariff lines. If restrictions on these few tariff lines were maintained, a large share of current trade could escape liberalization.[9] Conversely, a large number of tariff lines may be devoted to a small amount of actual trade. For example, around a quarter of all HS tariff lines deal with agricultural products, which may account for only a small portion of actual trade.[10]

Trade flows provide an alternative to tariff lines in establishing the threshold of trade for which restrictions must be eliminated. Thus, for example, the elimination of internal restrictions could be required with respect to 95 per cent of all trade flows between the FTA parties. However, using trade flows as a criterion is also problematic. First, actual trade flows are distorted by trade restrictions and do not necessarily reflect the likely trade volumes if restrictions were eliminated.[11] Second, difficulties arise in applying this criterion. For example, a threshold of 95 per cent of all trade could be measured either as a proportion of aggregate trade flowing between the parties or as a proportion of each party's individual trade with the other. To take the simplest case, where there are only two FTA parties,[12] suppose that Country A exports to Country B are valued at US$95 million, and Country B exports to Country A are valued at US$5 million. Using an aggregate measure, the two countries would need to eliminate internal trade restrictions on 95 per cent of the total trade, valued at US$100 million. The parties would have discretion as to which part of the total trade to liberalize,[13] and they could even agree simply that Country B would eliminate all restrictions on Country A imports. In contrast, using an individual measure, each country would have to eliminate trade restrictions on 95 per cent of the imports from the other country.

The question of how to calculate trade flows in applying a quantitative approach to 'substantially all the trade' could be of particular importance in the case of North–South agreements, where the parties may wish to liberalize trade unequally. Using an aggregate measure, developing countries might be able to benefit from elimination of restrictions on a greater share of their exports to a developed country party. Alternatively, WTO Members might consider it preferable to prescribe individual measurement, in order to prevent one FTA party from forcing another, in a weaker bargaining position, to accept a lower degree of liberalization.

In order to measure 'substantially all the trade' between FTA parties 'in products originating' in those parties under Article XXIV:8(b), rules are required to determine whether goods 'originated' within the PTA. Such rules are also needed in connection with a customs union if the parties choose to eliminate restrictions not with respect to substantially all trade between them but only with respect to substantially all trade in products originating in the parties' territories.

Rules of origin are used to decide in which country goods are produced and, therefore, in an FTA setting, whether they qualify for a tariff preference.[14] In FTAs, the parties often adopt special rules of origin to determine which goods qualify for preferential treatment in the FTA. The preferential rules may apply much stricter qualifying conditions than the rules of origin generally used in MFN trade.[15] Thus, goods that are deemed to originate in one FTA party under the general rules of origin may not be treated as originating in that party under preferential rules of origin. Such special rules of origin may, therefore, narrow the scope of trade that is liberalized within an FTA. This has led some Members to suggest that the measurement of 'substantially all the trade' should take into account preferential rules of origin. For example, 'all the trade' within an FTA in products originating in the FTA parties could be measured using MFN rules of origin, while the proportion that is liberalized could be measured using the preferential rules of origin applying within that FTA.[16]

2. Interpretation in dispute settlement

Although the Members have yet to agree on a meaning for the term 'substantially all the trade', panels or the Appellate Body may be called upon to interpret the term in dispute settlement. So, far, neither the Appellate Body nor any panel has provided a detailed interpretation of this notion. In *Turkey – Textiles*, the Appellate Body noted that 'substantially all the trade' is not the same as all the trade, but that it 'is something considerably more than merely some of the trade'.[17] Therefore, the relevant amount of trade falls somewhere between some and all trade among the FTA parties. Beyond this, the disputes provide little guidance. In order to prove that NAFTA complied with Article XXIV:8(b) in *US – Line Pipe*, the United States submitted evidence that NAFTA eliminated 'duties on 97 per cent of the Parties' tariff lines, representing more than 99 per cent of the trade among them in terms of volume'.[18] After reviewing the evidence, and without offering any views on the meaning of 'substantially all the trade', the panel held that the United States had established a prima facie case that NAFTA met the definition of an FTA under Article XXIV:8(b).[19] The Appellate Body took the view that it need not address this finding and declared it to be of no legal effect.[20]

It is perhaps unrealistic and inappropriate to expect that panels or the Appellate Body will develop a refined formula for identifying 'substantially all the trade'. For instance, it would be difficult for a panel to find a textual basis for a finding that a precise threshold of 90 per cent is never 'substantial' but that a precise threshold of 95 per cent always is. If the clarification of this notion is left to panels and the Appellate Body, it is more likely that they will develop a flexible test premised on the word 'substantial', which indicates that the elimination of internal restrictions must cover a very considerable proportion of the trade between the parties. The words 'all trade' will also be important, as they identify the broad base against which internal liberalization is to be measured. In each case, panels are likely to reach a conclusion based on the specific facts at issue, probably taking account of the qualitative and quantitative factors discussed by the Members.

Eliminating 'Duties and other Restrictive Regulations of Commerce'

A second question arising from the definition of FTAs is which trade restrictions are to be eliminated. According to Article XXIV:8(a)(i) and (b), the parties to an FTA must eliminate duties and ORRCs on substantially all the trade. WTO Members have frequently discussed the words 'duties and other restrictive regulations of commerce', without reaching any agreement on their meaning. Similarly, no panel or Appellate Body reports to date have interpreted these words. While the words 'substantially all the trade' dictate how much trade must be liberalized within an FTA, the words 'duties and other restrictive regulations of commerce' describe the types of restriction to be eliminated. Evidently, elimination of a broader range of restrictive regulations will result in a higher level of liberalization within the FTA, in accordance with the purpose of the exception in Article XXIV:5.

What seems important in determining which regulations constitute ORRCs is not the form of a regulation, but its effect on commerce. The requirement of elimination applies only to regulations that have a 'restrictive' effect on commerce, irrespective of whether the regulation imposes duties or takes some other form. Article XXIV:8 does not state expressly what kind of restrictive effect is intended. Virtually all regulations affecting goods have some kind of 'chilling' effect that restricts trade in those goods. This is equally true of border regulations, which chill imports, and marketplace regulations,[21] which chill trade in domestic and imported goods. It seems rather unlikely, though, that Article XXIV:8 was intended to encompass all regulations that have a restrictive effect on trade, however small. It is worth noting that the PTA Understanding refers to the 'elimination *between the constituent territories* of duties and other restrictive regulations of commerce'.[22] This suggests that the regulations to be eliminated under

Article XXIV:8 are those restricting the cross-border movement of goods between the FTA parties. The focus of internal liberalization under Article XXIV:8 is, in other words, on restrictions that adversely affect imported or exported goods, with the goal being to create a market among the parties that is border free rather than regulation free.

So what types of restrictions are duties or ORRCs pursuant to Article XXIV:8? By definition, border restrictions apply solely to imports, imposing restrictions on the cross-border movement of goods, and they are certainly ORRCs. These include import bans, quantitative restrictions, and the many administrative rules regulating importation. Sanitary and phytosanitary (SPS) measures prohibiting the importation of goods would also be ORRCs. ORRCs are also likely to include marketplace regulations that adversely affect imported goods, as compared with domestic goods, but such regulations would likely be already proscribed by the WTO national treatment obligation.[23]

Much discussion among academics and WTO negotiators has focused on whether trade remedy measures are ORRCs. Measures adopted under Article VI (anti-dumping and countervailing measures) or XIX (safeguard measures) of GATT 1994 are not expressly identified in the bracketed phrase in Article XXIV:8 ('except, where necessary, those permitted under Articles XI, XII, XIII, XIV, XV and XX'), which is discussed further below.[24] The exclusion of trade remedy measures from this phrase could mean that trade remedy measures are simply not ORRCs (in which case there was no need to include them in the brackets and they are not subject to the elimination requirement). However, it could also be that they are ORRCs and their exclusion from the brackets means there is no express right to maintain them (in which case they should be eliminated on substantially all the trade between the FTA parties).[25]

The text of Article XXIV:8 contains little support for excluding trade remedy measures from the measures that need to be eliminated, that is, duties and ORRCs. Anti-dumping and countervailing duties are described as 'duties' in Articles II and VI of GATT 1994, as well as in the Anti-Dumping Agreement and the Subsidies and Countervailing Measures (SCM) Agreement. These 'duties' are imposed, in addition to ordinary customs duties, on the importation of products. Moreover, the very purpose of these duties is to restrict imports of specific products. Under Article XIX of GATT 1994, safeguard measures involve the modification or withdrawal of a market access concession for imported goods. The purpose of safeguard measures is, therefore, also to restrict imports. The restriction on access takes the form of either a duty or a quantitative restriction. Again, there is little reason to suppose that safeguard measures are not ORRCs.[26]

Internal Restrictions that may be Maintained

1.   Restrictions on an 'insubstantial' portion of trade

Under Article XXIV:8, the FTA parties need not eliminate all ORRCs; they must simply eliminate ORRCs on 'substantially all the trade' between the parties. On the remaining portion of trade, the parties are entitled to retain all ORRCs of any type (provided that they are not otherwise inconsistent with WTO rules), including trade remedy measures and other measures not listed in the brackets. But difficult questions remain.

If the FTA parties decide to retain the possibility of imposing trade remedy measures on each other, the FTA is likely to include a general authority for each party to impose such measures in specific cases in the future. This general authority, of itself, might be regarded as an ORRC on all the products that are potentially subject to trade remedy measures at a later stage. In this case, restrictions would be deemed to remain on all the products potentially subject to trade remedy measures. To comply with the requirement to eliminate restrictions on substantially all the trade, FTA parties would have to confine the general authority to a defined group of products representing no more than an insubstantial portion of trade.

Alternatively, it could be argued that the general authority does not, in fact, restrict commerce; it merely enables a potential future restriction, which might never be realized. On that view, the general authority is not an ORRC and need not be limited to particular products representing an insubstantial portion of trade. Rather, specific measures imposed pursuant to the general authority are ORRCs and must be limited to such a portion.[27] This approach is also problematic. It would leave undefined and uncertain the number and type of ORRCs that could be imposed within the FTA and, hence, the proportion of trade subject to ORRCs. As a result, the consistency of the FTA with the conditions of the exception in Article XXIV:5 of GATT 1994 would vary, depending on the number and extent of trade remedy measures imposed at any given time. It would be impossible to state definitively, based merely on the FTA itself, whether it was justified under the exception.

2.   Other restrictions expressly permitted

Although Article XXIV:8(b) states that, in an FTA, restrictive regulations of commerce must be eliminated on substantially all internal trade, an exception to this requirement operates, 'where necessary' for 'those' ORRCs 'permitted under Articles XI, XII, XIII, XIV, XV and XX'.

Some WTO Members have suggested that the bracketed list of measures is illustrative only. In other words, measures apart from those 'permitted under Articles XI, XII, XIII, XIV, XV and XX', such as trade remedy measures, may also be implicitly included in the list and maintained within an FTA.[28] This argument has not won the support of all Members. In any case, since the bracketed list provides an exception to the general rule of elimination of ORRCs, it would normally be interpreted in a manner pre-cluding the addition of other measures. This approach is consistent with the Appellate Body's statement in *Turkey – Textiles* that the bracketed phrase allows parties to maintain measures 'otherwise permitted under Articles XI through XV and under Article XX of the GATT 1994'.[29] While not a definitive ruling on this issue, this statement suggests that the Appellate Body would read the bracketed phrase as containing an exclusive list of the ORRCs that may be maintained in an FTA.[30]

In *Turkey – Textiles*, the Appellate Body recognized that this exception to the general requirement of elimination of ORRCs offers 'some flexibility' to the parties to a customs union (and presumably also an FTA) to maintain certain types of ORRCs.[31] However, the Appellate Body cautioned that this flexibility is limited by the requirement that ORRCs be eliminated with respect to substantially all internal trade. In addition, the exception applies only 'where necessary', although the text provides no guidance as to when it is necessary to maintain restrictions. In *Turkey – Textiles*, the Appellate Body developed and applied a necessity test to the exception for PTAs in Article XXIV:5 of GATT 1994. A similar test could also be applied to the bracketed phrase in Article XXIV:8. In that context, to the extent that the formation of an FTA would be prevented if an ORRC listed in that phrase were eliminated, it could be regarded as 'necessary' to maintain the ORRC.

An interesting and, as yet, unresolved question is whether products subject to ORRCs listed in the brackets are part of the 'substantial' or 'insubstantial' portion of trade. The question can be illustrated by example. Suppose a WTO Member maintains quantitative restrictions, under Article XII, on imports of all steel products from partner countries in an FTA. No duties or other restrictions are imposed on steel imports. In measuring whether ORRCs have been eliminated on substantially all the trade in the FTA, should steel products be counted as trade on which ORRCs have been eliminated (the substantial portion of trade) or as trade on which ORRCs have not been eliminated (the insubstantial portion of trade)?

The straightforward – and stricter – view is that trade in any product subject to an ORRC has not been liberalized, and the product cannot form part of the substantial portion of trade on which ORRCs have been elimi-nated. In this view, the substantial portion of trade is confined to products that are subject to no ORRCs at all; conversely, a product that is subject to any ORRC, including an ORRC listed in the brackets, must form part of the insubstantial portion of trade.[32]

This reading is, however, problematic. The list of ORRCs in brackets includes, among others, restrictions maintained pursuant to Article XX of GATT 1994. Article XX provides a general exception to all GATT 1994 obligations. In certain circumstances, Article XX allows Members to promote governance priorities – such as public health and environmental protection – that conflict with WTO rules. WTO-consistent SPS measures are also covered by Article XX[33] and, in all likelihood, so are most WTO-consistent technical barriers to trade (TBTs). There is broad recognition in the WTO Agreements, and among WTO Members, that Members should have discretion to pursue these other priorities, subject to the conditions governing the exceptions to WTO rules. However, if a product subject to health restrictions permitted by Article XX necessarily formed part of the insubstantial portion of trade on which ORRCs had not been eliminated, this would constrain WTO Members' right to pursue health objectives. In a customs union or an FTA, a WTO Member would be able to promote health only through internal restrictions on the 'insubstantial' group of products. As well as being questionable in terms of State sovereignty, this reading of Article XXIV:8 would be at odds with the text of Article XX. Article XX(b) states that 'nothing in this Agreement shall be construed to prevent the adoption or enforcement by any Member of measures . . . necessary to protect human, animal or plant life or health'. If Article XXIV:8 of GATT 1994 meant that Article XX health measures could only be maintained on the insubstantial portion of trade, that interpretation would 'prevent' the adoption or enforcement of health measures on 'substantially all the trade', contrary to Article XX.

An alternative reading follows from the structure of Article XXIV:8(b). This provision requires that an FTA eliminate all ORRCs – except those bracketed – on substantially all trade. The bracketed exception is located immediately after the phrase 'duties and other restrictive regulations of commerce' and, together with this phrase, defines the universe of restrictions that must be eliminated with respect to substantially all trade. Thus, for products comprising substantially all trade, all ORRCs must be eliminated except those listed in the brackets. This reading, therefore, creates three categories of product under Article XXIV:8:

- First, products that are subject to no ORRCs at all. These products form part of the 'substantial' portion of trade with respect to which all ORRCs have been eliminated.
- Second, products that are subject to no ORRCs, except for one or more of those listed in the brackets. These products also form part of the 'substantial' portion of trade with respect to which ORRCs, other than those listed in the brackets, have been eliminated.

- Third, products that are subject to ORRCs that are not listed in the brackets. These products must represent no more than an 'insubstantial' portion of trade, with respect to which ORRCs need not be eliminated. These products may also be subject to ORRCs listed in the brackets.

Under this reading, WTO Members would be entitled to maintain, 'where necessary', any of the ORRCs listed in the brackets with respect to any product. In addition, they would be entitled to maintain any ORRCs with respect to an insubstantial portion of trade. This reading of Article XXIV:8 would, therefore, avoid the problem of constraining Members from maintaining measures permitted under Article XX.

RESTRICTIONS ON THE EXTERNAL TRADE OF THE FTA: ARTICLE XXIV:5(B)

Introduction

As we have seen in the previous section of this chapter, Article XXIV:8 of GATT 1994 imposes certain conditions on the restrictions imposed by FTA parties on trade within the FTA. In addition, Article XXIV of GATT 1994 imposes conditions on the restrictions applied by FTA parties in the external trade of the FTA.

Under Article XXIV:5(b), an FTA will not qualify for the FTA exception under Article XXIV:5 if, broadly speaking, the 'duties and other regulations of commerce' imposed by the FTA parties on other WTO Members are higher or more restrictive than before the FTA was formed.

Specifically:

> [T]he duties and other regulations of commerce maintained in each [of] the constituent territories and applicable at the formation of [an FTA] to the trade of [WTO Members] not included in such area . . . shall not be higher or more restrictive than the corresponding duties and other regulations of commerce existing in the same constituent territories prior to the formation of the free-trade area . . .

The Meaning of 'Duties and Other Regulations of Commerce'

1.   Structure and context of the relevant provisions

The words 'duties and other regulations of commerce' in Articles XXIV are reminiscent of the words 'duties and other restrictive regulations of commerce' in Article XXIV:8(b), examined earlier in the context of the conditions imposed on internal trade restrictions. The key difference is that the word 'restrictive' is absent in the context of external trade. However, although this is not formally part of the definition of 'other regulations of commerce' (ORCs), Article XXIV:5(6) is concerned with the 'restrictiveness' of ORCs.

It addresses ORCs applied in respect of trade with WTO Members that are not party to the FTA. In the remainder of the discussion in this section of the meaning of 'duties and other regulations of commerce', we use the words 'external trade' or 'trade with third countries' as a convenient way of referring to trade with WTO Members that are not party to the FTA.

2.   Examples of regulations of commerce

FTA parties could impose various measures that could potentially constitute ORCs, including:

- border measures regulating either the import of goods from third countries or the export of goods to third countries; and
- marketplace measures that may be applicable: solely to goods of third countries; to goods of both third countries and FTA parties; or solely to goods of FTA parties.

(a) Border measures   It seems clear, and relatively uncontroversial, that the ORCs relevant to Article XXIV:5(b) include border measures applied to imports from third countries, as these measures are certainly imposed on, or applied to, external trade. These measures include customs duties and similar charges, import prohibitions, quantitative restrictions, and administrative rules regulating importation. Administrative rules might include rules of origin used to distinguish between imports of goods originating in an FTA party and those originating in a third country, and prohibition of imports from third countries that do not comply with certain SPS or TBT standards. Moreover, these measures are ORCs whether they are applied individually by one FTA party or, in the case of a customs union, by all parties.

Border measures that restrict exports from FTA parties to third countries are more problematic. During the Uruguay Round, one proposal was that the words 'duties and other regulations of commerce' should be interpreted to cover 'all border measures taken in connection with importation or exportation which have a differential impact on imported products as compared to domestic products'.[34] This proposal was rejected due to, among other things, the inclusion of the word 'exportation'. This might suggest that the negotiators did not agree that ORCs included export measures.

A further difficulty with interpreting ORCs as including border measures on exports is that such measures are generally applied by FTA parties to their own goods when destined for third country markets[35] and therefore cannot be described as being applicable or applied 'to the trade *of*' third countries within the meaning of Article XXIV:5(b). However, in the context of customs unions, Article XXIV:5(a) refers to measures 'imposed . . . in respect of trade *with*' third countries. This language might be broad enough to encompass export measures. This could mean that, on the one hand, export measures are not relevant to the determination under Article XXIV:5(b) of whether the parties to an FTA impose higher or more restrictive ORCs on other Members; but, on the other hand, export measures are relevant to the determination under Article XXIV:5(a) of whether the parties to a customs union impose higher or more restrictive ORCs on other Members. It is unclear whether the drafters intended this distinction.

(b) Marketplace measures   During the Uruguay Round, a second proposal was for 'duties and other regulations of commerce' to be interpreted as covering 'all duties and charges and measures imposed on or in connection with importation or exportation'.[36] This proposal was also rejected, primarily because of differing opinions as to whether ORCs include internal measures such as sales taxes and price controls. In the end, no agreement was reached on an authoritative interpretation of 'duties and other regulations of commerce', and no explicit guidance was included as to whether these words cover internal or 'marketplace' measures.

Article XXIV:5(b) refers to ORCs 'maintained in . . . and applicable . . . to the trade of' other WTO Members. This wording might extend to marketplace measures. However, the use of the word 'trade' (as opposed to 'goods') may well signify that the focus is not on the treatment of goods of other Members within the FTA but on the treatment of such goods at the border.

Some Members have argued that certain marketplace measures imposed by FTA parties solely on goods originating within the FTA might restrict external trade and therefore be relevant ORCs under these three subparagraphs.[37] Examples of such measures, drawn from existing FTAs, include the application of lower SPS or TBT standards[38] on internal FTA trade or the replacement of anti-dumping measures within the FTA with competition rules.[39] These harmonized rules apply solely to goods from FTA parties; the normal WTO rules apply to goods from third countries.[40]

It is difficult to know how to treat measures that apply solely to goods from FTA parties but may have a distortive effect on trade with third countries. ORCs are described as measures, 'applicable . . . to' (Article XXIV:5(b)). The verb 'apply' suggests that relevant ORCs are measures that directly regulate trade with third countries and not measures that merely have an indirect effect on trade with third countries. This perhaps indicates that marketplace measures 'imposed' only on goods from FTA parties are not ORCs and, therefore, do not need to be included in determining the level of restrictions on external trade in any FTA under Article XXIV:5(b). Moreover, these harmonized rules arise from internal liberalization within the FTA, which some have argued means that they should not be regarded as barriers to trade with third countries.[41] However, it is difficult to reconcile this with the twin purpose of the FTA exception in Article XXIV:5, given that these harmonized rules may well distort or restrict trade from third countries.

External Restrictions not Higher

Article XXIV:5(b) calls for a comparison between two sets of ORCs: those 'existing' prior to the formation of the FTA, and those 'applicable' at the formation of the FTA. The comparison is between the ORCs applied after the formation of the FTA and the 'corresponding' ORCs applied before formation. The use of the word 'corresponding' suggests that specific ORCs should be compared as they applied before and after the formation of the FTA.

This view is consistent with the nature of economic integration in FTAs. As with parties to customs unions, FTA parties must eliminate most 'duties and other restrictive regulations of commerce' on substantially all internal trade. However, as stated above, FTA parties have no obligation to adopt common rules for external trade, and parties to an FTA typically continue to impose their own external trade regimes.[42] Therefore, Article XXIV:5(b) prevents an FTA party from using the formation of an FTA as an opportunity to increase the burden of any individual ORC it imposes on external trade. In Article XXIV, such an increase in burden is essentially deemed unnecessary to the formation of an FTA and is inconsistent with the purpose of Article XXIV of minimizing the restrictive effects of FTAs on external trade.

Article XXIV:6 envisages increases in specific bound rates upon the formation of a customs union and provides a procedure for negotiating a 'compensatory adjustment' for the affected Member. In contrast, no provision in Article XXIV envisages any increase in specific duties upon the formation of an FTA. This supports the view that a WTO Member may not make any ORC more burdensome upon the formation of an FTA. Nevertheless, other provisions of GATT 1994 or other covered agreements could conceivably provide a justification for the introduction of new restrictions by FTA parties. For instance, if the parties to an FTA decide to harmonize the SPS/TBT framework within the FTA and, in the process, one or more of the parties introduces new SPS measures or TBTs, the parties could justify the new restrictions under the SPS Agreement or the TBT Agreement, even if these restrictions would normally be regarded as relevant ORCs under Article XXIV:5(b). The introduction on the formation of an FTA of a new ORC that is justified by other WTO provisions should not prevent the FTA concerned from benefiting from the FTA exception under Article XXIV:5 – WTO rules entitle the Member to adopt the ORC whether or not it joins the FTA.

THE LIKELIHOOD OF LEGAL CHALLENGE

One might imagine that, given the uncertainties identified above and the enormous number of FTAs concluded or being negotiated, FTAs are at substantial risk of challenge. Certainly FTAs can be challenged, either through the Committee on Regional Trade Agreements (CRTA) or through the dispute settlement mechanism. However, neither mechanism looks likely to begin effectively enforcing the rules.

Committee on Regional Trade Agreements (CRTA)

WTO Members have a duty to notify the WTO of their decision to enter into FTAs.[43] These notifications are received by the CRTA.[44] The CRTA is required to, among other things, 'carry out the examination of agreements in accordance with the procedures and terms of reference adopted by . . . and thereafter present its report to the relevant body for appropriate action'.[45]

The CRTA has the power to determine that an FTA is inconsistent with the rules. It may: 'make such reports and recommendations to contracting parties as they may deem appropriate'.

However, the CRTA has never made a decision that an FTA was inconsistent with the rules. Indeed, the reports that the CRTA makes on the FTAs it reviews are adopted notwithstanding the often divergent views on their consistency with the rules.[46] The only consensus that has been achieved on an FTA's consistency with the rules was the customs union between the Czech Republic and the Slovak Republic after the breakup of Czechoslovakia. Given that 211 notifications have been made received, the sustained lack of serious enforcement is disturbing.

Dispute Settlement

While WTO Tribunals clearly have the competence to determine claims of the inconsistency of a RTA with the WTO Agreements,[47] a legal challenge is unlikely for a number of reasons. One is that Members may consider that WTO Tribunals will avoid determining the ambiguities identified above and therefore not wish to engage in the costly process of bringing a dispute. Given

> the uncertainty surrounding the precise legal frontiers between consistency and inconsistency with the multilateral rules, apart from exceptional cases, it is unlikely that a panel will find itself on firm legal ground to provide a definitive statement on the law itself. [For example, they might state] the burden of proof has not been met, or evidence provided has not been effectively refuted and request additional proof from the complainant.[48]

WTO Tribunals are skilled at avoiding answering unnecessary questions but are likely to be able to avoid resolving some key questions where the WTO inconsistency of an FTA was at issue. A stronger reason is that, since all but one WTO Member is party to an FTA, and many FTAs could be WTO inconsistent, a situation of 'cooperative equilibrium' has developed, where to avoid challenge, Members do not challenge other Members' FTAs.[49]

CONCLUSION

In a global trading system, where FTAs have become a central tool of trade policy, and where they are growing rapidly in number and complexity, the exception in Article XXIV:5 of GATT 1994 plays a crucial role in ensuring coherence between multilateral and regional trade policy. This exception seeks to ensure that FTAs work to the benefit of the global trading system by promoting a net increase in trade liberalization. Yet questions remain on almost every issue of importance concerning this exception.[50] Without answers to these questions, the value of Article XXIV in shaping regional trade policy is diminished. Moreover, the risk that FTAs work to undermine trade liberalization at the multilateral level increases. In this chapter, we have explored some of the questions surrounding Article XXIV, evaluating possible options, and always keeping in mind the underlying purpose of the FTA exception. We have examined the views expressed by Members, panels, and the Appellate Body, as well as the text of WTO Agreements. We have also drawn on the way FTAs work in practice. The conclusion must be that Article XXIV is mired in doubt. Until the WTO makes further progress in this area, the WTO-consistency of most FTAs will be uncertain and Members will have difficulty determining the best way of structuring FTAs in a WTO-consistent fashion.

NOTES

1. WTO Agreement, Preamble.
2. GATT 1994, art I; GATS, art II.
3. Decision on Differential and More Favourable Treatment, Reciprocity, and Fuller Participation of Developing Countries, GATT Document L/4903, BISD 26S/203 (28 November 1979) (Enabling Clause). As a decision of the GATT contracting parties, the Enabling Clause forms part of GATT 1994. See para 1(b)(iv) of the language incorporating GATT 1994 into the WTO Agreement.
4. www.wto.org/english/tratop_e/region_e/summary_e.xls calculated as the sum of notifications occurring after 1 January 1995 relating to the enabling clause, GATS art V and GATT art XXIV as at 15 September 2006.
5. In 1995 there were 62 operative PTAs, in 2000 that number had increased to 104 and by 15 September 2006 the number was 211, www.wto.org/english/tratop_e/region_e/summary_e.xls.
6. See Appellate Body Report, *EC – Tariff Preferences.*
7. New Zealand has even suggested, in view of the many difficulties surrounding the word 'substantially', that the word should be 'removed' from Article XXIV:8: WTO Committee on Regional Trade Agreements, *Note on the Meetings of 16-18 and 20 February 1998*, WT/REG/M/16 (18 March 1998) para 115.
8. WTO Committee on Regional Trade Agreements, *Coverage, Liberalization Process and Transitional Provisions in Regional Trade Agreements: Background Survey by the Secretariat*, WT/REG/W/46 (5 April 2002).
9. For instance, the European Communities has pointed out that in agreements involving the Faroe Islands, 'well under 50 tariff lines accounted for about 80 per cent of the trade'. Norway, likewise, has observed that in a Faroe Islands–Norway FTA, all of the trade between the two parties was conducted under just 10 tariff lines. WTO Committee on Regional Trade Agreements, *Note on the Meetings of 16-18 and 20 February 1998*, WT/REG/M/16 (18 March 1998) paras 118 and 125.
10. WTO Committee on Regional Trade Agreements, *Note on the Meetings of 23-24 September 1998*, WT/REG/M/19 (16 October 1998) para 18.
11. See generally WTO Committee on Regional Trade Agreements, *Communication from Australia*, WT/REG/W/22 (30 January 1998) and Add. 1 (24 April 1998). See also WTO Committee on Regional Trade Agreements, *Note on the Meetings of 16-18 and 20 February 1998*, WT/REG/M/16 (18 March 1998) para 112.
12. The situation becomes even more complicated for PTAs with three or more parties.
13. See WTO Committee on Regional Trade Agreements, *Communication from Australia – Addendum*, WT/REG/W/22/Add. 1 (24 April 1998).
14. The WTO imposes limited disciplines on rules of origin under the Agreement on Rules of Origin.
15. Preferential rules of origin are not subject to the general obligations in the Agreement on Rules of Origin, although they are subject to certain transparency requirements in the Common Declaration with Regard to Preferential Rules of Origin in Annexe II of that Agreement.
16. See, for instance, WTO Committee on Regional Trade Agreements, *Note on the Meetings of 6-7 and 10 July 1998*, WT/REG/M/18 (22 July 1998) para 19.
17. Appellate Body Report, *Turkey – Textiles*, para 48 (original emphasis).
18. Panel Report, *US – Line Pipe*, para 7.142.
19. Ibid., para 7.144.
20. Ibid., paras 198–9.
21. Marketplace regulations regulate, for example, the distribution, transport, marketing or sale of goods.
22. Emphasis added.
23. GATT 1994, art III.
24. See section 'Other Restrictions Expressly Permitted', pp. 242–5.

25. WTO Negotiating Group on Rules, *Compendium of Issues Related to Regional Trade Agreements – Background Note by the Secretariat (Revision)*, TN/RL/W/8/Rev.1 (1 August 2002) para 74.
26. The panel in *Argentina – Footwear* assumed that safeguard measures are 'duties and other restrictive regulations of commerce' under Article XXIV:8: paras 8.96–8.97. The Appellate Body reversed the panel's findings on Article XXIV: Appellate Body Report, *Argentina – Footwear (EC)*, para 110. However, this aspect of the panel's findings on Article XXIV was not examined by the Appellate Body nor specifically declared to be an erroneous interpretation of Article XXIV:8.
27. This seems to be the approach suggested in Panel Report, *Argentina – Footwear (EC)*, para 8.97. See above n. 26.
28. WTO Negotiating Group on Rules, *Compendium of Issues Related to Regional Trade Agreements – Background Note by the Secretariat (Revision)*, TN/RL/W/8/Rev.1 (1 August 2002) para 75. The WTO Secretariat has observed that '[t]he drafting history does not indicate why Articles XI–XV and XX were included in the list of exceptions while others, in particular Article XIX, were not included' (WTO Committee on Regional Trade Agreements, *Systemic Issues Related to 'Other Regulations of Commerce': Background Note by the Secretariat (Revision)*, WT/REG/W/17/Rev.1 (5 February 1998) para 6).
29. Appellate Body Report, *Turkey – Textiles*, para 48.
30. It may be that certain measures permitted under Article XXI of GATT 1994 in connection with essential security interests are also permitted by Article XX, perhaps as necessary to protect human, animal or plant life or health, or even public morals.
31. Appellate Body Report, *Turkey – Textiles*, para 48. The Appellate Body was examining a case involving a customs union and not an FTA. However, the text of Article XXIV:8 is the same in this regard for customs unions and FTAs.
32. It is not clear whether the advocates of this approach take the view that the only restrictive regulations that may be applied to any product are those mentioned in the brackets. Contrary to this view, we have suggested that the parties are free to retain any restrictive regulations they wish on products representing an insubstantial portion of trade because Article XXIV:8 requires only the elimination of restrictions on the substantial portion of trade.
33. See SPS Agreement, art 2.4.
34. WTO Committee on Regional Trade Agreements, *Systemic Issues Related to 'Other Regulations of Commerce': Background Note by the Secretariat (Revision)*, WT/REG/W/17/Rev.1 (5 February 1998) para 10.
35. Export measures may also restrict the re-exportation of (processed) goods imported from third countries.
36. WTO Committee on Regional Trade Agreements, *Systemic Issues Related to 'Other Regulations of Commerce': Background Note by the Secretariat (Revision)*, WT/REG/W/17/Rev.1 (5 February 1998).
37. WTO Committee on Regional Trade Agreements, *Note on the Meetings of 6-7 and 10 July 1998*, WT/REG/M/18 (22 July 1998) paras 40–46.
38. The application of two different SPS or TBT regimes – one for internal trade and another for external trade – may mean that the external regime is inconsistent with the SPS or TBT Agreement. For instance, if more stringent rules are applied externally than internally, that could well indicate that the external rules are more trade-restrictive than is necessary or that different restrictions are being applied in similar circumstances. See SPS Agreement, arts 5.5, 5.6 and 6.1 and TBT Agreement, art 2.2.
39. See WTO Committee on Regional Trade Agreements, *Inventory of Non-Tariff Provisions in Regional Trade Agreements: Background Note by the Secretariat*, WT/REG/W/26 (5 May 1998).
40. Canada has argued that preferential rules of origin cannot be ORCs because they are directed to the internal trade of the PTA and not the external trade (WTO Committee on Regional Trade Agreements, *Note on the Meetings of 6-7 and 10 July 1998*, WT/

REG/M/18 (22 July 1998) para 28). However, preferential rules of origin apply equally to all goods in order to determine their origin, even though the result will be preferential treatment for goods treated as originating in the PTA.

41. See WTO Committee on Regional Trade Agreements, *Note on the Meetings of 3-5 November 1997*, WT/REG/M/14 (24 November 1997) para 8.

42. There may be situations where the formation of an FTA does result in modification to the external trade regimes of the parties. For instance, the parties to an FTA may harmonize certain internal restrictions, such as SPS measures, and in consequence modify the corresponding external restriction.

43. GATT Art XXIV.7(a). The language in this Article suggests that it is a prospective obligation, but for most of its history, notifications to the CRTA have been made after the establishment of the PTA. WTO Members have recently agreed to a new transparency mechanism which provides for early announcement of any RTA and notification to the WTO (much of the mechanism arguably reflects existing obligations): JOB(06)/59/Rev.5

44. The CRTAs was established by a decision of the General Council on 7 February 1996: WTO Doc WT/L/127.

45. WTO Doc WT/L/127, p. 1.

46. Mitsuo Matsushita, Thomas Schoenbaum and Petros Mavroidis (2006), *The World Trade Organization: Law, Practice, and Policy*, 2nd edn, Oxford: Oxford University Press, p. 560.

47. PTA Understanding, art 12 'The provisions of Articles XXII and XXIII of GATT 1994 as elaborated and applied by the Dispute Settlement Understanding may be invoked with respect to any matters arising from the application of those provisions of Article XXIV relating to customs unions, free-trade areas or interim agreements leading to the formation of a customs union or a free-trade area'.

48. Matsushita, Schoenbaum and Mavroidis 2006, p. 585.

49. Ibid., p. 587.

50. For example, does the exception extend to GATT-inconsistencies arising from the elimination of internal trade restrictions only if these inconsistencies were necessary to the formation of the PTA? Does it justify a departure from the obligation under the Agreement on Safeguards to impose safeguards on all imports of the relevant product from all sources? How should 'substantially all the trade' between the PTA parties be measured in assessing whether internal trade restrictions have been sufficiently reduced? Do the parties to a customs union have to harmonize not only border measures but also marketplace measures applied to goods of other Members?

Index

/